MANAGING BY COMMUNICATION

Managing by Communication

WILLARD V. MERRIHUE
Manager, Community and Business Relations
General Electric Company, New York

McGRAW-HILL BOOK COMPANY, INC.
1960   New York   Toronto   London

MANAGING BY COMMUNICATION

7890-VBVB-987

41495

Preface

This book had its genesis several years ago when the author was asked to distill, from a long and exciting career in customer and employee communication, a series of lectures on the uses of communication by managers for the benefit of students in the Graduate School of Business at Columbia University in the City of New York.

Out of this experience has evolved, by dint of stern discipline and many midnight watts, the following comprehensive treatment of a vital aspect of the management process which is too little understood and inadequately practiced.

This book is directed primarily to executives in American business and industry. It should be equally helpful, however, to administrators of medical, educational, and charitable institutions, as well as to the growing number of managers in local, state, and Federal governmental components.

Particularly, it is hoped that the business-oriented treatment of this subject will motivate American universities to include a much more basic and practical treatment of the philosophy and practice of business communication in the curricula of their graduate business schools.

The author has eagerly followed many a fresh trail to undergraduate schools lured on by the semantics of a catalogued curriculum which indicated a realistic treatment of business communication. Invariably, the course concerned itself primarily with public speaking, report writing, and conference leadership.

v

Currently, most business schools give far less than adequate treatment to the subject, although it is one of the most essential and complex of the skills which must be mastered by the successful business executive.

Particularly in business and industrial enterprises, one observes a great and growing need for a codification of the principles and practices of business communication. This is attested by the stream of visitors from all over the world who come, year by year, to the company with which the author is associated, to learn more about this vital and fascinating subject.

For this reason, the author offers no apologies for dipping so deeply into the pool of research and experience to be found within the General Electric Company where he has spent his entire career and has been privileged to participate actively in much of the research and codification and teaching of the subject.

This book has been designed to help managers at all levels from first-line supervision to chief executives better to understand how to get work performed through people.

Particular emphasis has been placed, however, on the use of communication in managing employee, community, and union relations work, or industrial relations work, to use a common terminology. The management of industrial relations work in the modern business enterprise or institution represents the newest of the clearly differentiated business functions. Highly able talent is to be had for the bidding in the other primary functions of the business enterprise such as research, engineering, manufacturing, marketing, and finance. Conversely, there is a dearth of top professionals who can develop a positive philosophy of relations work and a body of acceptable practices adequate to cope with complex "people problems" of the enterprise.

It is hoped that this treatment of the subject may make a significant contribution to the maturing of this new profession.

There has been no intent to delve deeply into communication theory, nor to write as a theoretician or specialist in the complex social, political, and economic areas treated; rather the concern has been with the practical uses of the communication process within the business setting.

The author is deeply grateful for the contributions of numerous associates within the General Electric Company to the development of the philosophy and practices which form the basis of this work: James E. Barron, William J. Barron, Joseph M. Bertotti, Clarence J. Dover, Richard Eells, Dr. G. Roy Fugal, Clayton P. Fisher, Virgil B. Day, Fred N. Neal, Joseph T. Klapper, Edward J. Kneeland, William Scholz, Dr. Herbert H. Meyer, Dr. William A. Schwarzbek, Harold F. Smiddy, and J. Stanford Smith.

To Ralph J. Cordiner, chairman of the board, especial acknowledgment is made for his brilliant contributions to the development of a science of professional management which is the basis for management work within the General Electric Company and which is referred to repeatedly within this volume.

One of the heaviest contributors, of course, is Lemuel R. Boulware who, as vice-president of public and employee relations, developed, as a "way of life" within the company, the dynamic and positive philosophy of employee, community, union, and public relations which gives this work so much of its substance.

At the same time, I should make it clear that the responsibility for the material included in this book is entirely my own. Although I have tried to acknowledge the many sources from which I have gained information, background, and comments, this is not meant to imply the specific endorsement of these persons or of the General Electric Company.

Along more personal lines, I am thankful to Viola De Rosa and Madeline Neuhaus for their assistance with the manuscript and to Mrs. Catherine Durrell for her superb craftsmanship as a proof reader.

I am especially grateful to my wife Gay for her encouragement, her helpful critiques—and for her assumption of complete responsibility for the indexing.

Willard V. Merrihue

Contents

Part 1. Introduction

The role and potential of communication as a management tool must be reexamined in the light of a series of rapid changes in American business: increasing size and complexity of units; increasing specialization, decentralization; technological progress; increasing social consciousness; influence of unions; antibusiness propaganda.

Communication defined; communicating without words; the need to convey meaning accurately; factors that influence meaning. The frame of reference. Management's listening habits. How to listen more effectively. Essential elements in communicating.

Part 2. The Manager's Role in Communication

Analysis of the work of a professional manager; integrating versus the classic concept of "directing" places high premium on communication skills; integrating a business through communication; the communicative work of a manager; the responsibility of managers to speak up in defense of their enterprise and of the entire business system; communication is an interpretive process.

The basic problems in developing satisfactory employee relations; application of marketing principles to employee relations work; selling a company's "social product" versus selling its "economic product"; developing

ix

an improved social product; employees' needs at the work place; fulfilling these needs through individual man-manager relationships; early failures in motivating supervisors to sell social product; the role of communication; the need for economic education; a case study in merchandising a company's employee relations philosophy and program.

Nature and extent of communication depend upon eight basic factors; a comparison between the old and the "new look" in collective bargaining; the three acts in the "old look" pattern; a new management philosophy in collective bargaining described; the advantages of mature negotiations versus horse trading; the distinction between union relations and employee relations; the role of communication in "new look" collective bargaining; the utilization of new look bargaining in a small company—a case study; communication, a new management dimension.

Importance of community relations; a successful four-step approach; good corporate citizenship must be constantly communicated; twelve steps to good community relations; community opinion surveys; tailor-made programs for specific groups; civic leader mailings; press, radio, and TV relationships; local newspaper advertising; radio and TV programming; speakers bureau and film library; the "open house" and special plant tours; employment office and reception centers; corporate and employee participation in civic activities; economic education; plant-community relations council.

Comparative failure of the one-way-street community relations approach; the business climate concept—a *quid-pro-quo* approach; criteria of a good business climate; four steps to an improved environment for business; appraising the local and state business climate; determining goals, planning the work; communication, civic participation, political action, contact with and support of courageous legislators; multiemployer action.

Part 3.   The Supervisor's Role in Communication

Anatomy of the first-line supervisor's job; factors limiting foremen's ability to communicate; helping supervisors to communicate effectively; profile of a successful communicator at the supervisory level; top management's interest, support, and reward are essential.

Selection interviewing; orientation of new employees; initial job instruction; transmitting policies and procedures; assignment making; communication characteristics of most effective and least effective supervisors.

Informal and formal methods of communicating praise, censure, and progress; importance of formalizing and communicating performance appraisals; how to conduct resultful performance-appraisal discussions, give advance notice, compare accomplishments with targets, agree on next year's goals, review how managers can help draw out employees; the need for training the appraisers; importance of rating hourly employees.

Formalized sharing of information with employees; objectives, methodology; "Employee Round Tables" described; nature of information communicated; some do's and don't's; employee evaluation of information sharing.

Part 4. Principles, Techniques, and Media of Communication

Attitudes versus opinions; the process of opinion change; eight tentative principles: (1) drawing conclusions, (2) emotional versus factual appeals, (3) sleeper effect, (4) credibility factor, (5) effect of known motives, (6) selective exposure, (7) personal involvement, (8) group influence; importance of primacy in opinion change and retention.

A published code of personnel administration; establishment of a beneficial climate for communication; integrating middle management into communication process; development of formal company policy on communication; design features of an effective oral-communication network—downward, laterally, and upward; building the written-communication structure; written communication for management personnel; for nonsupervisory personnel.

Special-purpose employee meetings; counseling; informal employee contacts; recognition and special award meetings; supervisors' home visits; formal training courses, grievance processing; communication advisory councils, public address systems; telecommunication; family night; managers' luncheons; walking the shop and office. Pitfalls of oral communication: the Allport-Postman "chain loss" demonstration; the filter effect and circuit losses in oral communication; need for supplementing with written communication; proper utilization of both classes of media.

(A) Written communication for management: administrative communication, special management bulletins, the management newsletter, formal management reports, supervisor's handbooks, special publications.
(B) Written communication for employees: the employee bulletin, employee newspaper, monthly house organ, daily news digest, letters to new employees, letters to employees' homes, payroll-envelope inserts, employee booklets, reading racks, annual financial reports, individualized benefit reports, bulletin boards, audio-visual media.

Management's weakness—unilateral communication; barriers to upward communication; review of upward communication techniques: (1) organization structure, (2) management accountability for bilateral approach, (3) motivation of intermediate and first-line management, (4) formalized procedure for "problem-solving," (5) counseling, (6) good listening habits, (7) rumor clinics, (8) question boxes, (9) the suggestion system, (10) exit interviews, (11) attitude surveys.

Measurement of short-term and long-term communication programs; specific measuring techniques reviewed: (1) feedback, (2) attitude surveys—objectives, methodology, and use in measuring communication results, (3) nondirective depth interviews, (4) the Employee Relations Index (ERI), (5) surveys by outside organizations.

Part 5. Specific Management Uses of Communication

The philosophy of participative management; "employees support what they help to create"; case studies of successful participative projects: Ansul Chemical, Steel Improvement and Forge, Johns-Manville, Pitney-Bowes, New York Central, General Electric (four studies); three essential steps in achieving goals through employee participation.

The necessity for change in a business enterprise; change sets up a countervailing force; "resistance to change"; the resultant multibillion dollar loss; key to problem is the way changes are introduced; suggestions for introducing change; changeover to electric accounting in an insurance office. A three-step plan for administering change: technical, personnel, and communication planning. Elements of the communication plan. Case studies in communicating change. Training to develop expertness.

Contents

Case studies in the perceptive use of communication in typical business crises; hurricanes, storms, floods; reductions in work force in face of falling business or rumors thereof (three studies); illegal work stoppages; strike threats; union organizing campaigns.

Need for a mature and complete strike-termination plan; principles of such a plan; setting up a planning task force; assignments to functional managers; announcing the decision to take the strike; ten steps to take before strike deadline. Case study of a strike quickly and successfully terminated at a defense plant. Communicating about strikes to employees.

An essential quality of leadership is courage. To speak or not to speak up on controversial issues—two conflicting philosophies. An appraisal of management thinking in fifty-six companies on pros and cons of risk-taking communication. The amazing contrast between union and management house organs. Silence—the losing strategy of businessmen. Regaining a valuable birthright. Employees respect leaders with the courage to speak up.

The increasing importance of planning in business enterprises. Thinking ahead in the communication field. A gap exists between the attitudes and actions of employees and their managers. How the employee communication process narrows the gap. Three distinct types of communication work required. Importance of developing a three- to five-year plan of employee communication. Reconciling diverging ideological issues. Specific areas of misunderstandings and opportunities for interpretation. Du Pont and Ford case studies. Conclusion.

PART ONE

Introduction

CHAPTER 1

Communication's New Role in Business

Could it be that the chiefs of American business have heard the legend of Ganduki?

Ganduki was a newly chosen warrior chieftain of an African tribe in a remote fastness in the vast Belgian Congo. Much irked by the poaching and sporadic raids of a persistent chieftain of a rival tribe, Ganduki called together his warriors and, after a six-day march, liquidated the troublesome tribe in a brilliant coup distinguished by its strategy and his own personal courage. On the long trek home, Ganduki was sorely troubled, despite the great victory and the booty and the slaves his warriors were bringing back. A man of action, but inarticulate, he would rather wage another battle than face up to the victory speech his tribe would expect upon his return. So, calling upon his medicine man, Bo-Gobi, he prevailed upon him to communicate the magnitude and the brilliance of the victory to the home folks.

And so it was. After hours of feasting, Bo-Gobi mounted an ivory dais and began the narrative of the battle. As he warmed to his task to the rising crescendo of the throbbing drums, the gaudily painted, spear-waving warriors leaped and howled in the eerie light cast by the roaring fire. And when he had completed his tale, Bo-Gobi was caught up in the arms of his tribesmen, and with a mighty shout, they hailed him as their saviour and newly elected chief.

In a somewhat similar vein, the tale is told of a reputed political system in one of the smaller islands of the Samoan group. It seems, so we are told, that all the men on the island are chiefs (the women, of course, do all the work). But there are two kinds of chiefs, the regular chiefs who are powerless but who are in the majority—and the talking chiefs who run the island.

All authoritarian governments or organizations—whatever their claim to legitimacy—sooner or later gather about them the instruments of power, including the control of the communication network.

Our society and culture, conversely, are based on the voluntary association of free people for the purposes of government and for producing for each other (the "consent theory" of Rousseau and Locke). The essentials for this approach are freedom of speech and decentralization of communication. In sum, the foundation for communication and a democratic society are one and the same.

In our Western society, the democratization of work organizations lagged behind the democratization of the process of government. This is not surprising. Our forefathers migrated to this country largely to escape authoritarian government; thousands of years of bitter experience with kings, monarchs, and other tyrants were responsible for the wisdom that went into the writing of our Constitution. On the other hand, when our framework for self-government was developed, our forefathers were producing largely for self-consumption. It was not until long after the advent of the Industrial Revolution in the nineteenth century, when men began producing for each other on a large scale, that they began to think about more democratic methods of work-group leadership and group dynamics.

Gradually we have learned that leadership in work groups cannot be long effective unless it is by persuasion rather than by command.

We have learned the hard way that, in the long run, we cannot get effective work accomplished in groups, corporations, armies, churches, or governments, unless we can get it accomplished by individuals.

We now see clearly that individuals working in groups work best when each can see clearly the objective of the group of which he is a part, when each understands both his work and his teamwork responsibilities.

Our prime tool for providing this insight and understanding is communication.

The past decade should be chronicled by historians as the age in which businessmen discovered communication as their principal tool, first, to build understanding and cooperation by the employees they were trying to lead within their enterprise, secondly, to project their leadership among the employees and the publics they served, and thirdly, to discredit their detractors (many of whom are sterile nonproducing talking chiefs stalking the public forest).

The American business leader's appreciation of the importance of communication has been further heightened by a series of changing conditions within industry and within the sociopolitical environment in which business operates. Let us pause and look at some of these changing conditions. They are the basis for many of the strategic concepts of communication usage that will be dealt with later:

THE INCREASING SIZE AND COMPLEXITY OF BUSINESS

American business enterprises are constantly growing in size and complexity. Ignoring the relatively few which are mushrooming for tax and speculative purposes, we find that they grow by virtue of these principal forces at work:

1. The increasing demand of a public pleased by their product, prices, service, and business integrity.

2. The desire, stimulated by competition, to diversify in order to sell a more complete line to a public which holds in high regard their present products.

3. The need to achieve greater stability of employment and operating efficiency by supplementing highly seasonal lines.

This growth in unit size is nowhere near as alarming as some would have us believe. Mostly, it is a natural evolution of the American business economy. For example, a well-known industrial company was enjoying about 25 per cent of the industry market for its product back in 1925. At that time it did an annual volume of business of 340 million dollars and provided jobs for 85,000 employees. Thirty years later, its gross volume was 3.25 billion dollars, produced by 220,000 employees, but its percentage of the over-all market in which it had historically been the leader dropped and the number of competitors had increased by more than 600 per cent. Despite its growth in sales, the company simply had kept pace with the natural growth of the country, as measured by the market position. These same forces should result in the enlargement of practically all business enterprises. Obviously, every increment in growth increases the difficulty of communication. The informal contacts between owner or manager and employee are greatly diminished.

In organizing to handle the growing enterprise, the manager resorts to longer spans of control (horizontal types of organization with more people reporting directly to him) or vertical organizations with a number of levels of management separating the owner or professional manager from the production employees. Communication, like the water at the delta of a river, finds the channels complex and filled with sedimentation. Size alone, therefore, is forcing the manager to engineer his communication conveyor lines as scientifically as his product flow.

INCREASING SPECIALIZATION OF BUSINESS

The miracle of mass production is a result of increasing specialization and a division of highly skilled work into subdivisions of work which require less skill. This increased specialization lessens our intuitive understanding of the other fellow's job, problems, and interests. Specialized vocabularies, instructions, data, and reports emerge. There is an increased compartmentalization of supervisors, professional workers (engineers, accountants, scientists), and even of employee groups working on the same product. Managers are discovering that most of their problems in administering the enterprise result from their failure to integrate the business through planned two-way communication.

DECENTRALIZATION

As enterprises grow in size, they tend to build or buy plants in widely separated parts of the country in order to put payrolls into important new markets, to get closer access to raw material resources, and to tap new sources of available labor. The current trend in management is to make these new plants as autonomous as possible in order to push decision making out and down to the level where the best decisions can be made. These outposts are then provided with various services by staff units located at headquarters. This is an effective device for making the dispersed enterprise more manageable. However, it puts a great new premium on better-planned and more effective communication.

NECESSITY FOR CONSTANT TECHNOLOGICAL PROGRESS

Management of mass-production enterprises, as distinguished from small businesses specializing in crafts, conducts a ceaseless quest to take more and more direct human labor out of the manufacture of its product. This it must do to survive in the fiercely competitive American market place. In 1850, 65 per cent of the work in this country was performed by human beings and work animals; 35 per cent by water, wind power, and machinery. Today, machines perform 98½ per cent of the work; human workers perform 1½ per cent. The beneficent effects of this application of technology are familiar to all, taking the drudgery out of industrial work, shortening working hours, providing more leisure time. Most importantly, the long-range result is the creation of *more* jobs to make, sell, and service the increasing flow of goods that results from this process, also the spawning of entirely new businesses to cater to the increased leisure time of the population.

Despite these apparent benefits, almost every move by managers to change methods or introduce new machines or technology encounters opposition from the employees or their union representatives, ranging all the way from passive resistance to refusal to come up to expected output, and sometimes to costly strikes. This human reaction to progress has a thoroughly normal psychological basis. As will be discussed later, employees may subconsciously recognize that progress is based upon change, yet so fear the immediate disruptive influences of change, that they instinctively resist it. Accordingly, the more prescient managers turn to communication to pre-inform employees of the change and explain the reasons for the change. It is surprising how often resistance is replaced by cooperation when management takes the time to factor in the human consideration by means of intelligent and properly timed communication.

THE INCREASING SOCIAL CONSCIOUSNESS OF INDUSTRY

Adolph A. Berle, Jr., professor of corporation law at Columbia University,[1] sketches the metamorphosis of capitalistic institutions from enterprises interested solely in business for business' sake to social and quasi-political institutions and he gives some examples to prove the steady emergency of a praiseworthy corporate conscience.

Mabel Newcomer, professor of economics at Vassar College, also documents this encouraging trend: [2]

It seems quite possible that the professionalization of big business will, in the long run, make an important contribution toward solving the so-called problem of big business. . . . We have continued to hope that big business could be controlled for the public good. Professionalization of leadership . . . appears to offer one possible route to this end. The critics used to talk about the "heartless and soulless" corporation. Some of them today are discovering the "corporate conscience."

The progressive development in this century of a management philosophy which increasingly recognizes the dignity of the indi-

---

[1] Adolph A. Berle, Jr., *The Twentieth Century Capitalist Revolution,* Harcourt, Brace and Company, 1954. See also his earlier treatment, A. A. Berle and Gardner C. Means, *The Modern Corporation and Private Property,* The Macmillan Company, New York, 1933.

[2] Mabel Newcomer, "Professionalization of Leadership in the Big Business Corporation," *The Business History Review,* 39:1, pp. 54–63, March, 1955.

vidual is evident to all unbiased observers. The primary function of a large business enterprise is economic but not exclusively economic. The small private proprietor or entrepreneur may, for self-preservation, function exclusively as an economic entity, but as his enterprise evolves into an institution in society, it becomes a multifunctional entity or, as some writers describe it, a social and quasi-political institution. The managers of such institutionalized enterprises read, work, analyze, and experiment empirically in an attempt to bring their relations skills somewhere within range of their technical know-how. They are sent back to school to learn relations-centered management. Advanced management refresher courses of thirteen weeks and six weeks, such as those given at Harvard and at Columbia's Arden House, to name but two, deal largely with humanized management. Unfortunately, they are still short on the study of formalized communication. This is surprising because all human relationships are established through some form of communication, or lack of it.

Today's managers, in addition to their own research work, are increasingly turning for help to the congeries of human relations skills to be found at such institutions as Michigan, the Massachusetts Institute of Technology, Harvard, Northwestern, Stanford, Pennsylvania, and many others.

This new assumption of social responsibility is dramatically reflected by the American Telephone and Telegraph Company and the General Electric Company. In its Bell Telephone Laboratories, famous for research in the physical sciences, AT&T has established a new department for research in the social sciences. Three main areas of inquiry, communication, motivation, and personal and organization effectiveness, are being explored by a group of social scientists recruited from leading universities. In its announcement, AT&T stated: ". . . It is an experiment to see if the benefits of basic research that have contributed so much to the development of the material side of the business can be extended to people—in the continued improvement of their relations with each other and with their work."

The General Electric Company has recently established a behavioral research service "to undertake experimental studies pertaining to employee effectiveness within normal . . . working life situations." The long-term research program bears upon many fields of social psychology including in particular motivation processes, thinking processes, decision processes, learning and development processes, communication processes, social interaction and social structure, and individual assessment. Studies are pursued both by the service's own staff of social scientists and by university personnel for whom the company provides situations suitable for research and, in some cases, financial support. The entire program is periodically reviewed by an advisory panel composed of leading social scientists.

In the General Electric Company, all officers and managers as well as key "individual contributor" employees, are being enrolled in the company's "institute of advanced management" at Crotonville, New York.

The participants leave their jobs for three months to study fundamental concepts of the work of a professional manager as seen through an emerging company-oriented philosophy.

One aim of the program is to stimulate study of managing as a "distinct kind of work." Further, it aims to give participants the opportunity to think through management situations in terms of concepts and principles which, taken together, are beginning to constitute a philosophy of the company as a business enterprise. The program is divided into four main categories:

1. Philosophy of the company as a business enterprise and how this relates to a "theory of the firm."
2. Basic concepts and elements of managerial work.
3. Teamwork among decentralized components of the company.
4. New managerial tools.

INFLUENCE OF THE UNIONS

A major factor influencing managers to reappraise their communication has been and still is the growth and power of unions. Union membership grew from three million in 1925 to 18.4 million in 1958. Although it shows signs of leveling off at about one-quarter of America's total number of people in the work group, it is a potent force indeed.

Unions reached their ascendancy in the decade from 1935 to 1945 under the shelter of the prolabor Wagner Act. Like all past recipients of too much power, including employers, some unions abused it. The voices of employers were largely muted because they misinterpreted Section 8A of the Wagner Act as imposing rather rigid restrictions on their right of free speech in labor matters.

The imbalance of power between unions and employers created by the Wagner Act was partially rectified in 1947 by the passage of the Taft-Hartley Act. The amended national labor law stressed equal rights of expression to both unions and management, subject only to reasonable restrictions.[3] Obviously, nothing is more appreciated than the return of something which one has thought was previously denied. Communication immediately moved up in priority on the agenda of all thoughtful managers.

Nevertheless, labor unions today too often out-communicate management in smartness of strategy, in timing, and in volume. They award scholarships and fellowships to enable their members to match training with managers. They employ top-flight professional talent and send members to university-conducted summer schools constantly to heighten the influence of their communication.

ANTIBUSINESS PROPAGANDA

A familiar phenomenon and a prime reason why management is improving its communication skills is the increasing propaganda of antibusiness groups and of political philosophies bent on changing

---

[3] National Labor Relations Act (Taft-Hartley) Section 8C.
"The expressing of any views, arguments, or opinions or the dissemination thereof, whether in written, printed, graphic, or visual form, shall not constitute or be evidence of an unfair labor practice under any of the provisions of this Act, if any such expression contains no threat of reprisal or force, or promise of benefit."

both the American economy and our system of government and, hence, the entire "business climate."

One of the most perceptive analyses of the source and nature of the unceasing attacks on our modern industrial civilization is that of John D. Glover, professor of business administration of the Harvard Business School. In his introduction, he states: [4]

The target of the criticism is clearly something more than just a particular, if uncertain, group of corporations, be it more or less extensive. Essentially, it seems to me, the common bond among the critics is their opposition to departure from some sort of an "ideal" way of things in which economic life, political life, and social life is based upon independent, unorganized, unrelated, and even isolated individuals. This ideal is embodied in the individual as the economic unit, the political unit, and the social unit. "Colossi," "mammoth corporations," and even "larger companies" are merely the more obvious, outstanding manifestations of deviation. For some critics, all "modern business" and even the "ordinary businessman" represent a deviation from his "ideal." They are an embodiment of this deviation. They are among the principal prime movers of this deviation.

It is the deviation from the "ideal," and everything associated with this deviation—in reality or in fancy—which is the ultimate object of the criticism directed against "big business." This criticism expresses *reaction* against the modern industrial revolution.

Lest any "ordinary businessman" who reads this be in doubt, when it comes right down to it, the critics are not just talking exclusively about "corporate empires," or even "large companies." They are talking about *you.*

Many of these critics hold positions of importance in government, educational institutions, the press, radio, TV, in publishing houses, in labor unions, and religious organizations. Because they are dedicated to their cause and are highly skilled in the art of setting ideas in motion, they pose one of the most serious threats to the survival of our free-market business enterprises and their ability to serve the American people effectively.

[4] John D. Glover, *The Attack on Big Business,* Harvard University, Bureau of Business Research, Boston, 1954, p. 7.

THE BEST INTEREST OF THE ENTERPRISE

In reality, management need look for no further justification than this for employing the top communication talent available to teach its organization the modern skills and techniques of administrative and interpretive communication.

Peter Drucker states the impelling need for more and better employee communication in this way: [5]

> To measure work against objectives requires information. . . . Management must try to convey this information—not because the worker wants it, but because the best interest of the enterprise demands that he have it. The great mass of employees may never be reached even with the best of efforts. But only by trying to get information to every worker can management hope to reach the small group that in every plant, office, or store leads public opinion and molds common attitudes.

All the recent evidence indicates that employees work more effectively and with greater job satisfaction when they understand not only their own job objectives and accountability but the objectives of their work group and of the over-all business enterprise. They need to know not only the over-all objectives but the short-range goals that have been planned to achieve such objectives.

Yet employee-attitude surveys disturbingly reveal that one of management's poorest skills is its ability to interpret its good intentions, its goals (and their values to everyone), in a timely and meaningful manner to the workers on whom it depends for the successful attainment of such goals.

The effect of the foregoing factors on the thinking of those who direct business enterprises is strikingly illustrated by a study conducted by Purdue University which addressed a series of questions to fifty presidents to obtain their views on in-plant communication. The composite "we believe" of this group can be condensed as follows:

[5] Peter Drucker, *The Practice of Management,* Harper & Brothers, New York, 1954, pp. 306–307.

A definite relationship exists between communication and employee productivity.

Labor disputes and strikes are definitely linked to breakdowns in communication.

Many factors contribute to communication breakdowns; but the greatest single factor is inadequate use of communications media.

Oral communications are at least as important, or more so, than written ones.

All managers cannot communicate effectively. While natural talent is a factor in the possession of this ability, it is not the only one. Far greater communicative ability can be developed through training and experience.

Communication training of some type should be offered to management personnel—at all levels, from the president on down.

The authority that the communicator has by virtue of his position in the firm has an effect on how his ideas will be received.

The effectiveness of management personnel is greatly dependent upon their ability in oral communication.

In sum, many factors are motivating American business leaders to devote top priority to the complete overhauling and aggressive implementation of their communication philosophies, policies, and practices. Among the more important are the democratization of work organizations; acceptance of the concept of leadership by persuasion rather than command; the growing size and complexity of business; increasing specialization and subdivision of skills; the trend to decentralization as an organizational and operating concept; the necessity for constant technological progress and the resulting "resistance to change" which this engenders; the increasing social consciousness of industry, with its great new emphasis on human relations; the rise in power of unions and their aggressive and skillful use of communication; the ideological assault on employers and attacks on business by all types of critics who are among the nation's most skilled practitioners of antibusiness propaganda; and the need for communication in "the best interest of the enterprise" so that business may serve the balanced interests of customers, share owners, employees, suppliers, distributors, and all citizens.

CHAPTER 2

The Communicating Process

As individuals, we started to communicate a few seconds after our formal entrance into this world. Although we probably don't remember the incident, it can be identified precisely by the obstetrician who delivered us. It occurred when he held us by our feet and administered a sharp slap on our rump. The purpose of this slap? To cause us to inhale and start the process of breathing. The result of the exhalation was probably a faint yelp. This early, then, did we start the first phase of communicating.

In the ensuing days we quickly and empirically learned that certain behavior on our part conveyed crystal-clear meaning to our mothers and usually, though not always, resulted in certain behavior on their part which was pleasing to us because it satisfied our needs or wants. That was the complete process of communicating.

Communication defined

We are now ready to define communication. Some social scientists are content to define it as an exchange of information. The American Management Association defines it as "any behavior that results in an exchange of meaning." A special committee on communication in business and industry (National Society for the Study of Communication) tentatively defines it as follows: "Communication is a mutual exchange of facts, thoughts, opinions or emotions. This requires presentation and reception, resulting in common understanding among all parties. This does not necessarily imply agreement." [1]

Although all these definitions are apt, they refer to communication in general. The author's concept of communication as it should be practiced in business usually encompasses the complete cycle which started with the baby's behavior. In this context, communication may perhaps best be defined as "any initiated behavior on the part of the sender which conveys the desired meaning to the receiver and causes desired response behavior from the receiver." [2]

Business communication should be purposeful. Its purpose, preponderantly, should be to transmit information and understanding from one person to another, or to a group, to achieve cooperation and action. In social communication, we may be content merely to convey meaning. (I love you. I am tired.) In business, downward communication should almost always seek employee action, response, or motivation, to assure and reassure employees (to reduce uncertainty), to strengthen or change employee attitudes, or to get desired action on the part of managers if the communication is upward.

Note that the key word in this concept is "meaning." Let's examine that word. What is "meaning"? It is what the sender hopes to convey to the receiver. An exchange of meaning is usually accomplished by language (words) transmitted orally or in writing. When we use words, we engage in the first order (or level) of communication. But meaning can also be conveyed by tone, facial or hand expressions, by deeds, or by silence, in which not a word is transmitted or spoken in the conventional sense. This is known as the second order (or level) of communication.

Communicating without words

Bleached bones along the wagon trail, smoke signals from the hills conveyed portentous meaning to our forefathers heading west-

---

[1] *Journal of Communication,* 4:1, spring, 1954.
[2] Communication is a two-way process and the sender may be either the manager or a subordinate.

ward. The helmsman of a ship entering a harbor and seeing a black buoy knows its meaning (B.P.O.E., black to port on entering). He knows he must keep the black buoys to the port of his ship to stay in the channel. Perhaps one of the most famous nonlanguage devices for conveying meaning in our times was Churchill's finger V.

Both words and seeing may be absent in conveying meaning. A deep-throated growl from the Stratford Shoals Lighthouse in Long Island Sound means but one thing to hundreds of thousands within hearing—the Sound is enveloped in fog.

Silence particularly can be a frightfully effective behavior to convey meaning. We usually knew the meaning when a school associate suddenly began ignoring us with studied silence. We daily observe in business the insecurity occasioned by the usually un-intended omission of a greeting by our superior—the insecurity ranging in degree from mild uneasiness to panic. In this case, we misread a meaning from an unexpected behavior.[3]

Another familiar business phenomenon is the application of social pressure by a group upon one of its members by simply ceasing to speak to him or include him in their conversations. Among produc-tion workers, for example, such behavior very often conveys to him that he violated the code or ethics of the group by exceeding the group-imposed limitation on work output. The meaning of the silence is usually clear indeed.

In fact, astute supervisors, counselors, and staff personnel people rely on shifting communication patterns to reveal group moods, cross currents, and developing problems.

Or take another example of language-less communication familiar to many workers in business and industry. An employee arrives at work to find unexpectedly that his desk and other equipment have been moved from a private office to an open clerical area. To him, and to most of his associates who were not party to the decision, this very often means he has been demoted or his status

---

[3] Some years ago, Metro-Goldwyn-Mayer released an amusing, but pointed, short feature illustrating this phenomenon. It was entitled, *The Boss Forgot to Say Good Morning.*

lowered in comparison with his associates still possessed of private offices.

Finally, we are all familiar with the fact that gestures and facial expressions are often fraught with meaning and therefore a distinct form of communication. How easy to understand the meaning of the expression on certain secretaries' faces when asked to "take a letter" at five minutes to five!

It is of prime importance to every businessman to be alertly aware of the power and pitfalls in the nonlanguage type of communications. With this awareness, he can avoid many personal worries. More importantly, he can understand, analyze, and remedy many human relations mix-ups when mistaken meaning is the crux of the problem.

We can now see clearly that effective or faulty exchange of meaning can exert a constructive or destructive force in everyday life and in business.

FACTORS THAT INFLUENCE MEANING

How much and how accurately meaning is conveyed in communication depends on a number of factors, including:

1. *The functional relationship between the sender and the receiver.* Is it that of an accountant communicating to a personnel worker? Very often they differ sharply in their policy thinking and their sense of values. Likewise, the goal of the salesman to please the customer with custom-made products is incomprehensible to the manufacturing man who knows the cost advantages and speedier manufacturing time of a standardized line of products; then, too, traditionally, staff and line men have had great difficulty in conveying desired meaning to each other.

2. *The positional relationship between sender and receiver.* Is it that of an oldtimer authoritatively instructing the newcomer? Is it that of president speaking to a workman?

3. *The group-membership relationship.*[4] Is it that of management

---

[4] See Paul Pigors, *Effective Communication in Industry*, National Association of Manufacturers, New York, 1949, p. 17.

speaking to management or to a member of a union which is overtly hostile to management?

4. *Differences in heredity and prior environment.* Are the backgrounds of sender and receiver relatively homogeneous? If not, meaning will be difficult to convey. Status in life powerfully shapes ideas and attitudes.[5]

People do not live in a vacuum until they meet us. Their minds are not clean slates on which we may freely write. On the contrary, beginning at birth, they have been busy absorbing ideas and attitudes to which they cling with great devotion. Their ideas and attitudes reflect their status in life. They are related to what kind of people they are. It makes a difference whether they are rich or poor, old or young, Christian or Jewish, city or farm, men or women, management or non-management, professional or laymen, Republicans or Democrats, etc.

5. *Differences in formal education.* What is the capacity of the audience to understand and comprehend the message? Do the same words mean the same thing to the Ph.D. and the employee who quit school at the seventh grade? Recognizing this barrier to correct understanding, some companies carefully tailor communications to make them meaningful to all employees above a certain grade level.[6]

6. *Past experience.* What has been the quality of the human relationships between sender and receiver? If the sender has exploited the receiver or passed the buck or failed to give credit due or to back him up where such action was called for, then dislike and suspicion can distort all intended meaning. The same may be true if *past* employers or supervisors other than the sender have been the transgressors.

7. *Emotions.* The current emotional state of the sender and receiver can determine whether correct meaning is exchanged or whether all meaning will be blocked by an insurmountable barrier.

[5] *Communication in Industry,* Employers Labor Relations Information Committee, Inc., New York, 1954.
[6] Rudolf Flesch, *The Art of Plain Talk,* Harper & Brothers, New York, 1946; *The Art of Readable Writing,* Harper & Brothers, New York, 1949. The latter deals with the measurement and design of readability.

8. *Misunderstanding of words (the vagaries of semantics)*. Too many people believe that words are precise instruments for conveying meaning. Words alone do not convey meaning. Only people can convey meaning through their use of words. Disraeli said: "Words are but empty vessels into which I pour meaning."

It will readily be discerned that the foregoing factors, in reality, describe the respective frames of reference of the sender and of the receiver of any communication. The frame of reference of a receiver determines how he will interpret a particular communication; that is, how much of the sender's true meaning is comprehended.

Elmer L. Lindseth, president, Cleveland Electric Illuminating Company, relates the following illuminating experiment to point up the importance of a common frame of reference between sender and receiver:

On the matter of communicating without a common frame of reference, let's try a little experiment. I have it from M.I.T. I'll describe a simple situation; see what it means to you.

A man was walking along. He looked down at his suit and saw a hole in it. In a minute he was dead.

What picture comes into your mind? What did I communicate to you? If I led you to the conclusion that the man was walking along a street, that the hole was a bullet hole, and that he died of the wound, you have reached the conclusion of the vast majority. You're normal. But your conclusion is not what I intended. The facts are these: The man was a deep-sea diver; he was walking on the ocean bottom; the hole was in his diving suit; he died by drowning.

Each of us translated this little story in terms of his own frame of reference. It is easy to see how different the results can be. I communicated the information in one context, you received it in another, and certainly we failed to achieve effective communication.

Dr. Joseph Klapper, consultant, communication research, General Electric Company, relates the following on the variant meanings of words:

The phrase "on the Fritz," which conveys to a northeasterner that something is not working, is totally meaningless to many southeasterners, who would instead say that the mechanism in question "had tore up." "Dropped eggs" may suggest an unholy mess to most Americans, but in Boston, no other order would produce eggs elsewhere described as "poached." An "evening" appointment occurs, in most places, sometime after dusk, but in certain parts of Tennessee, Texas, Georgia, and Mississippi it would take place between noon and six. Such terms as "old" or "rich" mean one thing to the ten-year-old child of an indigent laborer, something else to a 35-year-old executive, and still something else again to a newly retired man of 60 who has previously discovered and exploited vast oil fields. What a given word conveys, in short, is often dependent on local speech patterns, individual experience, and the general social or economic position of the hearer.

This is by no means a complete list of the factors that influence meaning, but these may help explain why so often a manager's sincerest attempt to communicate may backfire or fail to produce the desired behavior response.

MANAGEMENT'S LISTENING HABITS

Management spends millions to communicate, but pennies, if anything at all, in research on how best to exchange meaning accurately. A suggested beginning for such research would be an appraisal of management's listening habits.

Most of us do not know how to listen. Yet how much or how accurately meaning is conveyed by us or to us depends greatly upon the quality of our listening habits.

Ten illustrations of bad listening habits are offered by Dr. Ralph Nichols, professor of speech at the University of Minnesota and a national authority on listening habits. He suggests that we analyze our listening habits with this check list:

1. Science says you think four times faster than a person usually talks to you. Do you use this excess time to turn your thoughts elsewhere while you are keeping general track of a conversation?

2. Do you listen primarily for facts, rather than ideas, when someone is speaking?

3. Do certain words, phrases, or ideas so prejudice you against the speaker that you cannot listen objectively to what is being said?

4. When you are puzzled or annoyed by what someone says, do you try to get the question straightened out immediately—either in your own mind or by interrupting the speaker?

5. If you feel that it would take too much time and effort to understand something, do you go out of your way to avoid hearing about it?

6. Do you deliberately turn your thoughts to other subjects when you believe a speaker will have nothing particularly interesting to say?

7. Can you tell by a person's appearance and delivery that he won't have anything worthwhile to say?

8. When someone is talking to you, do you try to make him think you're paying attention when you're not?

9. When you're listening to someone, are you easily distracted by outside sights and sounds?

10. If you want to remember what someone is saying, do you think it is a good idea to write it down as he goes along?

(If you answer "no" to all these questions, then you are that rare individual—the perfect listener. Every "yes" answer means that you are guilty of a specific bad listening habit.)

Robert K. Greenleaf, director of personnel research, American Telephone and Telegraph Company, in a paper entitled "Behavioral Research," lays great stress on the development of better listening behavior on the part of management. He says:

I believe that the first step in good communication—anywhere—is listening. In planning, deciding and communicating on matters concerning how people think and feel and act and grow, one has only two general ways of getting at the data on which to manage:—observing and listening. . . .

Listening . . . might be defined as an attitude toward other people and what they are attempting to express. It begins with attention, both the outward manifestation and the inward alertness. It includes constructive responses that help the other person express both his thoughts and his feelings. . . . The good listener tries to hear everything that is said, not just what he expects or wants to hear. . . . And good listening communicates something which is almost universally good.

Carl Rogers proposes a dramatic experiment [7] that management might well install, especially in its interminable conferences, in order to learn the discipline of listening and to accelerate the exchange of meaning:

. . . The major barrier to mutual interpersonal communication is our very natural tendency to judge, to evaluate, to approve (or disapprove) the statement of the other person or the other group.

Although the tendency to make evaluations is common in almost all interchange of language, it is very much heightened in those situations where feeling and emotions are deeply involved.

Accordingly, Rogers proposes this solution:

1. Listen with understanding.
2. Next time an argument occurs between two persons, institute this rule:

Each person can speak up for himself only after he has first restated the ideas and feelings of the previous speaker accurately and to that speaker's satisfaction.

Surely such a discipline would provide the finest type of basic training in perceptive listening for our managers and supervisors.

ESSENTIAL ELEMENTS IN COMMUNICATING

By this time we should be aware of the fact that effective communication, far from being simple, is much more complex than we had thought because of the difficulty of getting across one's true meaning and because of the fact that communication is a two-way street with many blockades.

We have implied before that effective communication must be planned. Let's look at some essential steps in the planning of an important communication:

1. *Know your objective.* Is it to gain understanding of a new policy or

[7] Carl R. Rogers, Centennial Conference on Communciations, Northwestern University, October, 1951, as cited in *Harvard Business Review,* July–August, 1952.

procedure? Is it to get action such as more suggestions? Is it to change attitudes? Is it to precondition employees in advance of some change? Is it to refute false charges by union officials? Is it to dispel fear caused by false rumors? Sharpen your objective. The sharper the focus, the better the result.

2. *Identify your audience.* You may wish to use not only different language but different media to reach your engineers from those you would use in reaching your shop people.

3. *Determine your medium (or media).* How best to communicate your message? Orally? If orally, will you go down the line of command man-to-man or by group meetings? If printed, will you use the plant house organ or the public press or letters to employees' homes?

4. *Tailor the communication to fit the relationship between sender and receiver.* Is the relationship climate one of fear and distrust, or one of confidence? Is the receiver preoccupied, under emotional strain, fearful of impending layoffs? Are the employees accustomed to getting communication from you, the sender? (If you act differently from the way they expect, they will be bewildered or suspicious.) Is the receiver or are the receivers *able* to respond with the behavior response you desire?

5. *Establish a mutuality of interest.* Can your objective be expressed in terms of self-interest to the receiver? Are you tuned in on his wavelength? Can he clearly see that your proposal or policy has something in it for him? Does it promise to fulfill one of his basic needs: to be superior, secure, socially acceptable, healthier, safer, etc.? Empathy, the ability to see the other person's point of view, is a priceless ingredient of effective communication.

6. *Watch your timing.* It can often make or break the effectiveness of your communication. Do you wish to beat the grapevine? Should not your management employees receive the message first? Should not your employees receive it before they see it in the local press? Should the letter to employees' homes be sent on Monday? Perhaps Wednesday would be better.

7. *Measure results.* Use readership or recall surveys or other feedback devices to ensure that mutual understanding has been achieved, to check if desired response has occurred, and to improve the planning of your next communication.

In its "Ten Commandments of Good Communication," the American Management Association stresses the urgency of careful planning in its first commandment: "Many communications fail because of inadequate planning. Good planning must consider the goals and attitudes of those who will receive the communication and those who will be affected by it."

The good communicator, through instinct and training, subconsciously considers these factors in day-to-day communication and very consciously considers them in each of his important planned communication programs, whether it be the semiannual meeting with each employee to review his performance and progress, or a mass appeal to all employees.

PART TWO

The Manager's Role in Communication

CHAPTER 3

How the Modern Manager Uses Communication

To understand fully the importance of communication to the manager of a business enterprise or of any of its components, we must begin by analyzing the managerial process. Many standard texts break the process down into six subparts: planning, organizing, assembling resources (personal and capital), directing, and controlling.

In manager-development instruction in the General Electric Company, all the work of a professional manager (those engaged in the profession of management) is subdivided into four major categories: planning, organizing, integrating, and measuring. Conspicuously absent are the terms "direct" and "control," which were rooted in the old proprietorship concept where the owner was presumed to have the *right* to direct and control.

Brantley Watson, vice-president of human relations, McCormick and Company, Inc., contrasts the old and the new leadership philosophies in this way:

Under this point of view (a "control" philosophy of management) employees are thought of as a commodity to be bid for, developed, and protected as any other commodity—primarily to serve the purposes of the organization. Emphasis in employee relations is, therefore, on control of employees, and such employee benefits as may be provided are granted largely as an expedient or as a paternalistic gesture.

A contrasting view might be called a "cooperative" philosophy of management. Under this philosophy, business management accepts its responsibility as a trusteeship, serving the interests of stockholders, consumers, the public, and employees alike. Responsibility for the welfare of all members of the organization is recognized as inherent in the management function, and not as an expedient. The emphasis in employee relations, then, is not on the arbitrary control of employees through authoritarian methods, but on the development of teamwork, on soliciting ideas, on participation, on considering each employee as a member of the organization rather than as being merely employed by it.

MANAGEMENT BY COMMUNICATION

Today's developing concept of leadership, exercised largely by persuasion rather than by command, places a great new premium on communication. Three of the elements of a manager's work, planning, organizing, and measuring, are heavily dependent on employee communication; the fourth category, integration, is almost synonymous with communication.

The quality of planning, of organizing, and of measuring, for example, is largely determined by the quality and speed of information flowing *inward* (from customers, public, government, unions, share owners, and the local community) and downward, upward, and laterally to, from, and between employees and the various intermediate levels of management. Likewise, to be successful, the manager must see to it that the results of such planning, organizing, and measuring are made known, understood, and acceptable to all parts of the enterprise through competently planned and executed communications.

It is in the integrating work of the manager, however, that we perceive the true importance of communication. Harold F. Smiddy, General Electric's vice-president of management consultation services, defines the integrative process as the "reuniting, harmonizing, synchronizing and blending of the portions of the work which were divided and separately assigned in planning and organizing."

Note the high communication content defined or implicit in the following condensed listing of the specific steps in the work of integration as conceived by the General Electric Company:

1. Interpreting the work of a professional manager; that is, interpreting his total job so that the team may help him do it.

2. Listening, making it easy to get frank communication to the manager. Utilizing the principle of feedback to improve the manager's job of integration.

3. Obtaining sincere voluntary acceptance of assignments, responsibility, relationships, and accountability (essentially developing understanding).

4. Creating and maintaining a friendly, cooperative, dynamic, and productive working climate.

5. Encouraging individual self-development.

6. Relating the interest of the individual, his department and his company to the interests of the industry, community, nation, and world.

7. Achieving successful, economical, profitable, integrated performance by all individuals and components.

Note the key words in the foregoing types of work which a manager performs in integrating his enterprise: interpreting, listening, developing understanding, creating proper climate, encouraging, relating, etc.—all are facets of the communication process.

Peter Drucker describes the manager's prime tool in managing, communication, in this way: [1]

The manager has a specific tool: information. He does not "handle" people; he motivates, guides, organizes people to do their own work. His tool—his only tool—to do all this is the spoken or written word or the language of numbers. No matter whether the manager's job is engineering, accounting or selling, his effectiveness depends on his ability to listen and to read, on his ability to speak and to write. He needs skill in getting his thinking across to other people as well as skill in finding out what other people are after.

Professor Alex Bavelas and Dermot Barrett draw the following significant analogy in depicting the role of communication in a business: [2]

[1] Peter F. Drucker, *The Practice of Management,* Harper & Brothers, New York, 1954, p. 346.
[2] Alex Bavelas and Dermot Barrett, "An Experimental Approach to Organizational Communication," *Personnel,* March, 1951, p. 368.

It is entirely possible to view an organization as an elaborate system for gathering, evaluating, recombining, and disseminating information.

It is not surprising, in these terms, that the effectiveness of an organization with respect to the achievement of its goals should be so closely related to its effectiveness in handling information. In an enterprise whose success hinges upon the coordination of the efforts of all its members, the managers depend completely upon the quality, the amount, and the rate at which relevant information reaches them. The rest of the organization, in turn, depends upon the efficiency with which the managers can deal with this information and reach conclusions and decisions.

This line of reasoning leads us to the belief that communication is not a secondary or derived aspect of organization—a "helper" of the other and presumably more basic functions. Rather, it is the essence of organized activity and is the basic process out of which all other functions derive. The goals an organization selects, the methods it applies, the effectiveness with which it improves its own procedures—all these hinge upon the quality and the availability of the information in the system.

The communication work of an executive

The late Dr. Irving J. Lee, one of the most competent students of communication in business, arranged to have some of his students sit all day in the office of cooperating executives to make notes on the types of communication utilized to perform the day's work. Their findings are summarized in the following communication log of a business day in the life of a typical manager: [3]

1. Giving information to subordinates
2. Interpreting department policies and instructions (on request)
3. Instructing on what and how to work
4. Making assignments to subordinates
5. Following up or checking on assignments or general work progress
6. Getting information
7. Advising subordinates at their request
8. Correcting subordinates for mistakes
9. Praising subordinates

[3] Irving J. Lee and Laura L. Lee, *Handling Barriers in Communication,* Harper & Brothers, New York, 1957.

10. Stimulating subordinates to continue or increase effort
11. Leading conferences to get advice or sell a conclusion
12. Persuading someone not responsible to you
13. Negotiating with equals
14. Conciliating or mediating disputes between subordinates
15. Small chit-chat
16. Speechmaking inside and outside the business

In view of the foregoing, can we not conclude that we manage primarily by communication?

MANAGEMENT'S RESPONSIBILITY TO SPEAK UP

Thus far we have discussed the importance of communication in the planning, organizing, integrating, and measuring of the internal work required to operate a business enterprise. But communication has a much larger role to play. Business is not a closed system operated in a vacuum. Rather, business is conducted in an environment. Many of the major deterrents to success are to be found in the social and political environment in which it must operate.

To operate successfully, the business must please people at a profit. It must please its employees, its customers, its suppliers, its share owners, and the local community or communities in which it operates.

However, the management of any business enterprise will not long succeed in pleasing its many publics if its deeds do not deserve approbation or if, in the presence of good deeds, it fails to carry on a continuous program of interpretive communication. A businessman, after first seeing that his house is in order, must have the courage to take a public stand and speak out against all self-seeking detractors of his business, whether they be demagogues, misinformed politicians, powerful union officials, or that minority of intellectuals who plan their "new society" on a foundation of economic fallacies.

Particularly must the attitudes of our intellectuals be factored into management's long-range communication planning because it is they who provide the leadership, for good or ill, in the political, economic, and social crusades that periodically mark the history of any free country.

Crusades may produce needed adjustments in a free system—or they may destroy or tragically restrict freedom. How hazardous such leadership, based on untested economic theories, may be to the cause of freedom, is suggested by William Schlamm, ex-Communist, who later repudiated the doctrine in his provocative book, *The Second War of Independence*.[4]

Schlamm believes that "contrary to the general consensus of opinion, all brands of totalitarianism, and especially Bolshevism, are not social expressions of economically distressed underdogs, but rather diseases prevalent among rather well-fed intellectuals." He considers that such "totalitarian lunacy . . . is relatively fifty times" more common among intellectuals and professionals "than among the poverty-stricken Okies, the needleworkers, or unemployed miners."

This is particularly dangerous, Schlamm believes, because it is among the professionals and intellectuals that opinion leaders are found. "Within every society," he points out, "be it ever so democratic, there is a relatively small group of intellectuals who give that society its tone and character. What 1,000 professors, writers, bishops think, write, preach is handed on by 300,000 teachers, journalists and ministers, to the other Americans and forms the consciousness of the entire nation."

Recent research indicates that opinion leadership and the flow of influence is probably not as simple as Schlamm suggests. It appears, for example, to be more "horizontal" than "vertical." The great majority of people seem to be more influenced by members of their own groups than they are by national leaders, clergy, and other supposed founts of influence. But these everyday opinion leaders—people "like ourselves" who nevertheless influence us—apparently get their ideas from the mass media and from other opinion leaders

---

[4] William Schlamm, *The Second War of Independence*, E. P. Dutton & Co., Inc., New York, 1940.

slightly higher up the economic or intellectual scale.[5] The ultimate origin of the ideas has not been pinpointed by the research, but it would seem likely to lie where Schlamm suggests, among the intellectuals, the writers, and the media.

This situation is not to be deplored but it must be recognized. The security of American democracy as well as our economic system depends in important measure on our protecting the right of intellectuals to develop and publicize their ideas.

William J. Barron, counsel for the public and employee relations services of the General Electric Company, stated the case admirably in an address to the community relations representatives of the company in 1958.

The real genius of our Anglo-Saxon democracy which has made possible the free enterprise system is immeasurably attributable to the honor and respect which we not only instinctively, but also consciously and deliberately, have accorded to those who entertain social, economic and political philosophies in conflict with our own. I think there is something magnificent and expressive of our way of life in the term applied to the minority party in England's House of Commons. The minority party is, as you know, referred to as "His Majesty's *Loyal* Opposition." I suggest to you that in a democratic free society every organization concerned with broad political or social issues will have the wellsprings of its inner sources strengthened and refreshed to the extent it encourages within it a function akin to that performed by "His Majesty's Loyal Opposition."

Instead of denouncing the critics among the intellectuals, business management must accept the challenge of winning their understanding and acceptance of the system. So far, we seem able to promote our system only on the pragmatic argument that it works better than any other, which of course, it does. But it does have a sound intellectual base and this must be understood and explained.

If business were to take a fraction of the money it spends on so-called institutional advertising to the public in mass media and

5 For a review of pertinent research, see Elihu Katz, "The Two-step Flow of Communication: An Up-to-date Report on an Hypothesis," *Public Opinion Quarterly*, 21:1, pp. 61–78, spring, 1957.

utilize it thoughtfully through direct contact to gain the understanding of these idea multipliers and innovators, the devolution of this country from the outstanding model of free enterprise to an undistinguished, unproductive semisocialist state would be sharply inhibited. Business leadership is on trial largely because it has contented itself with the use of communication (and a very inadequate and unskillful use at that) to operate its enterprises with a premium on short-term results, without due regard to its external environment, and with its sights on the wrong target.

As will be pointed out subsequently, business communication of the future will involve strategic considerations of the highest order: it will start with being sure that actions are sound and in the public interest; it will involve surveys of the ideological market, planning short- and long-range goals, planning of the ideological product, and merchandising the needed understanding and information product through modern marketing techniques and the development of much more precise methods of evaluation and feedback.

An interpretive process

Communication, as the author and his associates see it, is not a constricted concept of getting work performed by people through listening and talking and writing to them. Neither is it a concept of manipulating people through hypnotic semantics. Rather, communication is a process which both affects and is affected by the deeds and attitudes of management, on one hand, and the employees and public on the other. It is essentially an interpretive process. This implies that the successful business communicator—like the successful translator of languages—must not only know the languages of both the senders and the receivers, but must also have a sympathetic understanding of the backgrounds, the attitudes, and aspirations of both. Communication, then, is a broad conception equaling, in its magnitude and importance to the business, such other accepted or upcoming practices as automation, decentralization, or operations research and synthesis.

It is the purpose of this book to help businessmen see above and beyond the innumerable techniques of employee and public communication, to help them perceive the essential purpose of the process—which is to assist managers to manage more efficiently, and with greater understanding, support, and approval of those managed—and finally, to show businessmen how planned communication can be applied both inside and outside the business in the attainment of optimum long-range profit, growth, and survival objectives.

CHAPTER 4

Use of Communication in Improving
Employee Relations

American businessmen have distinguished themselves particularly in the areas of invention, production, and distribution. They have no peers and they move with sure-footed competence in the familiar business functions of market forecasting, product innovation, new-product planning, assembling resources (equity capital, manufacturing facilities, and labor force), engineering design, production mechanization, automation, dynamic pricing, distribution, and credit financing. It is only when they come face to face with the problems generated by employee, union, and community (public) relations that they become uncertain and frustrated. A vice-president of the General Electric Company, Lemuel R. Boulware, whose unique and successful approach to the problems in this complex area of public and employee relations has been termed "Boulwareism," points to the crux of the problem in these words:

We are great physicists, chemists, engineers. We are phenomenal manufacturers. We have been fabulous financiers. We are superb in individual selling and mass marketing. Yet as the *whole* man of business—the manager and leader—we are condemned. When we try to merchandise the over-all economic and social consequences of our operations, we fail.

People like—and respect—the results of our separate professional skills. But taken as a whole, our activities are too likely to be regarded by a majority of the public as anti-social.

Why do we find ourselves in this situation? With our customers, stockholders, vendors approving of us, to be sure—but with too many of our employees and their allies—the unions, the government, too often the educators and clergy, too much of the public—in other words our real bosses—not only not respecting and liking us, or even appreciating or understanding us, but not even crediting us with good intentions—with being on their side, whereas we thoroughly believe that being on their side is being on the side of what's good for all.

People just don't think that the jobs we provide are what they ought to be. They don't think that the economic and social consequences of our activities, and the system back of our activities, are what they ought to be for the good of each community and of the nation.

They think that we are smart, skilled, technically honest, but coldly selfish and not on the side of employees and the public. Yet we are the same people who give largely those same people the products and prices they like.

Whose fault is this? I think we are going to find it's solely the fault of us businessmen. What can be the matter? What ought to be done? And who ought to do it—this undone task, the business leader's larger job?

In our Company, where we have all these questions, we decided that we would have to try to do something about it, and that we certainly must not continue to take these puzzling problems lying down—or go on about our customary pursuits being technically successful there, while appearing to be failing in the larger and the only really important sphere of true personal accomplishment and real social usefulness.

We determined to try to draw on our sales and general management experience to discover what were all the things which we did to make us successful in the product sales field but which we were not doing in the job customer and community relations field.

THE MARKETING APPROACH APPLIED TO EMPLOYEE RELATIONS

Using this analysis of a basic problem facing most American businesses as a backdrop, let us now examine step by step the manner in which the General Electric Company applied familiar marketing principles to the development of a basic employee relations philosophy and program.

In marketing its products, the company conducts market research to find out what the customer wants changed or improved in the product, what he expects in terms of guarantees and in service, and the approximate price that will attract his business. The researchers come back with the bad news and they and the product planners get busy with their engineering, manufacturing, and finance associates. Invariably they come up with what the customer wants at the price he will pay.

Using the same market-research approach, the company studies the basic needs and wants of its job customers through polling the supervisors and the employees, listening carefully to the union, and surveying community practices. Next comes the product-planning phase of designing better jobs to keep them up to competitive standards. Perhaps local salary and wage inequities must be corrected, or supervisors must be shown through example and training how to improve their relations with their subordinates; perhaps better market forecasting and production scheduling must be achieved to make the jobs steadier, or sloppy procedures in administering benefit plans must be corrected.

In this way an improved job is designed that will be more attractive and salable to the employees or job customers.

After the company has designed and produced a new economic product, such as a refrigerator or television receiver, it brings in the sales force and trains it carefully on how to introduce and sell the new product. Each salesman is equipped with certain printed information, such as descriptive leaflets and price lists. Analogously, the company has a sales force available to sell its job customers inside the plant on the newly improved jobs. This sales force consists of supervisors primarily, but also the doctors, nurses, cafeteria workers, benefit plan administrators, and all other service employees. And just as was the case in the product field, this in-plant sales force is provided with printed materials describing the improved job to help them to do better personal selling of the job to the employees.

In marketing economic products, it would be unthinkable to send the sales force out to do the selling job barehanded. Preceding their very first contact with the customer, the advertising and sales promotion department supports them with communication in mass media, point-of sale displays, and so forth.

Likewise, inside the plant, employee newspaper articles, press releases, letters to the home, and materials for supervisory meetings are utilized to help the supervisors interpret the improved jobs to the employees.

In the best of companies, some products develop weaknesses, break down, and fail to give satisfaction. In the economic product field, these are referred to the product service department, which attempts to fix the product or replace it.

Likewise, enlightened managers, regardless of whether their plants are unionized or not, accept the responsibility for seeing to it that the job product is "right" and for establishing workable procedures to perform prompt "job-repair" service.

This is the marketing approach to industrial relations. Looked at in this light, a manager is able to give much better direction to his industrial relations activities because he is on familiar ground where he is competent and confident. Furthermore, in using this approach, he instantly sees the importance of using communication to keep his job customers sold on their jobs and less vulnerable to competitive advice to walk out, sit down, or strike.

In pursuing this job-marketing approach to employee relations, the General Electric Company surveyed the likes and dislikes of its employees and discovered that these were the principal features that they wanted in their jobs:

1. Good pay and benefits
2. Good working conditions
3. Steady work
4. Good bosses
5. Fair promotion practices
6. Respectful treatment
7. Full information
8. A belief in the importance of the job
9. Rewarding associations on the job

NOTE: These features are not listed in the order in which they are prized by employees. The Chamber of Commerce of the United States reports [1]

Employees of 24 different companies were asked to rate the following ten items in accordance with their importance to them individually. The first column below indicates the order of preference as indicated by employees; the second column, the order in which their foremen rated them. Note the degree to which the foremen, who theoretically should have the greatest understanding of the preferences of their subordinates, misjudged the things that count most with employees:

Job element	Employees' rating	Foremen's rating
Appreciation of work done	1	8
Feeling "in" on things (full information)	2	10
Help on personal problems	3	9
Job security (steady work)	4	2
Good wages	5	1
Interesting work (belief in importance of job)	6	5
Promotion	7	3
Management loyalty to workers	8	6
Good working conditions	9	4
Tactful disciplining (respectful treatment)	10	7

It is obvious that there is nothing in these employee preferences that is at variance with an enlightened company's policies and intent. Yet as every executive knows, there is often a wide disparity in the quality of the various job features as designed at top policymaking level and that which is received by the job customer or employee. The difference, of course, is in the unevenness of administration of personnel policies and practices by hundreds of supervisors and their neglect to sell the good features of the jobs provided

[1] *Economic Intelligence,* Chamber of Commerce of the United States, Economic Research Department, Washington, D.C., November, 1957.

by their company (an unevenness, by the way, which is rarely eliminated by the advent of a union).

THE IMPORTANCE OF MANAGER-MAN RELATIONSHIPS

Good employee relations are not achieved by enlightened policies administered collectively, rather they are a resultant of all the individual manager-man relationships developed between each supervisor and each employee supervised. The following constitutes the General Electric Company's *intentions* in the field of manager-man relationships. They are the essence of the company's "do-right-voluntarily" philosophy. They are taught in supervisory-training courses and constantly communicated to both supervisors and employees:

1. Treat employees with respect—don't push them around. Both by your manners and by your looks, show your interest in each employee as an individual and as an esteemed associate. Convey to him that he's important and needed.

2. Avoid favoritism, or the appearance of favoritism, like the plague. Play fair on your promotions, work assignments, overtime distribution.

3. Let each employee know what is expected of him and that you expect the best from him. Insist on high work standards.

4. Enforce fair, firm, and uniform discipline. This builds an atmosphere of security. (Give the employee the maximum latitude in performing his work—don't supervise him too closely—don't oversupervise him.)

5. Improve your ability to commend him and correct him.

6. Tell him in advance of changes that will affect or seem to affect him. Explain the reasons why.

7. Keep him informed on the things he should know about his job, his department, his company, and the economic facts of life.

8. Listen closely to what he's trying to tell you.

9. Be a man of your word—keep your promises.

10. Back up your men and give credit generously.

11. When he has personal troubles, be available and helpful.

12. Let each employee know regularly where he stands with you. Let him know "how he's doing."

13. Develop techniques for the reverse procedure; that is, determine where you stand with each of your employees. In other words, "How'm I Doing with My Associates?"

The first efforts of the author's company to plan, develop, and market its new nine-point job with its emphasis on manager-man relationships were directed at first-line supervision. A dramatic and intensive three-month training program was developed to train the supervisors to make sure that they properly gave all nine job elements to their associates and then to sell the superiority of the over-all product. The effort failed and rightly so. The foremen enthusiastically embraced the idea but then awakened to the painful realization that their own supervisors had not received the training. Not only was the second level of supervision failing to provide the nine-point job for the front-line supervisors, but it was failing to provide the permissive climate so vital to the success of the concept.

This failure led to a new approach. It started at the top and worked downward. The influence of the top officers was enlisted. "Do right voluntarily" became a guiding principle all down the line. Year by year by personal precept, by training, and by communication, the basic job product was improved and its good features communicated.

Progress was painfully slow and much more remains to be done. This is understandable. All progress in relations between human beings is slow. One only has to look at progress in family relations or international relations to realize the encouraging pioneering taking place in this and thousands of American business enterprises.

The supervisors did not quickly accept their responsibility for selling the improved job. Good deeds, they felt, spoke for themselves. The idea of having to keep pointing out the good content of the nine-point jobs was to them a strange, new, and questionable concept.

Educators tell us that learning takes place fastest when the new knowledge can be related to old knowledge or to currently accepted beliefs.

Dr. Claude Robinson, chairman of the board of the Opinion Research Corporation, and a strong advocate of the marketing approach to industrial relations, helped to facilitate the learning process and to gain management acceptance by advancing the following analogy:

In marketing economic products, he pointed out, American businessmen have been fabulously successful through following this simple formula:

$$X \text{ plus } Y \text{ equals } MA$$

where X is an economic product, Y is merchandising effort, that is, oral and printed selling, and MA is market acceptance.

The same formula, he states, obtains in selling a social product such as a job, in this case:

X (social product) plus Y (oral and printed selling) equals
EA (employee acceptance)

American businessmen are unexcelled in their ability to apply merchandising effort to an economic product. Why is it, then, that they have for so long overlooked the necessity of selling their social product—the material and human values of the jobs they provide, the unexcelled standard of living they have made possible?

The General Electric Company believes (and ceaselessly practices its belief) that communication has been one of the missing links in the failure of business to sell its social products—and that it is an indispensable supplement to the intelligent planning of, and design of, improved social products.

MARKETING A COMPANY'S SOCIAL PRODUCT

While trying constantly to improve its job product through market research and product planning, it keeps continuously communicating the results of this technology. Not uniformly and by no means as speedily as had been hoped, its supervisors at all levels, and particularly its top managers, are learning in ever-increasing numbers to communicate more articulately and effectively the values not only of the job product but of other social products which flow from the operation of the enterprise.

The company soon discovered that it had competition in selling its social product, every bit as intense (although too often lacking the ethics) as that encountered in the economic-product field. The segments of society which constitute this competition for the favor of employees communicate incessantly to the effect that business does not care for the welfare of the employees and does not share fairly the rewards of production.

Their sales arguments are familiar to all. Wages are too low, profits too high. Wages can be increased without price increases and in the absence of corresponding productivity increases. Wages should be paid according to a so-called ability-to-pay.

"Logic," [2] says Stuart Chase, "is the process of drawing a conclusion from one or more statements or propositions, called premises. If the premises are assumed to be true—whether they are or not—the logic can be technically correct" (and the conclusion false).

Because of the economic illiteracy of too many of the American people, a long list of specious economic premises are assumed to be true. But rather than fight the perfectly logical conclusions that are drawn, we must go to the core of the problem and correct the misinformation which is the basis of widely held premises.

The author's company accordingly came to the conclusion that all of its good deeds (X) and the communication thereof (Y) would fail unless (1) its deeds would, in fact, measure up to sound economic analysis; (2) unless it could somehow help its employees understand the rudiments of business economics; and (3) unless its employees had some sound basis for evaluating the fairness of the countless decisions the company had to make if it was to continue to operate in the balanced best interests of its employees, its

[2] Stuart Chase, *Guides to Straight Thinking*, Harper & Brothers, New York, 1956.

customers, its share owners, its suppliers and distribution associates, and the rest of the public.

The methods being employed to explain the relationship of wages, prices, taxes, profits, savings, capital risk, retained earnings, productivity, and standard of living, etc., are not unlike those employed by an ever-growing number of businesses and are not within the scope of this book. Suffice it to say that although massive one-shot courses in economics are helpful for initial orientation of employees, best results are obtained when the economics of the business are integrated into all the media of communication as a business way of life.

A CASE STUDY IN FORTHRIGHT COMMUNICATION

The Timken Roller Bearing Company is another of the rapidly growing list of companies which imaginatively utilizes a skillful employee and community communication program to merchandise a highly successful employee relations program.

Herbert E. Markley, Timken's assistant to the president, describes the program in the simple, forthright, powerful language that characterizes all of this company's employee communication.[3]

We have approached employee relations as we would any other (management) problem; that is, to treat it positively. . . . We are convinced that planning in this field must be just as forward and as imaginative as in a sales program or in the designing and manufacturing of a product. This means that we have to be looking years ahead and not just to the end of the next negotiations.

We think our employees, their families and the public must be informed about the results, implications and consequences to them of any course of action the company may follow either voluntarily or from being forced by a union.

A further conviction which we have is that well-informed employees will act in a way which contributes to our mutual best interest. We intend to see they are informed. The public is also interested in what a large employer in the community does. The influence of a neighbor on an

[3] *Vital Speeches of the Day,* June, 1957, p. 532.

employee cannot be discounted. Our hope is that trouble can be avoided by expecting people to reason logically if they have the facts. If in spite of all efforts trouble still comes, it may be minimized if employees and the public have a complete understanding of the circumstances.

. . . it is possible to sell the company just as well as we sell products. . . . This kind of approach cannot begin just before negotiations. It must go on continuously so that employees learn to have confidence in what management says.

After describing in detail how his company develops its employee relations program and continuously interprets it through communication, Mr. Markley lists the following results attributable to the harnessing of good deeds and forthright interpretation:

1. Because we regard a contract as just that, we have not lost a day in wildcat strikes since 1946.

2. We avoided the industry strike of 1956 and the short one of 1955. Even in 1952 one of our unionized mills continued to work. The local president himself worked throughout.

3. We have been able to keep out of our contract any kind of clause providing for union participation in management decisions.

4. Our productivity has improved.

5. Employees and citizens in the community are now saying to us they are beginning to see the wisdom of many of the things we have done, where once they criticized.

6. We believe our program has helped to improve living standards of our employees and of others in the community who benefit indirectly.

7. Our new employees still have a choice of whether or not to be a union member.

8. Our customers have benefited by uninterrupted deliveries.

9. Our stockholders have benefited by reduction in work stoppages and the profits made from increased sales to customers to whom deliveries were made without interruption.

In summary, the pattern of two companies which have developed a unique "theory of the case" in their employee relations, may be capsuled as follows:

1. Develop and practice a code of conduct for relations with employees; that is, "do right voluntarily."

2. Constantly redesign the job package (X) to encompass the maximum expectations of the job customers within the economic limitations imposed on management as a trustee for all the contributor-claimants of the business. Pay particular attention to the nonfinancial features (fair promotion practices, full information, good bosses, etc.).

3. Constantly interpret the constantly maintained good features of the product through the most modern merchandising methods, with heavy reliance on mass communication (Y).

4. Combat all spurious sales arguments by anyone seeking to mislead employees both by direct factual rebuttal and by developing the wider economic awareness which can equip the employees to evaluate wisely.

CHAPTER 5

Use of Communication in Union Relations

How extensively and how skillfully a manager uses communication in the conduct of his union relations depends upon a number of factors.

1. The type of union that represents his employees.
2. The type of contract.
3. The pattern of collective bargaining. Does he bargain independently with his union or is he circumscribed by industry-wide bargaining such as is prevalent in the steel and other industries?
4. Whether the employees place their major reliance and trust in the union or the managers that represent them.
5. Whether there is a gentlemen's agreement not to communicate before or during negotiations.
6. Whether there is an agreement to communicate jointly always.
7. The tradition, or lack of it, of communicating to employees on any and all subjects.
8. The willingness to permit the union to seize the initiative in communicating with employees and the public.

A common phenomenon on the American collective-bargaining scene is the utilization of advance and skillful communication by certain union officialdom to precondition employees, the public, government officials, and employers themselves to the inevitability of radical new demands for guaranteed annual wages, shorter work week, profit sharing, and rebates to customers before taxes, etc. Negotiations are aggressively conducted by such union officials in

50

the newspapers long before the gathering around the bargaining table. In the face of this, the employers too often remain silent despite the fact that their employees are anxious to learn their views regardless of whether they will find themselves in agreement.

Because these factors, as well as management philosophies and practices vary so widely, there is no one standard pattern of communication among American companies.

THE ORTHODOX PATTERN OF COLLECTIVE BARGAINING

In order to obtain the background requisite for a consideration of communication tactics, it may be useful to examine two widely varying schools of collective bargaining philosophies.

These two divergent philosophies have been compared by Allen Weisenfeld, secretary of the New Jersey State Board of Mediation, and Monroe Berkowitz, assistant professor of economics at Rutgers University, in an analysis entitled: "A New Look in Collective Bargaining." [1]

The authors first describe the orthodox method of collective bargaining which has been historically employed by the majority of employers as follows:

Collective bargaining has been likened to a theatrical production—it has many of the aspects of a play. Generally, it takes place in three acts. It has overtones of comedy and undertones of tragedy. It frequently has both a hero and a villain. It begins sedately and crescendos to a climax.

Typically, the first act of the collective bargaining play opens with the presentation of union demands. These are fully discussed in an atmosphere that is reasonably free from tension. The second act deals with the "shaking down" of the issues. The company makes its reply to the union demands. Most of them it rejects, some it accepts and on others, it moves forward tentatively. Progress is evident, though possibly slow. Tension mounts as the deadline of contract negotiations approaches.

Act three is, of course, the climax of the production. The demands

[1] "New Vistas in Mediation," *Proceedings of the Fourth Annual Conference, Association of State Mediation Agencies*, Ithaca, N.Y., June, 1955.

which the union had initially presented for trading purposes, and perhaps because political exigency indicated their presentation, are narrowed to "this is the least we'll take." The company's initial offers presented in Act Two are now dressed up in a "package" representing substantially the company's best response to the union. The differences between the union's "rock bottom" offer and the company's "package" remain to be hammered out. Positions are firming; stalemate appears inevitable. In the closing moments of the drama, it is not infrequent for a government mediator to enter the scene, after which, by dint of his efforts and some hard bargaining by the parties, an agreement is reached and a treaty guaranteeing peace for a fixed period of time is signed. The play is over. It is a success. The respective parties return to the workaday world.

Most companies have been satisfied with this state of affairs. Once the contract is concluded, management heaves a sigh of relief and is content to turn its attention to production, sales and more serious problems.

This, of course, is an oversimplification of orthodox collective bargaining, but essentially it is a rather accurate chronology of a widely employed union relations procedure. Obviously, communication is sparingly used, and it is stereotyped. A brief announcement of impending negotiations, heated oral and written communication between the bargaining agents, an occasional report to employees, either singly or jointly, depending upon prior agreement, and an announcement of a *fait accompli*, namely, the agreement or the final results of the haggling. Weisenfeld and Berkowitz then proceed to describe the opposite end of the negotiating pole which they term "a new look."

A MATURE APPROACH TO COLLECTIVE BARGAINING

More recently, however, a new management philosophy has made its appearance. This "new look" in collective bargaining threatens to tear the traditional script into shreds and substitute an entirely new plot which violates all the dramatic unities. . . . This is something much more than a new negotiating technique; if it can be carried through, it promises to revolutionize collective bargaining and, perhaps, the whole position of unions in the economy.

Weisenfeld and Berkowitz call Lemuel R. Boulware "the recognized leader in this new management movement."

Because of the increasing economic impact upon our society of the consequences of the "old-look" collective-bargaining processes, it is important to all students of industrial management and labor economics to here record the facts concerning what is sincerely believed to be—and which in effect has proved to be—a more mature approach to the collective-bargaining process. The following description of the General Electric Company's collective-bargaining philosophy and the key role played by communication is excerpted from a comprehensive documentation of the process entitled "Year End Review in Employee, Plant Community and Union Relations" published December 31, 1954, and distributed to all management personnel.

We think all this [the historic three-act approach to collective bargaining] is out of keeping with the change from bargaining as a "class struggle" to bargaining as a joint search for what is accurately and honestly in the fair and balanced best interests of all concerned.

To be sure, some may yet for a while associate bargaining with horse trading, or with downright deceit, or with the flea-bitten eastern bazaar type of cunning and dishonest but rather pointless haggling.

But the objective of competent and honorable "collective bargaining" is for employees to get for their individual contribution no less and no more than what is fairly coming to them in keeping with what is the balanced best interests of all.

Thus, our bargaining has as its objective the most mature approach possible by management and union representatives; to arrive at the facts and then take the action which will be in the balanced best interests of all. We don't want any more or any less than what's right for anybody. We are seeking the facts and sound conclusions. We don't care where the facts come from, or when. We are not concerned with credit or face-saving. We just want to do right.

We have to be fair with all the union officials involved. In the first place, any favor to one over the other would be unfair to the other officials—no matter how big or small is the bargaining group involved. And, also, any variation that resulted in our treating one group of employees unfairly for what they do at their jobs, as compared with any or all the other groups of employees, would certainly be a very unfair or incompetent or unfortunate kind of bargaining.

When it comes to making offers, the only way we know to do this ably and honorably is:

. . . to study all the evidence all year long as to employee compensation and benefits,

. . . to study all the applicable union statements made meanwhile,

. . . to listen to the union demands made in negotiation,

. . . to consider carefully these demands along with all other old and new information available or that may become available,

. . . to make our offerings at the proper time and voluntarily include absolutely everything our research from all sources, including unions, has indicated should be included to measure up to what's fully right by every reasonable standard,

. . . to discuss fully with the unions, and

. . . to make promptly any modifications in our offers that are indicated as right by any new light on the subject from any source.

Incidentally, we are always freshly amazed when a top union official now and then will claim—despite his direct experiences with us—that this is a "take it or leave it" program and that our efforts at "doing right voluntarily" represent some sort of challenge to the whole usefulness and survival of unions. For nothing could be farther from the facts.

In the first place, this is no "take it or leave it" program as the experience of every union official with it must make him admit to himself. Every one of our offers has stated we would be glad to change on learning of any valid reason why we should—and that was the truth, as proved in practice. One of the early offers was accepted within a day or two for the surprisingly and completely acceptable offer it was. But in every other case we can now recall, we have made any number of modifications in our original offer—some substantial, some minor.

What one particular group of top officials is really complaining about is that we voluntarily come so close to what's obviously right that they can't make it appear that we have been dragged unwillingly to make substantial changes through pure force. Apparently they want us to adopt the outmoded "cooperating" method of making a very low offer we would know is not right and then be publicly bludgeoned up to what's right.

We believe there is no demand on them [top union officials], from the employees, to stage a great emotional or political victory to get more than what is right or more than is willingly available if that's right. We believe—and we think our employees believe—that any good union official of theirs has a better and nobler function to perform than trying to persuade or force us to help fool our employees about something we are perfectly willing to do and should be fired if we weren't willing to do.

Communicating a company's determination

A key feature in the successful (up until the present) application of this philosophy has been a clearly announced and proved determination of the company to take a strike rather than to be forced to do what is not believed to be right. On its attitude toward strikes, the "Review" has this to say:

We do our level best to see that no employee ever has a valid reason to strike—and we mean "valid reason" from *his* standpoint on the basis of all the facts.

Yet we would defend to the last our employee's right to strike voluntarily of his own choice—regardless of how we may have failed to convince him of what we believe to be the facts.

But likewise, if the strike instrument is available to the one for what he feels is a just cause, the other should also be permitted to stand the strike in order to keep from being forced to do what he believes to be wrong for the balanced best interests of all those for whom he is responsible.

The real complaint is that the strikes called here by the official in question have been unrewarding. But that has been because, when all the initial charges and emotions have had a chance to clear up, our employees and their families and neighbors have realized the issues had been misrepresented or misunderstood and the strikes were not the kind of activity they thought proper in their own interest as well as in the interests of others affected.

To try to clear up the misinformation at such times we take as a matter of honorable duty.

The codification of the company's philosophy on collective bargaining ends on this hopeful note:

We are particularly impressed with the new generation of union leaders now coming up through the local ranks where we do have unions. They are intimately conversant with what we are trying to do to lay a foundation for peaceful fair-dealing and rewarding association with employees and with employee representatives who are businesslike. . . .

They give every evidence of welcoming the higher grade pursuit thus opening to them as the dignified and responsible representative who can look forward to dealing in unemotional and accurate facts as opposed to any necessity or fashion of conducting themselves in the old rabble-rousing manner amid the old false charges that we in management are greedy and brutal and have to be bludgeoned into doing any least thing that is good. . . .

From men of this type we hope will soon emerge the kind of top union leadership which will match the growing knowledge, sophistication and maturity of their membership and will live up to their great opportunity for good as opposed to following the less constructive paths of some of their predecessors.

Our entire program of mutual study and public discussion of the facts—and of honest, forthright, non-artful bargaining—is intended to encourage the development and aid the influence of such honest, direct and responsible union leaders. In contrast, our program is bound to be somewhat discouraging to any who want to go back to the old double-standard or "flea-bitten eastern bazaar" type of bargaining. . . .

. . . there is every reason why both parties will eventually come to the bargaining table with a fairly common set of facts about a common objective—with both sides later frankly stating publicly that they found themselves initially in such admittedly substantial agreement that they only had to work out the remaining small differences in an atmosphere of confidence and good will.

There have been some companies which have attempted to apply this type of bargaining to their own situation very much as one might apply a new façade to a building. The results have been disastrous because of failure to understand that employee confidence is essential and can be gained only by constantly trying to earn that confidence by deeds as well as words.

The innovator of the "new look" is dedicated to the policy of *trying* to "do right voluntarily" in its relations with its employees. This is not to imply that employees unvaryingly receive the full range of job satisfaction that the company intends they shall receive. Any manager knows only too well that a company's policies in the field of human relations are vitally dependent upon their administration at all levels of supervision and that supervisors, being human, will make mistakes or commit sins of omission when production pressures harass them.

The General Electric Company, however, is so deeply committed to the "do-right-voluntarily" policy from the top down, and works so hard at implementing it that the employees have quite consistently given the company a vote of confidence when national union officials have conducted a vote for a company-wide strike which, for a time, was almost annually.

A keynote of "new look" collective bargaining is *direct communication by management to employees* in order that they may be equipped to render independent judgment rather than being dependent exclusively on union sources.

Taking the issues to the employees

Don G. Mitchell, chairman and president, Sylvania Electric Products, Inc., has also stressed the need for greater management attention to employee relations and communication if it wishes to attain constructive union relations.[2]

[Today] it is more important than ever that employers distinguish between union relations and employee relations. It is true that the collective bargaining process must be carried on with a representative of the employees, but any employer who neglects employee relations as a separate subject, and who fails to be sure that his employees know the position that he takes on every issue, on every proposal, and on every phase of employee relations through a well-organized, well-maintained communication system, is going to increase the power of the labor union in his plant.

[2] Don G. Mitchell, "Address before the National Electrical Manufacturers Association," Atlantic City, N.J., Nov. 15, 1955.

The employer, in short, must not only deserve the confidence of his employees through his deeds, but he must provide them with reliable information to help them evaluate whether they are being dealt with fairly.

The role of communication in this pioneering approach to union relations is a key one indeed.

All through the year leading up to contract negotiations, the author's company communicates the good features of its jobs and its relations policies and its avowed intent to keep them up to top competitive standards. Salaries, wages, benefit plans, working conditions, promotion practices, and other features are compared with community and area standards.

In the best traditions of product marketing, every ethical opportunity is utilized to interpret the true value of the product (the pay, benefits, job security, human relations, etc.), and management's constant goal to improve the value. When a large order is received, in the face of particularly intense competition, it is interpreted in terms of the number of man-hours of work it will provide as well as the additional sales revenue involved. (There is no better way to teach the economics underlying management's continuing efforts to stabilize employment and create more jobs.) Upgradings of employees are publicized to emphasize management's desire to provide each employee with the opportunity to go as far as his talents and drive will permit. And so forth. This continual in-between-bargaining communication is also projected into the community.

Before negotiations, the company runs an advertisement in its employee house organs and the local city press. This message gives the date of the approaching negotiations, reaffirms the company's intent to do what is considered right for the employees, and reaffirms that no amount of pressure will cause it to do what is considered harmful to the balanced best interests of all claimants to the results of the company's operations.

Bargaining is conducted in the bright light of full publicity. Each evening the company sends a release to all interested segments of the press describing what happened during the day. Each evening—

or even during the day—the same material, in expanded form, is sent in a special management bulletin to key members of management down through the foreman level.

When the company has listened to the union's proposals and explanations for some weeks and then finally makes its offer to the unions, it is immediately publicized widely and dramatically in every conceivable in-plant and community medium of communication.

Both unions and employees are informed that the offer can become effective as of a given future date, provided the company and union representatives reach agreement on it within the announced period and work out appropriate adjustments of details. If a union does not sign by the announced effective date, the offer will become effective as of the subsequent date agreement is reached.

Very often one or more unions will fail to reach agreement—hoping by delaying or by threat of strike action to force additional concessions that will be competitively valuable in the political careers of the union officials. The company then takes the facts of the issue directly to the people with a full-scale communication program—informative in-plant meetings with employees, feature articles in house organs, letters to the homes, ads in the city press, etc.

The union officials, of course, counter with their particular kind of communication. This communication rather frequently tends toward intemperate language, transparent distortions, and extravagant claims in contrast with the more conservative, factual, and temperate communication of management. One union official has candidly remarked that employees realize that managers have to tell the truth and that, therefore, they are more inclined to believe management's reporting. As a result, the pressure on local union officials by employees who are convinced that the offer is a good one tends to bring earlier agreement on a contract.

When the contracts are signed, this company tries to keep its managers from reverting in joyous relief to their "metal-cutting and paper-shuffling" activities to the exclusion of continuing to carry out their relations responsibilities. It knows only too well that its employees will once again sit in judgment at the next bargaining session and will trust or withhold their trust in management to the degree that this trust has been earned.

"NEW-LOOK BARGAINING" BY A SMALL COMPANY

Many observers of this "new-look" union relations philosophy have commented that it can work only if the company practicing it is large, has contracts with a considerable number of unions, and is diversified both in product mix and plant location.

Let us, therefore, look at the conduct of union relations by a small company with one union, a homogeneous product, and only two plants.

The Gardner Board and Carton Company had two plants about 30 miles apart, one in Middletown, Ohio, and the other in Lockland, Ohio. It employed slightly more than 2,000 people equally divided between the two plants. Its employees were represented by an international CIO union which proved itself a strong union in its dealings with the company.

After the orthodox, old-look, collective-bargaining techniques had produced a steadily worsening situation despite the most conciliatory efforts of the management to develop constructive relations, the company "took a completely different approach to (its) labor relations." But let Vice-president Colin Gardner III tell it in his own words:

Instead of talking only to the union and passing on to them the responsibility of influencing our people, we decided we would talk directly to our people and make popular or understandable to them, the things we wished to accomplish, and let *them* influence the union. That was the most basic change in our new approach to Industrial Relations. We thought that if we did a *sound, fair* and *intelligent* job of developing our *policies* and the reasons therefor, we would get *employee* understanding or acceptance of them.

Effecting such a change necessitated quite a different philosophy of management in our company in one very important area. This was in the field of communicating with *our employees and other segments of the public* where we felt our leadership should be reasserted. Our new philosophy which had finally evolved as a result of these experiences, was founded on two fundamental principles: First, *living right*—which we had always tried to do. Second, telling our employees about it—WHICH WE HAD "NEVER" DONE.

Now to me, "living right" means doing at least three basic things:

1. Providing the leadership for employees by recognizing and dealing with their social and economic problems.

2. Recognizing that management must *live the truth*. This means that *when* management provides the leadership, it *must* take the responsibility *and credit* for its actions and not permit that credit to go by *default or intent* to any other group, nor shall it take any credit which is *not* deserved.

And in order to tell employees about how the management was performing, we had to recognize that they had a right to know the truth about those things which affect them, including our collective bargaining attitudes and proposals.

3. Recognizing that it is a responsibility of management to establish techniques to accomplish this. In other words, management must *tell the truth* that it is living, and keep employees informed about *what* it is doing and *why*.

So, we set about to develop a management organization at *all* levels, capable of providing the leadership for our employees. This involved, among other things, developing the abilities to influence employee thinking, particularly on matters which relate to the successful and continuing operation of the company. This we planned to accomplish through an adequate and effective system of communication. We felt this was *vital* to the success of our program.

The magnitude of the job and the need for consistent and constant daily application of the techniques of communication made it mandatory that the job be assigned to line management people, who had regular contacts with the employees. Therefore, the front-line supervisor is the *key* to our program. He is the contact between our people and the executive management. He is our salesman. Our entire organization above and beside him is dedicated to helping him . . . in addition, we select all new foremen primarily for their characteristics of integrity and leadership and train them in the technical knowledge—it is easier.

Now these same basic policies are also applied throughout the course of negotiating a contract. We take the initiative. We normally exchange proposals with the union at the first bargaining meeting.

We communicate actively with our employees all during the negotiations. This is done in two ways. The first and foremost way is oral communications between the foreman and his employees. The second way is *written communications*. For example, just before the opening of negotiations for a new contract last year, I wrote a letter to all employees which said in part:

"To ALL LOCKLAND HOURLY-PAID PEOPLE:

"On November 30, the contract between the company and the CIO Paperworkers Union Local 1009 will expire. Meetings to talk over a new contract will start next week. The first meeting will be on Friday, October 15th. There will be other meetings after that for the same purpose. When we meet on Friday, the company will make proposals to be included in a new contract. We will not hold anything back to be used later for 'horse trading.' We don't bargain that way. We believe you and your union representatives are entitled to know right from the start what our full proposal is on any matter . . . we will let you know what our proposals are as soon as we've talked them over with the union. . . ."

Now these communications also deal with the controversial issues of bargaining. [Space does not permit reviewing more of these excellent letters as bargaining progressed.]

. . . In addition to these letters, we provide our entire management organization with daily fact sheets during periods of negotiations, which report completely and specifically on each day's developments.

Our foremen pass this information on to employees, carefully detailing the management's position and the reasons therefor.

All of our superintendents and at least *one foreman* from each of our five main departments at Lockland attend our bargaining meetings. This gives them a first-hand view of the bargaining developments. This puts them on at least an equal basis with the union representatives who are present at the bargaining. It also serves to give the management bargaining group the benefit of the advice and counsel of our foremen and superintendents who have to live with the results of our bargaining. We also meet with *all* of our foremen between negotiating sessions for the purpose of ascertaining employee views on the company's position and conveying to them any new developments which may have occurred in-between bargaining meetings.

Now *you* must know that such an aggressive policy and method of operation raises some very pertinent questions, namely, what is the reaction of union leaders to such efforts on the part of our management? Don't they resent it and get angry and hence destroy any friendly relationships which might otherwise exist between these union leaders and our management?

Yes, certainly they do get angry, and resist, but they don't stay angry long because, as all of you know, unions are basically political in nature and their leaders cannot long afford to fight with management, when that is *not* the popular thing to do.

So in our company, when the management is right and produces the best solutions, our foremen have been able to sell these to the people in our plants, who do not then want their union leaders opposing such constructive actions on the part of management.

Now, simply making such a statement carries little weight, so let me illustrate with an example of something which took place in our plants after our negotiations for a new contract reached an impasse. The union officers, bargaining committee, and international representative recommended to the union membership that they reject our proposals. This was tantamount to a strike vote since the company had refused to extend the contract. Considering all the facts available to them, the union membership voted down the recommendations of their leaders and instructed them to sign the contract with us.

These union leaders were certainly angry. But yet three months after the conclusion of those negotiations, when we were badly in need of help at our Cincinnati plant, the union leaders came to us and asked if they could help us recruit. They told us that they wanted to run an ad in one of the local newspapers over their name, urging people to work at Gardner. We said we would appreciate their doing that. Let me show you that ad. [See Figure 1.]

That ad was written by the same man who led our strike in 1947, a man who was elected the president of the union in 1952 on a militant platform, and who still attacks us whenever he feels it is good politics to do so. But politically, it was popular for him to offer to help the management. Now we know he made more friends by doing this than he ever made by all the nasty letters he has ever written the management before or since, or the destructive actions he had taken from time to time to embarrass us. We do not believe that union leaders can effectively oppose a constructive, conscientious, honest, and fair management when the membership of their union *want* them to cooperate with such a management.

Here, again, we see the use of the basic formula (X plus Y equals EA) so successfully employed by managers in marketing their eco-

ATTENTION!
HELP WANTED!

The Gardner Board and Carton Company, one of Miami Valley's most thriving industrial establishments is in need of additional employees, both male and female, for their Lockland, Ohio Plants.

Few companies have as much to offer new employees as Gardner. Things worthy of your consideration available to Gardner employees are:

- A HISTORY OF STEADY YEAR ROUND WORK
- GOOD WAGES
- GOOD OPPORTUNITY AF- FORDED TO QUALIFIED EMPLOYEES FOR ADVANCEMENT
- HOSPITALIZATION INSURANCE
- GROUP LIFE INSURANCE
- AN EXCELLENT VACATION PAY PLAN
- SENIORITY RIGHTS

- ADDITIONAL COMPENSA- TION FOR WORKING NIGHT SHIFTS
- PAID HOLIDAYS
- JURY PAY SUPPLEMENTED
- EMERGENCY CALL IN PAY
- EMPLOYEES RETIREMENT PLAN
- PAID WASH UP PERIODS
- COST OF LIVING PAY PLAN FOR ALL

In addition to the above, Gardner employees have the added security of excellent Union-Company labor relations established through courteous administration and policing of sound Labor-Management principles and policies. The security and protection of a Collective Bargaining Agreement recently negotiated and signed by the Company and the Union to continue in effect for two years.

To people desirous of worthwhile steady employment, we unreservedly recommend Gardners at Lockland. The plants are located on Cooper Avenue, one block south of Lockland City Hall, Lockland, Ohio.

United Paperworkers of America
Local Union No. 1009, C. I. O.

Figure 1

nomic products, but strangely, so seldom used in marketing their social products: i.e., their philosophy, ideology, position, call it what you will.

All through the period leading up to negotiations, Gardner tries to live right (X, the product) and communicates (Y, the interpretation). Early in negotiations it makes the best offer (X) it believes it can in the best-balanced interests of all its contributor groups; then it communicates directly to its employees (Y) with signal success.

The key – direct communication to employees

If space permitted, the favorable experience of other companies in conducting collective bargaining on a base of full, free communication directly to employees could be cited. Yet these are the exception. Too many companies have turned over to their unions the leadership implicit in communication.

In summary, good human relations practices, continuously interpreted, are the foundation of successful collective bargaining. No manager can hope to communicate effectively unless he has established the climate, the rapport, the requisite credibility through consistently demonstrating that he does indeed care and that he intends to share fairly the rewards of production.

There is no magic in communication that will dispel deserved employee distrust of employers. "Confidence cannot be achieved by simple resort to selling techniques. The basic product must be worthy of the selling program if communication is to become truly a New Management Dimension." [3]

[3] Virgil B. Day, manager, union relations service, General Electric Company, "The Philosophy of Doing Right Voluntarily," Michigan State College, Personnel Institute Conference, October, 1954.

CHAPTER 6

Use of Communication in Improving
Community Relations

One of the prime attributes of a successful manager is his ability to operate with a proper balance of short- and long-range objectives. One of the more important long-range objectives is the development of sound community relations.

No matter how assiduously and wisely a manager conducts his employee relations inside the plant gates, he will fail unless he simultaneously invests the time and money required to develop deserved and favorable community attitudes toward the results of his operations as well as the means employed to achieve those results.

Let us see why this is so. Our employee, Bill, leaves the plant at 4 P.M. and heads for home and supper feeling rather good about his job, his boss, his associates, and his company (X plus Y equals EA).[1] After supper he drops in at one of the several community social organizations, or groups, of which he is a member and starts to communicate his satisfaction concerning the outfit that employs him. If the members of his group do not share his enthusiasm for his company, they quickly deflate him. He becomes insecure. Only the most rugged individualists can go counter to the norms of their groups. The almost universal tendency is to conform.

Whenever community neighbors are uninformed, through neglect

[1] X (good job) plus Y (interpretive communication) equals EA (Employee Acceptance).

of communication, or misinformed, through the communication of competition, we find this outside attrition of good in-plant relations occurring.

Business managers are discovering that it is impossible to operate a plant successfully without first deserving and then developing the respect, understanding, and approval of the local community. [X (good corporate citizen) plus Y (communication) equals CA (Community Acceptance).]

Community relations has been defined as "the management function which appraises and interprets community attitudes, identifies and relates company policies to community interests, initiates programs of action to earn for the company the respect and confidence of the community, and actively shapes conditions of mutual advantage to the community and to business."

Analyses of the most successful community relations programs reveal this four-step pattern of conduct and communication:

1. Live right inside the plant
2. Tell employees
3. Live right in the community
4. Tell the community

The "live-right-in-plant" course of conduct was explained in Chapter 4, as was the necessity for interpreting management's social products to the employees. It is repeated here for solid reasons. Recently a company that had been carrying on a most intensive and constructive community relations activity called in a group of social scientists to measure the results of its work. To its surprise, it found, despite its expenditures in mass communication, that the favorable attitudes toward the company had been largely shaped by word-of-mouth selling by satisfied employees.

Experienced managers know that good employee relations are the prerequisite of good community relations.

But good employee relations are not enough. Employees need the reassurance of their families and groups that their faith in their employer is well founded.

Hence the necessity to live right in the community. The business enterprise which sets out to earn the respect and approval of the community must live right by these criteria. It must be, in fact:

1. A good employer of local labor, so planning and running the business that it achieves maximum stabilization of employment

2. A friendly hospitable employer—granting *all* applicants for employment a fair, tactful, courteous interview—applying the same rules of courtesy to visitors as to guests in one's home

3. A good housekeeper, maintaining a clean plant in neat surroundings and with a systematic plan for abatement of offensive smoke, noise, odors, or waste products

4. A buyer of goods and services locally, to the maximum degree that is prudent

5. A good taxpayer, demanding justice but no bargains

6. A generous but not paternalistic contributor to local charities and capital fund drives

7. A good corporate citizen—actively participating to achieve good government, good schools, good churches, etc., and taking an active role in helping achieve a better community

8. A company which encourages all its employees to assume their individual citizenship responsibilities

But even such a code of corporate community conduct is not enough. Community-attitude surveys usually reveal that an action program of this type will fail to achieve a widespread, favorable reputation for the sponsor unless each aspect of the program is communicated continuously and skillfully.

The General Electric Company recommends to each of its plant managers a twelve-point communication program in order properly to merchandise the local plant's live-right efforts.

A brief enlargement of each of these techniques of communication to the community may be helpful.

1. Periodic opinion surveys to determine community likes and dislikes

The community-attitude survey is the starting step in any soundly planned community relations program. Just as the employer utilizes market research experts to study the needs and preferences of his market before planning any new product, so should he utilize market research techniques to appraise the attitudes of the community before designing any remedial action program.

The neighbors to be polled are selected on a scientific random sampling basis. The polling is done through personally conducted depth interviews. However, if expense is a serious factor, quite satisfactory results may be obtained through a mail questionnaire which has previously been tested through its limited use in personal interviews.

Many companies publicize the survey in the local press in advance of the starting date and a complete report of the findings is featured in the same media. The survey results are likewise communicated to the employees through in-plant media.

The question asked should be tailored to suit the requirements of the employer, but in general, consideration should be given to the following categories:

1. The adequacy of the company's wages and salaries
2. Awareness of the company's individual benefit plans and how they compare with those of other local employers
3. Extent and relative generosity of company and employee contributions to local charities
4. Extent and quality of company's participation in civic activities; ditto for its employees
5. Knowledge and acceptance of products or services produced
6. Community's appraisal of quality of products or services
7. Steadiness of work
8. Quality of labor relations
9. Quality of working conditions
10. Sources of most accurate information concerning company
11. Solicitation of spontaneous comments

NOTE: Employers who have acquired requisite skills through experience in community polling can personally conduct such surveys periodically to measure trends. An interesting variation of this "do-it-yourself" technique is the use of local teachers as the interviewers during the holiday seasons or summer vacation. This results in a valuable by-product, inasmuch as this important segment of the local public acquires a firsthand knowledge of the function and policies of a local business enterprise.

A survey of community attitudes is indispensable because of the clues it provides for better direction of the community relations program. However, as will be discussed in the next chapter, it must be supplemented by a complete appraisal of the business climate in the local community and state. Only in this manner can we formulate objectives and plans that will enable the business enterprise to measure up to its full potential for service in the community.

In essence, the community survey is a planned effort to discover how much your neighbors know about you, how they feel about you, and in what ways they would prefer to have you act differently. It provides a partial basis for your remedial program and a partial bench mark for measuring your community relations performance.

2. Interpreting your business to specific community groups

The skilled community relations practitioner tailors his communication to the specialized interests of specific local publics. Let us observe the operation of such a program with a typical local group, the educators, for example.

The starting point is a sincere interest in the problems and aspirations of this group and an earnest desire to be helpful from *their* point of view. Both employers and employees should actively support all worthy efforts to improve the educational facilities of the community and the quality, compensation, and status of the teachers. They should be encouraged to affiliate with and be actively constructive in school boards and PTA's. Many communities sponsor education-business days in which businessmen personally visit the schools to observe the quality of the faculty, the facilities, and the curriculum and to obtain a firsthand knowledge of the local school problems. Employers should vigorously participate in these education-business days.

The employer who makes this initial investment in understanding and empathy for this important community public is then in a position to solicit this group's interest and understanding of *his* problems and goals.

He can put the educators on his mailing list to receive his employee publication. He can mail, periodically, pamphlets which create a fuller understanding of his goals and accomplishments; he can solicit eager cooperation in the development of better and more adequate vocational training. Periodically, he can invite the teachers in a group to a plant visitation where they can observe firsthand his working conditions and the huge investment required to provide a job for a single employee. He can explain his benefit plans, his need for special skills in local graduates, the need for, and the role of, adequate profits.

He can do this job as an individual employer or he can participate in a group employer effort common in many communities which is known as business-education day. In this practice, the educators are divided into groups, each group being assigned to a specific employer's plant.

Solo or cooperatively, a prime requisite in planning is to provide ample opportunity for the frankest questioning by the educators.

A successful community relations program will embrace just such careful individual treatment of the clergy, physicians, dentists, lawyers, merchants, local government officials, and any other groups whose understanding, approval, and support for the local enterprise are sought.

3. Periodic mailing of pertinent information to civic thought leaders

Progressive employers maintain a civic mailing list for distribution of the company house organ, illustrative product and policy booklets, descriptions of benefit plans, significant speeches by company officials, and forthright expressions of employer views on any matter affecting the welfare of the company or the community, no matter how controversial.

4. Good relations with the local press, radio, and TV

Of prime importance to a successful community relations program is an understanding of the needs and unique problems of these mass conveyors of news and information to the local publics. No trouble should be spared to see that representatives of these media get, to the maximum degree practical, what they want when they want it. Of great aid to local editors is a list of home telephone numbers of a number of designated company spokesmen to aid the reporters in checking material after the plant is closed for the day.

Plant managers should be taught that the words, "no comment" are taboo and represent a priceless opportunity missed. Taboo also should be the pompous, hollow cliché, "a company spokesman stated. . . ." Can you picture any antibusiness spokesman missing a chance to sponsor, over his name, an opportunity to present his case or rebut the employer's case? They know that names make news!

5. Local newspaper advertising

The wise employer will supplement the news coverage accorded him (when his releases are *newsworthy*) with periodic paid advertisements in the local newspapers.

He will do this because only in this manner can the employer place a full unaltered presentation of an important message before the readers.

Some of the more progressive employers publish an annual report to their community neighbors in the form of a full-page newspaper advertisement. Titled with some such headline as, "Here's What the Kay-Ess Company and Its 1,200 Employees Meant to the Community Last Year," it presents a sectionalized illustrated story on wages, benefits, charitable contributions, civic activities, research, new products, etc. This is a dramatic and highly effective application of merchandising effort to the "live-right" course of conduct.

Other suitable subjects for newspaper ads are explanations of new contract settlements, invitations to open houses, wholesome effects on employees and community of the company's benefit programs, advance notification and economic reasons for impending layoffs, recruitment of employees, appeals to community for support in labor disputes, threatened strikes, secondary boycotts, illegal picketing, etc.

NOTE: The farsighted employer never waits until he is in trouble to initiate the use of any of these communication media in the community. He should expect little audience attention or interest in any medium unless he has used it naturally in normal times.

6. Radio and television

Local radio time is so relatively inexpensive that any plant, no matter how small, can justify its use as an institutional medium of communication. Many plant managers buy fifteen minutes of radio time while their workers are driving to work singly or in car pools. These workers seldom have time to read a morning paper and are grateful for local and national news and company news interspersed between musical recordings. However, such a medium should not be used as pure entertainment or as an employee benefit. It should be used as another very effective device to communicate (Y) the goodness of the jobs and other social products (X) to the employees, their families, and neighbors listening in.

This medium is also used at other intervals in the day or evening for news and sports. Some companies use radio as an excellent investment in good will to sponsor all home games of the local baseball team. Other employers sponsor religious programs on Sunday, to the great gratitude of the local clergy and thousands of neighbors.

Television is being increasingly used by the larger companies to win greater understanding and approval of the local business enterprise. Rates on some of the local TV stations are surprisingly low and the high audience impact of this medium makes it well worth consideration. In some cities a group of employers will cooperatively sponsor a program with each employer being given a certain evening to tell his particular story—a sensible method of speading the cost.

7. The speakers' bureau and film library

The speakers' bureau returns a double dividend to the progressive user. It provides a deeply appreciated service to the scores of civic groups in every town which are eager for speakers but cannot afford to pay them, and it is an excellent self-development and training device for employees.

The employer invites employees to volunteer for the bureau and to pick one or more subjects which may deal with the employees' vocations or avocations. A brochure listing the speakers and subjects is prepared and distributed to all civic groups. An employee in the industrial relations department schedules the speakers, as a part-time assignment. The bureau, although featuring talks of general entertainment and educational value, should include talks on various aspects of company policies, benefits, corporate conduct, human relations, business economics, etc.

The film library is a much older and more familiar service. A catalog of films describing company products, their manufacture and use, engineering and research, employee feeding, recreation, human relations, opportunities for advancement, company history, and basic economics is distributed to civic organizations, schools, church groups, etc., and the films loaned gratis on request. Appropriate films from other sources are also made available. Unusually effective with many groups!

8. The open house and special plant tours

Any family knows the friendliness and better understanding resulting from holding a periodic "open house" for neighbors and friends. Employers in increasing numbers are finding that these dividends accrue to their enterprise on a community-wide basis when the plant is thrown open for inspection by the entire community or by specialized groups.

The open house must be carefully planned and publicized far in advance of the date. Such problems as routes of the plant tour, training of tour guides, placement of interpretive signs on important machinery and processes, the serving of light refreshments, the choice of souvenirs, if any, balloons or caps for children, baby sitters, safety measures, etc., all deserve detailed planning, delegation, and follow-through.

The event should not alone entertain but should thoughtfully educate and should advance the broad community relations objectives of the company.

Many plants which manufacture products of special public interest have set up facilities for daily guided tours. By careful planning, they see to it that these tours win new customers for the firm's economic products and create a new awareness of the beneficial social products of the enterprise, as well as satisfying the innate curiosity of families as to where dad, mother, or brother works.

9. Employment office and reception centers

These two important adjuncts to any local business are vital communication centers and deserve far more thoughtful consideration than is often accorded. A shabby, uncomfortable employment office, staffed with brusque autocratic help, can undo all previously described attempts to develop good community relations. Every applicant for employment, whether or not accepted, should be treated with dignity and courtesy. He should be processed speedily and interviewed in a friendly, tactful manner, especially if not accepted. Even if he is not a prospective customer for the product, he probably has influence in some local group and he votes his approval or aversions at the polls.

Equally important in its first impressions is the main reception center or waiting room, where visitors, customers, and vendors register for plant visitations or official business.

In putting one's house in order as a prelude to initiating a community relations program, look to the employment office and the very important reception center *first*.

10. Civic participation

The utmost encouragement should be given to all employees to participate in civic activities. The top officers or managers should set the example through their own participation, through issuance of a clear, positive policy, and through procedural implementation which permits reasonable absence for short periods during working hours to perform useful civic work. By actively participating in community organizations, employees help to build a better home town; they help to create widespread understanding and favorable attitudes for their company and contribute to their own self-development.

Several thoughtful employers maintain a card index system to stimulate civic participation. The name and department of each employee active in a civic group is filed centrally. This enables the community relations representative to keep the employee's supervisor informed so that he may encourage the man or woman in specific terms. The index system is highly useful in civic fund drives and in many other ways. It can't be stressed too emphatically, however, that such a device must never be used to pass judgment on the type of voluntary civic organization with which employees choose to affiliate.

In no other country in the world do employers and employees give so generously and effectively of their time and money to improve their communities. Unfortunately, this invaluable contribution is all too often taken for granted by a community which progressively makes it more difficult for these same employers to grow and to be profitable. But this will be covered in the succeeding chapter.

11. Economic education

Businessmen, large and small, should reserve time in their busy work schedules to become more informed on how our American business system operates. Then, because they are interested in the future of their employees and community neighbors, businessmen must help them understand the system.

Businessmen must understand and help others to understand the separate, important, and interdependent parts played by the customer, the employee, the suppliers, the distributors and dealers, the share owner, and the government. Each of these contributor-claimants has a necessary part to play. Each must have an incentive to play his part well. The main problems in business stem from the widespread economic misunderstanding on the part of the public of the mathematics of our way of life—of the arithmetic of freedom itself.

Businessmen have to understand our free system of incentives and the vital role played by manual and mental work, by savings, by competition, by profit.

Businessmen need particularly to know about money—because that's the subject about which most people are fooled. They need to know about its origin, nature, and function; what *it* can and cannot do; what they can and cannot do to *it*. They need, especially, to understand inflation, that disease of money.

Businessmen need to understand taxes—not only direct taxes, but more especially the less obvious indirect taxes and how they are used to fool people about who is paying taxes and how much. They need to know and to make known that the public pays almost all corporation taxes in the prices that consumers pay.

As businessmen, they need to get the knowledge that will help them expose unsound and wasteful fiscal practices that dilute money, raise prices, destroy savings, insurance, pensions. They need to correct the belief that businessmen's responsibility to make a profit in order to survive is the reason for high prices.

These are only some of the "WHAT's" businessmen must learn. And then after they have mastered this understanding of our American enterprise system, businessmen must use all the ideas and techniques of modern mass communication in order to inform employees and community neighbors.

In short, we can "live right" inside the plant and in the community, and we can then skillfully communicate our good conduct, but we still will fail unless we can raise the level of economic understanding of our employees and neighbors. It is imperative that we help them intelligently to evaluate the problems facing businessmen in raising the standard of living and the decisions business leaders must make daily in order to operate in the balanced best interests of all contributors to any business enterprise—and why these contributors (customer-employees, suppliers, distributor-dealers, share owners, and the government) are all claimants to a fair share of the resulting product. We must prove that management is the trustee for each of these claimants—that if any one temporarily receives more than its fair share, all will suffer.

To get at this frustrating and enormously difficult problem, many companies give intensive courses in economics to employees and to community groups. They then encourage employees who have received such training to form community discussion groups. They work with local schools and colleges to upgrade their teaching of economics.

The important thing for any employer to remember is that economic education is not a one-shot job; rather, the economic interpretation of an employer's activities and results must be integrated into every communication issued. Only by such continuous intensive effort on the part of all employers in town can employees and the local public become sophisticated enough to avoid being fooled by demagogues and to dispel the mistrust that divides and subverts.

12. The plant community relations council

Many companies, which believe they are too small to afford a full-time community relations specialist, have set up a council with a rotating membership of managers and supervisors which periodically reviews and evaluates community relations activities and progress.

Larger companies will find rich values in enlisting the participation of a cross section of top management in such a council. It is not uncommon to see a company invest 8 million dollars in a new plant and then invest a few token dollars in the development of favorable community attitudes, or they will delegate the job to a part-time specialist low in the hierarchy, with no authority or backing.

This is not the case with successful farsighted managements such as the Ford Motor Company, which describes its community relations councils as follows: [2]

"On-the-scene" administration of the Company's community relations program has been effected by the establishment of a Community Relations Committee in Ford's home towns throughout the country. Members of the committees are top management men of whatever Company installations are situated in that community. Because the committees represent the Company rather than its individual divisions, they are the authorized bodies to handle those matters that concern the Company's relations with the community. Broadly speaking, it is the job of the committees to see that the Company is a good citizen of the community. Specific committee responsibilities include the following:

1. To maintain contact with community leaders and to meet with them periodically to discuss community problems.

2. To review requests for financial contributions, automotive equipment donations, Company memberships and management participation in community programs.

3. To plan and coordinate hospitality projects, such as open houses, civic luncheons and dinners, Company film premieres and special plant tours.

4. To forward Company literature, such as traffic safety pamphlets, copies of recent executive speeches and driver-training manuals, to persons who have a special interest in the subject matter.

5. To give local direction to the Company's public service programs, such as those described in the following pages of this booklet.

In addition, committee meetings provide a forum where individual managers can discuss those aspects of their normal operations that may have significance in community relations.

In the final analysis, good community relations cannot be achieved through a unilateral program initiated by a business enterprise, however comprehensive it may be. Good relations are a result of the inter-

[2] *Ford's Good Neighbor Policy,* Ford Motor Company, Community Relations Department, 1956.

action of the company and the community based on an appreciation by both of a *quid pro quo* in a modern industrial society.

Companies or institutions can exist only at the pleasure of the public. Companies and institutions alike must demonstrate continually that they are acting in the public interest and that they have the welfare of the community at heart.

At the same time, an awareness is growing that the two-way aspect of community relations demands certain basic contributions to the growth and profitability of local businesses on the part of plant communities. A promising new approach to identifying and earning the required contributions of local communities is discussed in the next chapter.

CHAPTER 7

Use of Communication in Improving the Business Climate

We have considered in some detail what an employer must do to deserve and win the understanding and approval of the community.

But if we are to stop right here, we shall indeed be guilty of a limited objective approach to our external communications.

There is another side to this coin. So let us ask the question which too few employers have had the temerity to ask. *What must the community do to make it possible for desirable employers to prosper and grow—and what must it do to attract new employers?*

Community relations, in order to justify itself as a business function worthy of the time and money it represents, must be a two-way, something-for-something process. Yet, historically, it has been largely a one-way defensive posture of winning friends and hoping for the best, if and when the employer needed understanding and support.

Slow strangulation of economic goose

Consider, if you will, what has been happening during the past several decades in many highly industrialized segments of our country. Here in community after community, the researcher will observe family-owned businesses and the regional plants of most of the country's largest corporations providing the leadership and a substantial part of the funds for improvement in economic, cultural, charitable, educational, religious, and other fields of civic endeavor.

81

Some of the best limited-objective community relations in the country are here to be studied.

Yet, concurrently, an apathetic citizenry in many of these same communities has permitted a gradual economic strangulation of its best golden geese. Extravagant government spending, discriminatory taxes, abusive administration of unemployment and workmen's compensation laws, featherbedding and spread-the-work schemes, secondary boycotts and jurisdictional disputes, organized resistance to improved machines and methods, failure to enforce the law impartially—all add layer after layer to the costs of doing business locally.

As a result, many enterprises have found it impossible to compete with firms in other locations. Some have moved away and started anew. Others have stayed but have been unable to expand and provide more job opportunities.

With the life-giving flow of payrolls restricted sharply by this ever-tightening tourniquet, the affected cities and states, prodded by powerful union influences, hastily passed ill-conceived restrictive legislation which only accelerated the disease. Still treating the symptoms instead of the virus, local government officials persuaded the Federal government to designate the affected city or region a "distress area" and thereby eligible for a blood transfusion of subsidy.

In many depressed areas there are, of course, basic economic forces inimical to the growth of certain industries, but the antidote for declining markets is not restrictive share-the-work or subsidy legislation which imposes rising costs. Not only is this the lethal overdose for the ailing industries, but it quarantines the area for badly needed new industries.

In most cases the plight of the distressed areas can be attributed primarily to bad local business climate and only secondarily to basic regional and national economic factors. The fault, of course, is primarily that of the employers in these areas. Some of them failed to live right in-plant and in the community and thereby became "hoist by their own petard." All of them failed to develop an awareness in their local communities of the two-way nature of the employer-community relationship—with the employer striving constantly to provide expanding numbers of steadier jobs in addition to being a responsible citizen, and the community, in turn, striving to maintain an equitable business climate in which deserving employers could prosper and grow.

CRITERIA FOR A HEALTHY BUSINESS CLIMATE

What constitutes an equitable business climate not only from the viewpoint of the business leader, but of the entire community? All of a sudden, states and communities are eager to learn because of the lively competition between the states to get their share of America's expanding business economy.

What criteria does a farsighted businessman use when he seeks a new location for his expansion—or considers whether he may risk remaining in his present location?

Putting it another way, what are a community's obligations to its employers? What kind of business climate fosters continued profitability and expansion of existing plants, attracts newcomers, and preserves and enhances the community's economic good health?

The United States Chamber of Commerce,[1] which is devoting increasing attention to this problem, lists the following criteria:

1. *Competitive Labor Costs.* The important consideration in labor costs is *cost per unit of output.* Contrary to a widespread misunderstanding, wage *rates* alone are not controlling. Labor costs can be affected by many factors—work attitudes and employee morale, artificial limitations on output, the frequency and intensity of work stoppages and slowdowns, acceptance of or resistance to new machines and methods, fringe benefits, susceptibility to training or retraining, and much else besides wage rates.

[1] "Getting and Holding Good Employers," *Report of the Committee on Economic Policy,* Chamber of Commerce of the United States.

2. *Harmonious Labor Relations.* Strikes, slowdowns, secondary boycotts, jurisdictional disputes, featherbedding, union leaders who act as masters rather than servants of those they represent—all these are symptoms of uneconomic labor-management relations. The picture is apt to be more favorable where genuine democratic processes govern union policies and demands and where labor legislation is written and administered in the public interest.

3. *Realistic Governmental Regulations.* Honest and intelligent administration of regulations which recognize the problems of industry is an important part of a community's effort to preserve good relations with employers. These include, particularly, adequate zoning and up-to-date building codes. Excessive and discriminatory regulation, especially if unfairly administered, is a red flag to employers. Refusal to enforce the law against politically powerful lawbreakers is likewise a glaring liability for a community.

4. *A Prudent Level of Government Expenditures.* Government spending on both the state and local level should be neither extravagant nor inadequate to meet needed community services such as education, highways, health, etc. A good educational system is a particularly important objective of local government.

5. *A Fair Tax Structure.* Equitable distribution of the cost of local government is essential to a good business climate. Employers should expect to pay their fair share of the tax burden, without special favors, but will certainly be repelled from communities which consider it "good politics" to tax business unfairly.

6. *Adequate Community Cultural and Recreational Facilities.* An attractive community is important to employees in these days of rapidly rising scales of living. Attractive living conditions are particularly important to highly trained workers, who are becoming more and more in demand.

7. *Progressive Attitudes in the Community and Its Leaders*—attitudes which reflect an understanding of the benefits of our economic system and the need for building a healthy relationship between employers and the community.

It should be borne in mind that many environmental factors which impose extra cost burdens on local employers originate at the state level. Accordingly, employers seeking new sites for their expanding businesses attempt first to measure the over-all business climate of the state.

Evaluating business climate at the state level

The following are some of the statistical indicators used by some employers in the first rough evaluation of the state's business climate:

1. Man days idle due to work stoppages, per million nonfarm workers (five-year periods)

2. Jurisdictional disputes per million nonfarm employees (available from U.S. Bureau of Labor Statistics)

3. Unemployment compensation employer contribution rates, adjusted for the level of insured unemployment (eight-year period)

4. Workmen's compensation payments, per nonagricultural employee (latest-year complete data)

5. Existence or absence of a labor relations act patterned after the Wagner Act

6. Existence or absence of a state right-to-work law

7. Business and license fees, as a percentage of total state general revenue

8. Per capita state taxes (latest-year complete data)

9. State indebtedness, related to growth trends over the last five years (latest-year complete data)

10. Government employment as a percentage of total employment (latest-year complete data)

11. Per capita expenditures for regulation of private enterprise (latest-year complete data)

12. Per capita expenditures for public assistance payments (latest-year complete data)

13. Voting records of state congressional delegation on key issues affecting business

14. Population in the fifteen-to-twenty-nine-year age group as a percentage of total population

15. Education expenditures per pupil, as a percentage of state income payments (latest-year complete data)

16. Enrollment in vocational education per nonagricultural employee (latest-year complete data)

17. Ratio of new housing to increase in population (five-year period)

18. Business failures as a percentage of total concerns in business

19. Population per local industrial development corporation

NOTE: Although these rough quantitative yardsticks are no substitute for exacting judicious qualitative analysis on a state-by-state, community-by-community basis, they do present a composite picture of the businessman's view of an equitable or nonequitable business climate. As such, they constitute a check list that should receive the thoughtful consideration of all state and community leaders and officials seeking to attract and hold good employers.

Auditing the local community

So much for the problem. Let us ask now, what should and *can* an employer do if he is operating in a costly, apathetic, or hostile environment? Should he "meet and eat" with his fellow employers, complain about the problem, delegate it to some association or committee, and then hopefully go back to the more familiar chores of production and marketing—believing he is on the way to a solution (which never arrives)? Shall he move to a newer area where the climate is temporarily more benign? Or isn't there some way in which he can approach this problem with the same keen analysis, planning, and execution he customarily employs in solving his other business problems? He most certainly can, as a number of employers bear witness.

The Employers Labor Relations Information Committee, Inc. (ELRIC), was formed several years ago to conduct research and to offer a consultation service to members in the complex field of improving relations between employers and their employees and plant communities.

One of the most valuable services it now provides is a new and extremely practical approach to the problem of improving the business climate which is known as the "Community Inventory" approach.

Although advocating no set pattern of action for every community, ELRIC strongly urges that the first step consist of taking a realistic inventory of the community's business-climate assets and liabilities. The following is excerpted from the ELRIC recommendations: [2]

"The Community Inventory" outlines a do-it-yourself management audit, not a public opinion survey. It consists of 108 questions to provide facts about four basic subjects of primary interest to management: (1) employees, (2) state and local governments, (3) community opinion-formers, and (4) management practices that influence the business environment. Taking "The Community Inventory" reveals the assets and liabilities your company shares with other businesses in the plant community—conditions that help or hinder your immediate operations or effect the long-range vitality of your business.

Here are a few sample questions selected from the Inventory:

On Employees

During the past five years, how many of your plant community's citizens have lost jobs because companies have moved away or reduced operations?

Is the labor supply adequate for your business and for the other business concerns in the community?

How responsible are your plant community's unions, as measured by the frequency of unauthorized strikes and slowdowns, by secondary boycotts and jurisdictional disputes?

On Government and Public Services

Are tax assessments fair to business?

Are the community's school buildings and equipment sufficient for educational needs?

Are there abuses in the administration of the state's statutory benefits, such as workmen's compensation and unemployment compensation?

What is the record of law enforcement agencies in matters affecting business?

On Those Who Influence Opinion

What is the attitude of local newspapers and radio and television stations on issues of interest to business?

[2] *Why It Pays to Improve Your Business Environment,* Employers Labor Relations Information Committee, Inc., New York, 1956.

Do union officials generally oppose the position taken by the majority of businessmen on civic matters, such as daylight saving time, bond issues, and other community questions?

Do local unions aggressively seek public support for unsound economic, social, and political objectives?

Do the community's clergymen indicate an understanding of business problems?

On Management Practices

What efforts has management made to stabilize employment, and have these efforts been properly communicated to employees and others?

Does your company support organizations devoted to good government?

Do you sponsor attitude surveys to learn how well the citizens understand the relations of business to their own welfare in terms of such questions as governmental regulations, taxes, wages, and profits?

Taking the Inventory provides a factual basis for appraising the present business environment and planning improvements for the future. This procedure is essentially the same as market research to determine factors related to the acceptance of your products, what advertising and selling problems must be solved and which are the most profitable markets. General impressions are not sufficiently accurate either for a market study or a "Community Inventory." Your "Community Inventory" will yield information any company needs, and a conscientious report based on it will reveal the facts necessary for an objective evaluation.

Weighing and measuring the facts requires a clinical approach. It involves checking every likely cause for a given problem, then mentally eliminating the factors that apparently are not the real causes. You challenge every fact by asking: "Is this *good* or *bad* in the business environment?" The clinical approach requires strenuous analysis and deliberate judgment, but it usually takes less time and effort than coping with emergencies. And it concentrates on basic causes.

After determining the problems in the business environment, you are in a position to decide realistically what attitudes and situations to modify —what problems should be, and can be solved.

One question is nearly always asked when management considers taking "The Community Inventory"—"After we've assembled the facts and figures, and have evaluated our problems, where do we go from there?"

Actually, where you go and what you do rests entirely with you and your associates. If you decide that any elements in your environment must be improved, you are now in a position to develop a program of corrective action.

FOUR STEPS TO AN IMPROVED BUSINESS CLIMATE

The General Electric Company recommends the following four-step solution to the problem to all of its plant managers as a method for managing their community relations activities with the express purpose of improving the local and state business environment.

Step 1: Make an appraisal of the existing business climate in your community and state

For this purpose, the local plant manager is provided with a *Guide to Making a Business Climate Appraisal*. This guide requires the answering of 187 questions in the following nine categories:

1. Community progressiveness
2. Government
3. Employee relations
4. People
5. Labor costs
6. Community services and facilities
7. Social, cultural, and educational institutions
8. Business citizenship
9. National issues

Each element of the climate is marked "good," "doubtful," or "bad." The bad elements are drawn off on a large work sheet and traced to the root cause. This leads to the second step.

Step 2: Determine your short- and long-range goals for improving the local and state business climate

Here are some typical short-range goals selected by plant managers:

1. Awaken a complacent community to an awareness of its problems.
2. Develop a public demand for *responsible* union leadership.
3. Enforce the law impartially.
4. Increase the supply of skilled labor.
5. Increase teacher compensation.
6. Develop public understanding of the role of productivity in producing a higher standard of living and of inhibiting inflation.

Here are some long-range goals:

1. Raise level of economic understanding.
2. Work for a modern building code without artificial "make-work" restrictions.
3. Prevent urban blight—support urban renewal.
4. Bring a college to the area.
5. Eliminate abuses in state unemployment compensation simultaneously with increasing the benefits paid.

Step 3: Plan, delegate, and manage the work necessary to achieve the goals

Having completed in Steps 1 and 2 the research required to set goals, Step 3 poses, by all odds, the most difficult task, namely, the determination and delegation of the kinds of work necessary to correct unsound conditions.

Let us analyze the approach of the more successful managers to this new and complex area of managerial work:

a. Gain employee support for the goals. Establish a mutuality of interest. Many employees represent the second or third generation in the plant community.

No matter how drab the town may appear to a newcomer, these employees embrace it as "our town." They are proud of, and have a deep-rooted loyalty for, their town and for their particular employer. They are willing to roll up their sleeves and help change conditions which threaten the growth or survival of their employer's enterprise; that is, they will if the employer will show them what needs to be done—and if *he* will provide the leadership.

The first element of work, then, is to meet with all supervisors and nonsupervisory employees in small groups to win understanding of the goals and a desire to support them. Obviously, if the goals are not in the balanced best interests of the employees and the community, they are not good goals for the employers.

An excellent example of such involvement of employees is to be found in a Providence, Rhode Island, plant. The general manager, after writing a series of letters on the business climate to the employees (in the weekly house organ), invited all supervisors and key exempt employees, on a strictly voluntary basis, to an eight-hour meeting outside the plant (half on company time and half on their time) to discuss improvements in the business climate.

The manager's objective was to create broad understanding of what employees could do as individual citizens to help the city and state attract more business and keep present employers from moving away—in short, to create more opportunities and a higher standard of living for themselves and the on-coming generation.

The employees were divided up into small groups, each with a chairman and a resource man. Each group discussed a particular aspect of the climate. They returned from the conference with a deep understanding of the problem and the realization of their own opportunity and obligation to help.

b. The second element of work which is planned and delegated is the work that can be accomplished through civic organizations. Customarily, hundreds of supervisors and nonsupervisory employees are members of one or more civic groups. Each of these groups has its own uniquely oriented goals. The League of Women Voters, for example, is working for permanent personal registration, to name but one goal; the American Legion may be supporting a Little League; the Junior Chamber may be building a new Boy Scout Lodge; the Rotary Club raising funds for a boy's club.

Employees are urged to become dedicated workers in these voluntary groups of their own choosing (and to the extent of their own interests) and to work for their organization's most desired goals because they are so important to the welfare of the community—but they are then urged to help their groups to understand how certain of the business-climate goals are directly related to their group goals.

c. *The third element of work required to accomplish local climate goals is the planned utilization of mass communication.* The goals, and the work needed to achieve them, are explained in the employee house organ, in management newsletters, in employee informative meetings, in the community newsletters, in fact, in every appropriate medium. In the General Electric Company, forthright discussion of all economic, social, and political issues affecting the well-being and survival of the business is fast becoming a highly effective way of life.

d. *The fourth element of work that must be considered by the plant manager for community betterment is the encouragement of individual participation by employees in the political field at the local, state, or national level—but particularly at the local level—in the party of their choice.* The professional manager has an innate distaste for direct political action. It is time-consuming. He feels woefully inept when he attempts to turn from the reasoned decisions of business to the emotional decisions of the political arena.

Historically, he has been content to be represented at state capitals and at Washington through his trade association, occasionally to contribute money to political campaigns, to appear on advisory committees, to let the professionals select the all-important local candidates, and to work late in his office or watch the returns on television while the professionals rounded up the voters precinct by precinct.

Whether businessmen know it or like it, the battle has now been joined.

Unless businessmen awaken now they must be prepared to settle for a business climate created and regulated wholly by the enemies of business and thus by the enemies of all whom business serves.

It need not be too late. The business community has the intellectual capacity, the resources, the genius for planning, organizing, and integrating, and the requisite leadership qualities to provide a moderating check and balance so essential in a democracy. It needs only to sense the urgency for action.

There are heartening evidences that the peril is at last recognized. Businessmen are attending in increasing numbers the schools for political training being conducted across the country by ECO (Effective Citizens Organization), a nonprofit, nonpartisan organization whose sole objective is to stimulate businessmen to become active and trained in the operation of the political party of their choice. The "faculty" consists of political scientists, local Democratic and Republican county chairmen, and party workers. The steps involved in affiliating and in becoming an influential voice in the party are precisely blueprinted.

ECO has also been the catalyst in stimulating individual employers and trade associations to develop their own courses in political sophistication and political training for businessmen. As a result of ECO's stimulus and assistance, an excellent course has been developed by the Chamber of Commerce of the United States to train thousands of businessmen in American communities in cooperation with local chambers. ECO similarly cooperated with the National Association of Manufacturers in developing its political training course called "Good Citizen." This course also is being used to train many additional thousands of businessmen. One of the most effective home-grown courses has been developed by the Manufacturers Association of Syracuse. This work was spearheaded by a businessman who attended an ECO workshop held at Princeton University. Highly useful to participants in any of these courses and to the general reader as well is a book by J. J. Wuerthner, *The Businessman's Guide to Practical Politics,* which ECO endorses. The book is published by Henry Regnery Company, Chicago.

In the General Electric Company, more and more of the top executives, managers, supervisors, engineers, accountants, scientists, and other professional employees are voluntarily participating in training courses to learn to exercise their role as citizens more effectively in the political party of their choice.

These are generally adapted from the basic ECO course and are in-plant political-effectiveness training programs open on a voluntary basis to all employees eager to develop greater competence in the local political arena.

This pioneering work is based on the premise that it is not enough for employees to understand and want the type of government that is in the balanced best interests of the majority; they must then be equipped to make this type of government a reality through exercising a respected voice in policy formation, in candidate selection, through helping to elect candidates of their choices, and through vigilantly making sure that their representatives satisfactorily represent them. They must be neither for business nor for unions, nor for farmers, nor race, nor creed, but for good government for all.

In every company, no matter how small, there are politically inactive employees who have an innate aptitude for politics, who have the time to be a precinct leader or a ward club chairman, or a party worker or an office holder. They need only to be encouraged, to be motivated and assisted in developing requisite competence.

Urging affiliation with the party of one's choice is not just lip service. The company believes political parties and candidates tend to run on about the same platforms and act about alike in office so far as matters affecting the ability of business to be useful are concerned. So the company genuinely hopes—but does not try to decree —that some of its managers and employees will find their particular free choices leading them to one party and some to the other, so that constituents and leaders in both parties will have better information about business and a resulting healthier attitude toward measures affecting the usefulness of business to buyers, sellers, workers, savers, and citizens.

Early results of this exciting new work by businessmen have been truly amazing. A metallurgist in a Middle Western company, not previously affiliated with a party, was elected a county chairman eight months after initial training. An employee relations manager became so self-motivated by the training that he organized a reform party organization and in seven months wrested control from a political machine which had been in power for twenty years.

The roots of the historic American aversion to big government and socialistic trends are sturdiest and deepest at the local community level. Here, then, and not at the state capitals or at Washington, is where citizens must take the leadership or retire in a confused unending retreat toward all-powerful centralized government. Direct political participation by businessmen at the local level is both an obligation and a privilege—and both major parties will be immeasurably strengthened and invigorated by such a transfusion of leadership.

e. The fifth element of work is the encouragement of managers and employees to become acquainted with and to make their wishes as individual citizens known to local, state, and national government representatives. But this liaison work is based on a new concept of political persuasion.

In the past decade, trade-union liaison with government representatives has been based on the premise that "the labor union is the *many* and business the few." The truth is that "business is the many, not the few." Accordingly, whenever a businessman writes to a political representative in defense of or in opposition to an impending issue or law, he should be encouraged to add ". . . and I am communicating these views to our employees and community neighbors in the hope that they also will express to you their personal views, whatever they are."

This action serves a most useful purpose. More often than otherwise, our government representatives would like to support new or reform legislation because, although backed by businessmen, it will obviously be of great benefit to the majority of constituents in the community. Some hesitate. The businessmen supporting the proposal seem to be a distinct minority especially if, as in the past, they remain silent while other voices are telling the employees, who stand to benefit by the legislation, that it is evil. Our politician wants to do what is best for the majority. He wants support from the many and not the few.

Businessmen can contribute to understanding on the part of their employees and neighbors on issues that affect the welfare of all— and votes for the government representatives who have the courage to do what is right in the balanced best interests of their constituents.

This concludes the review of the work planned in Step 3 to achieve better business-climate goals, many of which are essentially political in character. It cannot be emphasized too strongly that political training of business leaders and of employees and other beneficiaries of the business system is, per se, no guarantee of a wisely directed economy. Accordingly, such political training must be accompanied by a *full communication* of the factors essential to an attractive and prosperous community and state. This is the essence of better business-climate planning.

Step 4: Encourage other local employers to undertake this same type of appraisal, goal setting, and work planning

Impress upon them that the most effective business-climate development is that which is done between individual employers and their own employees working together on mutually agreed goals. To be sure, there is some work that may best be performed through joint action by a group of employers and some that can be delegated to business-sponsored organizations. However, the day is past when something as vital to the success of both business and the community can be largely delegated to committee work in trade and business associations. The accent today is on "do it yourself" in concert with all other employers who have the prescience to understand what is happening and the courage to do what must be done.

Here, then, is the soundest of approaches to the most frustrating problem that has faced employers in the past several decades. It is an approach they can understand. It is the professional management approach of plan, organize, integrate, and measure. It is work simplification applied to a manager's community relations work. It involves no great new expenditures over what an employer is now spending in time and money. It is simply getting the activities directed on specific targets.

The better-business-climate plan is the mature manager's plan for preserving and advancing his business through developing broad understanding of its values to all citizens. Although freedom of petition is not rejected, this approach does not rely primarily on lobbying, influence, special privilege, or special pleading. It relies on the common sense and self-enlightened support of informed employee and community neighbors exercising their constitutional rights as free citizens. And, as always, a prime tool of the manager is communication.

PART THREE

The Supervisor's Role in Communication

CHAPTER 8

Communication Responsibilities of the First-line Supervisor

The foreman's job is to get the work that is assigned to his unit accomplished by his employees in line with acceptable and pre-determined standards of time, quality and cost.[1]

This book began, quite naturally, with a consideration of the responsibilities of top executives, the president, his staff, and the top managers in the line organization. They establish the climate in which good communication flourishes. They set the policies; they determine the strategic uses of communication, and they encourage or discourage full, free two-way communication by precept and by positive or negative motivation.

At great risk of ignoring the crux of the problem, we skip to the bottom level of management, the first-line supervisor.

Middle management, of course, constitutes the most tenacious blockade to free-flowing communication up and down the chain of command but this problem will be dealt with later.

THE FOREMAN'S LUMP OF WORK

For purposes of this discussion, we will represent first-line supervision by the foreman because usually our biggest communication

[1] *Report of 39th Annual Session, Silver Bay Conference on Human Relations in Industry,* 1957, p. 27.

problem occurs in the production function, where normally we find the largest concentration of employees. First-line supervisors in production are customarily termed foremen. However, in principle, what we have to say here applies to all supervisors whether in factory or office.

Much has been written in recent years concerning industry's busiest man, the foreman. To appreciate fully the magnitude of his responsibilities, we need only look at the following outline of a training course for foremen in one of the departments of a typical industrial enterprise. As will be noted, the course was structured to develop fuller understanding of each responsibility listed in the foreman's position guide:

Item to Be Studied	*Number of Hours*
Purpose of the foreman's position guide	1
Planning and methods	2
Purpose of production schedules } Meeting production schedules }	4
Maintenance facilities	2
Employee relations	2
Labor relations	1
Wage rates	4
Personnel	2
Medical	1
Safety	2
Housekeeping	2
Quality control	2
Budgets—unapplied labor	1
Budgets—scrap and spoilage	1
Budgets—associated costs	2
Grievance prevention	2
Selection and training of employees	2
Relations of foremen to general foremen	1
Shop psychology	3
Communication	4

Another interesting view of the anatomy of a foreman's job is presented by George D. Halsey in his book, *Supervising People.*[2]

[2] George D. Halsey, *Supervising People*, Harper & Brothers, New York, 1953, p. 6.

His definition highlights the high communication content in the typical foreman's job. According to Halsey:

What	How	Purpose
Supervision is { Selecting / Interesting / Teaching / Measuring / Rating / Correcting / Eliminating / Commending / Rewarding / Harmonizing }	People { Fairly / Patiently / Tactfully }	{ In order to cause them to do their assigned tasks } { Skillfully / Accurately / Intelligently / Enthusiastically / Completely }

BARRIERS TO EFFECTIVE FOREMAN COMMUNICATION

The most persistent myth in business is that the foreman is the indispensable man in the communication chain. Ask any industrial relations director about employee communication and you will probably be exposed to the oldest cliché in business; that is, "the foreman is the key to effective employee communication."

The great paradox is this: we who most persistently argue that the foreman is the prime determinant of the quantity and quality of the communication flowing downward to the employee and upward from the employee just as persistently make it impossible for him to exercise his key role.

Robert H. Guest, associate director, Technology Project, Yale University, and his coworkers, decided to observe in detail each of fifty-six production foremen for a full eight-hour day. Each day the researcher recorded exactly what the foreman did, how much time the incident required, what action was involved, with whom it took place, where it happened.

The following is excerpted from Guest's preliminary report in "Of

Time and the Foreman," which appeared in the May, 1956, issue of *Personnel:*

The number of incidents ranged from as low as 237 per foreman to as high as 1,073 for a full day, exclusive of lunch. The average number of incidents was 583, which means that every 48 seconds of the day the foreman was doing something different. Some foremen averaged only 26 seconds per incident while others averaged close to two minutes. . . .

Obviously, these foremen had little idle time. They had to handle many pressing problems in rapid-fire order. They had to "take" constant interruption, to retain many problems in their minds simultaneously, and to juggle priorities for action. . . .

We also discovered that the first item to suffer was personal relations, generally regarded by personnel-minded people as an important function of a foreman's job. . . .

Important are the unpredictable operational factors, the things a foreman must face, minute by minute, which dictate how he allocates his time. Even the "best" foreman, when faced with absenteeism, mechanical problems, new operators, schedule changes, or material shortages, had to devote large segments of his time to this particular problem on a given day and at the expense of other important supervisory duties. The best selection and training techniques can hardly be expected to pay off, if the conditions of the job make it impossible for a foreman to discharge at all times the full scope of his responsibilities. . . .

As might be expected, foremen talked more with their own operators than with any other single group in the organization. Nevertheless, it was found that the average foreman spent less than five minutes per man per day. . . .

What clearly emerges from these detailed observations of the foreman's job is that there is considerable difference between what a foreman should do and what he can do. A foreman who has to jump from one operating emergency to another every 45 seconds has neither the time nor the inclination to practice the fine precepts he is exposed to in human-relations training programs. Indeed, such training may only serve to compound his own frustrations.

Overloading the transmission line

Winston Churchill is reputed to have said, "No generality is worth a damn, including this one." Perhaps it is a generality to state that most foremen do not have time to communicate. But hadn't we better find out what are the facts in our own companies?

If we knew as little about the sales performance of our dealers as we know about the communication performance of our foremen, our businesses would suffer slow strangulation.

Yet with little or no attempt to measure what happens at the end of the communication distribution line, we constantly overload the line.

The foreman is expected to communicate major changes in policies, practices, procedures, to explain intricate changes in wage payments, to extol new benefit plans and help get full participation, to interpret the new union contract, to interpret the goals of the managers, to conduct economic education, and to sell the merits of the free-enterprise system. All these with less than five minutes per man per day? Or ten? Or sixty?

It seems obvious in view of the foregoing that business must soon face up realistically to a choice between two alternate courses of action. Either it must bypass its foremen in the communication chain by relying largely on mass printed communication directly aimed at the worker, or it must restructure the job of the foreman to allow him time to carry out his communication responsibilities. The answer, more likely, will be a combination of the two.

Helping the foreman to communicate effectively

That industry is awakening to the problem was dramatically illustrated by an all-day meeting of eighty-four top executives in a seminar sponsored by the Employers Labor Relations Information Committee, Inc. (ELRIC) in New York City. The challenging assignment was stated as follows: "To What Extent Can Foremen Be Used As Communicators?" At the end of a day of intensive group discussion, the participants summarized their findings as follows:

1. The foreman too often has too many duties. This results in an imbalance between his function as a producer and as a communicator. For the best interests of the business, we must allow him time to communicate.

NOTE: These are not competing demands on his time. He achieves high production through effective communication.

2. The foreman cannot be a successful communicator of management information and attitudes unless he feels himself to be a real member of the management team with an adequate differential between his pay and that of the highest-paid employee supervised and the maximum possible job security. If he is subjected to layoffs or to temporary demotion to the hourly paid group during recessions, or if his treatment varies substantially from that accorded other managers, he cannot be expected to communicate management's philosophies and policies reliably.

3. The ability to communicate (that is, the creation of mutual understanding) is a key leadership qualification. Men who have no potential as communicators should not be selected as foremen.

4. Middle-management people are most responsible for the breakdown of two-way communication. They must be trained to understand and discharge effectively this important part of their work.

5. Communicating must be recognized as an essential part of the management process; it must be implemented by effective techniques, and opportunity, time, facility, and climate must be provided.

6. Communicating factual information is not enough. Listening as a part of business communication must not be ignored. Management must achieve three-dimensional communication: downward, upward, laterally.

7. Management must have confidence that given facts which are soundly interpreted, its employees will arrive at correct conclusions.

8. It is "feasible, practical, and desirable" for foremen to communicate on complex and controversial issues, but they must be given adequate help.

9. Foremen must be given both time and *incentive* to play their vital role as communicators. Particularly must they be given information promptly so that their employees will look to them first for the facts.

The course of action seemed clear to this influential segment of American industry. The foreman is indeed the key to effective communication, but he will be effective only if we are willing to accord him the status, the authority, the personal security, the time, the facilities, the assistance, the incentive, and the information necessary to exercise his key role.

The executive's goal of fulfilling two inalienable rights of employees working in a free society, namely, the right to know and the right to be heard, will not easily and quickly be reached. This is particularly true if the executive decides, as he surely must, to place such a complex task in the hands of the widely disparate human beings who comprise the foremanship groups.

The stakes are high, however. The ultimate goal that business seeks is fuller productivity through more effective motivation. The wellsprings of better motivation are to be found in the financial and nonfinancial rewards which business attempts to provide. The emphasis of the past two decades on financial rewards has not produced the desired improved motivation. The preponderance of evidence indicates that the *nonmaterial rewards,* including significant and challenging assignments and satisfying relationships with supervisors, will in the end provide the greatest motivation.

A good foreman communicator in action

In order to communicate effectively, the supervisor must first build satisfying relations with each employee supervised. He must be honest, sincere, considerate, and trustworthy. He must back up his people, fight for them. He must play no favorites, steal no credit.

He can be tough-minded, provided he is fair and dependable. He should show a thoughtful concern for his employees as individuals —helping them when they are deeply troubled—rejoicing in a wedding—consoling in a wake—unaffected fellowship at a ball game, picnic, a bowling match. Of these little things are good human relations compounded.

Where such man-manager relationships exist in a work group, effective communication, although still demanding skill, needs less pressure, or head, to keep it flowing. Downward communication is more effective because the communicator is highly regarded, respected, and trusted. Upward communication encounters fewer barriers because each employee feels free to discuss both work and personal problems with candor.

Millard E. Stone, vice-president, Sinclair Oil Corporation, examining the role of supervision in communication at an American Management Association seminar, emphasizes the interdependence of communication and human relations in this way: [3]

. . . We give the name "communication" to the process of imparting information and furnishing appropriate stimuli. This automatically broadens out the definition of "communication," so that it embraces much more than, for instance, words on paper or messages over a public address system. In fact, in terms of informing and stimulating people in relation to their work, communication means the sum total of all the contacts employees experience on the job—what is often called "human relations."

At General Electric, one operating department, with a reputation for extremely effective employee communication, sums up the responsibility of its foreman in the area of communication thus:

CHARGE TO THE FOREMAN

If you as a first-line supervisor hope to meet our standards in communicating with your employees, you will first need to:

1. Gain the confidence of your employees by:
   Being impartial and consistent.
   Making no commitments that you cannot fulfill.
   Making certain that all problems and grievances are answered promptly and correctly.
   Making the employees' shop problems your own—and *actively* representing your employees' interests to other levels of management.
   Making it clear that *we have grievance machinery that works!*
2. Gain the respect and the friendship of your employees by:
   According respectful treatment to each employee as an individual and esteemed associate.
   Showing sincere interest in their welfare.
   Displaying enthusiasm over their progress.
   Being considerate and helpful in all possible ways.
   Demonstrating a sincere personal interest in matters that are im-

[3] Millard E. Stone, *Supervision: Crossroad of Communication,* American Management Association, Special Conference on Supervision, November, 1956.

portant from their point of view—attending weddings, funerals, delivering pay and benefit checks in person when they are ill, attending social affairs together, family nights, etc.

3. Having thus established the proper climate for good downward communication to receptive employees and good upward communication from employees who feel free to discuss matters with you—you will need, and we will help you, to develop your skills in: listening; talking; selling.

4. Of all of the skills you will need to develop, none is more important than the ability to listen carefully, in order to achieve full understanding of the information received, to take action quickly based on this understanding, and to communicate the results of such action to the individuals involved.

Effective communication changes the attitudes and actions not only of the receiver, but of the transmitter. If our foremen can be taught and motivated to communicate freely and sincerely, they will not be the same foremen tomorrow that they are today. The more effectively they communicate, the more effective will become their relationships.

One of the surest paths to improved human relations and motivation is improved communication. If foremen can eventually be measured and rewarded significantly on the effectiveness of their communication, management will have discovered a long-sought device for improving its human relations.

CHAPTER 9

Fundamental Communication Work Performed
by Supervisor

The professional manager who aspires to helping his foremen or other first-line supervisors to become effective communicators (and who doesn't so aspire?) should first make sure that these supervisors have the time, the training, and the incentive to carry on the routine job-related communication work so essential in meeting their output goals.

Chronologically, the supervisor should be taught, encouraged, and helped to do the following job-related communication work:

SELECTION INTERVIEWING

In most businesses, a central employment office makes an initial screening of prospective employees and then refers one or more prospects to the supervisor for final evaluation. The interview too often is conducted in a hasty, slipshod, intuitive manner. Too much blame cannot be placed on the harried foreman if he has received no training in interviewing nor is permitted the time to make a careful selection. Unfortunately, the results of poor selection may plague the company for thirty or forty years. How often have we heard managers say, "How did he ever get on the payroll initially?" The answer is "You put him on, Mr. Manager, or your predecessor managers. It may be that you paid some attention to the selection process carried out in your spick-and-span employment office. But you forgot that, like an iceberg, whose major part is under the water and hence unseen, the more important part of the selection process was out of sight in the shop or office."

The face-to-face interview is perhaps the oldest and most widely used method of selecting employees—and it is still the most valuable single device used in employment. Application forms are often sketchy, incomplete, and can be readily falsified. Testing, at best, is restricted to a limited number of aptitudes or abilities and provides few valid measures of significant traits of motivation, personality, and character in a selection situation. Reference check-ups are noteworthy for their omissions, exaggerations, and other inadequacies. It is thus left up to the intensive interview to bear the burden of final selection of job candidates.

By its very nature, the interview is highly subjective. And it presents many special problems with which the interviewer must constantly cope. But no one has yet been able to devise any substitute method by which the same information can be obtained. Consequently, the interview will probably always remain the central feature, or core, of the employment process. Our goal should thus be to improve interviewing procedures, as well as to increase our facility in the use of the latest techniques.

Today the more progressive managers are giving "guided-interview" training not only to employment office personnel but, in a condensed form, to supervisors as well.

The author's company gives a one-week course in effective interviewing to central employment interviewers and a fifteen-hour course to its foremen. In the condensed course, the foremen are taught to regard the interview as a *planned conversation*. After a brief review of major interview pitfalls, the foremen are taught such fundamental techniques as these:

How to gain the applicant's confidence
The guided interview pattern
Keeping the applicant talking
Specific questioning techniques

Observant listening
Feedback as an interviewing technique
The chaining technique
Note taking
Use of interview rating form
Terminating the interview
Arriving at final selection decision

NOTE: Fuller information on scientific interviewing is available from the industrial division of the Psychological Corporation, New York City, which is assisting many of its clients in developing advanced techniques.

ORIENTATION

Once the employee has been selected, it is a prime responsibility of the supervisor to make the new employee feel genuinely welcome, to introduce him properly to his associates, to relieve the strangeness of the new situation, to stress the importance of the work, to give him the basic work rules.

Such orientation is not a one-shot proposition. It is a continuing process. To be effective, it must be given in small doses so that the employee can absorb it readily.

On first reporting to work, the new employee is concerned with such questions as these: "How much will I earn?" "Where will I eat lunch?" "May I smoke and where?" "What's my boss like?" These questions and anxieties must be satisfied quickly if the employee is to be effectively integrated into the work group.

The orientation process starts in the employment office but the real responsibility rests squarely with the supervisor. As a result, the orientation work is often divided up in some such fashion:

Orientation by Central Employment

All employees:
Knowledge of department and section, and work to be performed.
Performance standards.
Hours of work, pay days, and vacations.
Information on company benefit plans.

State workmen's compensation law.
Solicitation for company benefit plans.

Hourly employees
Starting rate and job rate.
Premium pay for overtime work.

Non-exempt salaried employees
Progression schedule for the job.
Absence allowances.
Premium pay for overtime work.

Orientation by supervisor
Welcome to company and job.
Show locker or coat rack and washroom.
Acquaint employee with cafeteria and other lunch facilities.
Show work place.
Review rate, hours, use of time cards.
Briefly describe individual and group work.
Review performance standards—why they are fair and reasonable.
Introduce to fellow workers.
Review tool-check system and location of tool crib, tools furnished by
employee, and tools furnished by company.
Briefly cover main safety rules and use of safety equipment.

The more progressive companies are giving close scrutiny to the
vital communication work involved in proper orientation of new
employees. They have learned that the impressions formed by the
new employee in his first critical period on the job profoundly influence his opinions, his attitudes, and his productivity. Accordingly,
they train both their central employment personnel and their
supervisors to do this job. They give the foremen a check list of
orientation duties to be administered the first day, the first week,
the first month, and then they install some built-in controls to see
that the job is thoroughly performed.

INITIAL JOB INSTRUCTION

Rare indeed is the individual who likes to do bad work, yet the
amount of money lost through poor on-the-job performance is ap-

palling. The reason for most "bad work" is not difficult to ascertain. Many employees never gain a clear picture of what is expected of them and what will constitute acceptable performance. The basic cause is often found in faulty initial job instruction.

Learners are seldom sufficiently impressed with the importance of the work they turn out or with the necessity for following standard procedures. Initial instruction is often performed in a hasty manner or turned over to one who has demonstrated little competence as an instructor. The time-worn excuse is frequently given, "We don't have the time!" Incompetent supervisors may also resort to the hackneyed "Experience is the best teacher." It may be, but it has proved to be the most expensive teacher.

Efficiently managed companies make a fetish of thorough initial job instruction. This includes the establishment of "training time-tables" to make sure instruction is scheduled and that the time for thorough instruction *is* provided. It provides for the development of "job breakdowns" to ensure a standard method of instruction, which in turn assures that no point of instruction, no "trick-of-the-trade," no safety point is overlooked during the instruction.

Many companies resort to the four-step procedure, or adaptations of this procedure, which was developed by the Training Within Industry Division [1] of the War Manpower Commission during World War II to train millions of green workers quickly and to provide experienced workers with new skills required to do far more complicated jobs than they had ever been expected to perform in the past.

Commonly termed JIT (Job Instruction Training), it follows this simple sequence:

1. Prepare the worker
    Put him at ease.
    Get him interested.
    Find out what he knows.

[1] This training work is now being provided by the Training Within Industry Foundation, Summit, N.J.

Position him.
2. Present the job
    Tell, show and demonstrate.
    Point out the key points.
    Give him the reasons "why."
3. Try-out performance
    Have him do the job for you.
    Have him explain the job to you.
    Continue until you know that he knows.
4. Follow-up
    Put him on his own.
    Encourage questions.
    Tell him whom to see for help.
    Taper off coaching as his skill increases.

When the sweeping claim, "This takes too much time," is subjected to analysis, it is found that effective instruction actually takes less time than hasty instruction. It results in jobs done right from the beginning. Employees pick up speed more rapidly because they have greater confidence in themselves, and as TWI surveys have demonstrated, there is an immediate and measurable reduction in scrap, accidents, and misunderstandings; hence, fewer employee relations problems. The same surveys established that there is a consequent improvement in both quality and quantity of work.

Adequate time and money spent on initial job instruction represent a blue-chip investment, but as so often happens in business, our cost-cutters overlook the obvious and cut funds for training, thereby creating financial losses that far outweigh the "savings."

TRANSMITTING POLICIES AND PROCEDURES

In order to get work performed most effectively, managers place great reliance on positional or administrative communication.

Charles E. Redfield thus perceptively describes this workaday communication: [2]

[2] Charles E. Redfield, *Communication in Management*, University of Chicago Press, Chicago, 1954, pp. 11–12.

A formal organization starts with a broad purpose or plan; this is sub-divided into activities, and the activities are assigned to positions. Structural relationships are established between Position A and Position B, not between Mr. Smith and Miss Jones. Since communication is the vehicle for carrying on relationships between positions, we find in any formal organization a phenomenon which can be designated as positional communication. The entire organization, as it appears on an organization chart, can be referred to as a positional communications network.

Positional communication is upset in practice, however, because positions are staffed with human begins with total personalities. The relationship between Position A and Position B does not exist apart from the relationship between Joe and Gertrude and the other folks in the office. Yet, although it is impossible completely to insulate a position from the incumbent's personality, administrative communication depends most of the time on positional behavior, including positional communication.

People in positions are required to communicate in accordance with their positional roles to a certain extent, and in connection with some matters they do so to a surprisingly great extent. However, positional communication can never be all-encompassing.

The General Electric Company, in an effort to free up its communication channels from the rigidities of positional communication, inserts the following significant statement in all position guides and organization charts:

Channels of Contact

While the organization structure and chart define lines of responsibility, authority and accountability, they do not indicate or limit CHANNELS OF CONTACT or FLOW OF INFORMATION between or among employees of the enterprise.

Organization policy permits and expects the exercise of common sense and good judgment, at all organizational levels, in determining the best channels of contact for expeditious handling of Company work.

Contacts and flow of information between people and components of the enterprise should be carried out in the simplest and most direct way practicable. In making such contacts, however, it is the duty of each employee to keep his manager promptly informed regarding any matters:

(1) For which his manager may be held properly accountable by others;

(2) As to which there are, or which are likely to cause, disagreement or controversy, especially between different components of the enterprise;

(3) Which require the advice of his manager or integration by his manager with other components of the enterprise; or

(4) Which involve recommendations for change in, or variance from, established policies.

Call it what we will, the burden of implementing this type of communication falls upon the already overloaded shoulders of the foremen. The downward flow of administrative communication is heavily freighted with assignments, orders, reports, policies, and procedures.

How effectively the foremen carry out this work depends on a number of factors: the emphasis placed on effective communication by the top officers or managers; the number of levels through which the information must pass positionally; the structure of the foreman's job; his innate ability and training as a communicator; the adequacy and clarity of information given to him to transmit; and whether or not there exist position incentives or measurements of the effectiveness of his work in this area.

Most progressive managers, however, employ one guiding principle. Although there is no substitute for face-to-face oral communication coming down the positional chain of command, this oral communication should be supplemented almost always with written communication. The underlying reasons for this policy are dealt with in more depth later.

Assignment making

One of the most important communication tasks of the foreman is the making of assignments. Except on paced machines, the foreman is constantly making assignments to his employees.

If the heads of business enterprises could measure the economic losses they suffer every day through slipshod assignments at all levels of supervision, more of them would be following the practices of American Telephone and Telegraph and other farsighted companies in providing specific training in assignment making.

AT&T retained the late Dr. Irving J. Lee [3] to conduct research in assignment making in business and to administer training to its supervision.

Dr. Lee built his training program around role playing in assignment making by certain of the participants, followed by critiques by the observers. Out of this he distilled certain fundamentals for improving the making of assignments which are roughly paraphrased as follows:

Content. Make instructions explicit. Include as much as possible of who, what, when, how much. If it is an important assignment, plan the content before calling in the man. Take enough time to do the job right, or you will pay for it in time consumed later to correct for hurriedness and vagueness.

Install some "built-in control," or check, in the assignment. Tell him when you make an assignment that you would like him to check with you when the job is half finished—or you would like to see an outline on Tuesday.

Invite questions on the assignment. Employees say that they are never asked for their ideas on how best to carry out an assignment; rather, they are simply told what to do.

Invitation to contribute. Ask the subordinate to contribute to the assignment: "Do you think of anything you can contribute to this that I have overlooked?" The failure to invite subordinates to contribute is a great source of inefficiency in business; it is also a source of resentment, poor morale, lack of interest. Less than 10 per cent of executives practice this.

Motivation. Failure to answer subordinates' unasked questions: "Why should I?" "What's in it for me?"

For example, many top secretaries say, "All he does is push buttons. He never seems to think that I can help him if he would only

[3] Irving J. Lee and Laura L. Lee, *Handling Barriers in Communication*, Harper & Brothers, New York, 1957, pp. 77–92.

ask me." Here is an example of motivation which appeals to pride: "You're the senior man and the best qualified—that's why I'm asking you to handle this particular job." Less than 10 per cent of all assignments carry any motivation. Of course, we shouldn't lay it on with a trowel, and we don't have to do it with routine orders or do it every time.

Increase time of every giving of orders by about 30 per cent. Instead of ten minutes, take thirteen minutes.

An amusing anecdote reflecting the inadequacy of many shop assignments is this: a new workman was given the assignment by his foreman to make a gear. The instruction was hurried, no feedback was employed to see if the operator understood thoroughly, and there was no check-back on the job. Ten days later the operator addressed this startling query to his foreman: "Look, Mr. Boss, I've got this much uncut metal left on the rim (indicates dimension of remaining stock with fingers). What I wanna know is this. Would you like one big tooth or two little teeth?"

The essence of motivational communication

A detailed observation of the way foremen communicate was conducted over a period of several months in the author's company and revealed this significant differentiation between foremen in their method of order giving.

The foremen under study were classified "most effective" and "least effective" by both their superiors and their subordinates, according to results achieved in their over-all jobs. In other words, the foremen were evaluated by looking at them from the bottom up as well as from the top down. The bottom-up evaluation is particularly important if we wish to assay the foremen's ability as communicators.

It was found that the "least effective" foremen gave three times as many authoritarian orders as the "most effective" group. The high group put a "reason why" into their orders three times as often as the low group.

These studies also indicated that the supervisor who anticipated questions and initiated communication to his employees had better morale in his group than the supervisor who gave information only when it was requested by his workers.

The General Electric Company periodically polls its supervisors to determine how best to help them discharge their communication responsibilities. The following abstract of a depth interview with one foreman shows an exceptional grasp of the problem.

As a foreman, here are my *receiving* needs; I need to receive communication concerning general Company developments, local department developments, and any and all information necessary to enable me to perform my function well. This includes information on matters affecting me as a foreman and/or my entire group. I want this to occur as oral communication from my general foreman at frequent (perhaps weekly) informative meetings, and as written communication emanating from the proper sources. I want written communication to be concise, clear, and accurate, and presented in the manner of a news story so that I could get the main thoughts by reading the first sentence or paragraph. I am able to decide quickly on the necessity for familiarizing myself with details in each particular instance.

I also want to receive communication from my men concerning problems, ideas, and suggestions arising from their work or the fact that they are employees of the Company, and concerning personal problems, as necessary.

As a foreman, here is my *giving* procedure: I pass all information received on to my men orally at regularly scheduled (usually weekly) informative meetings. In special cases only do I turn to written communciation.

I also pass all pertinent information upward to the general foreman. This includes a "feedback" of information from my men, either oral or written as the case may warrant.

We have examined here some of the primal communication work of a first-line supervisor: interviewing, orientation, job training, disseminating administrative communication, making hour-by-hour assignments. Two other types of communication work, performance-appraisal discussions and the conduct of informative meetings, are so important that they are treated separately in Chapters 10 and 11. Taken together, these constitute job-related communication work of the most basic type. It is folly to consider training supervisors in the more complex communication work until we have helped them with these fundamental problems.

CHAPTER 10

Communicating Praise, Censure, and Progress

It has often been stated that the supervisor who obtains the best from his employees is the one who creates the best atmosphere, or climate, of approval within which his work group operates.

He accomplishes this through the following methods:

1. He develops performance standards for his employees—and sets them high to stretch the employees.
2. He measures performance against these standards.
3. He consistently commends above-par performance.
4. He always lets employees know when they have performed below par.

When a supervisor consistently utilizes these methods of integrating his work group, his employees experience a sense of security. They know always "how they're doing" and where they stand with their superior.

One of the greatest needs of the employee is to know at all times if his performance is measuring up to his superior's criteria.

The supervisor's evaluation can be made through the first or second order or level of communication; that is, it can be formal (written or oral) or it can be communicated by gestures, silence, a pat on the back, or an approving poke in the ribs.

The more consistently praise and discipline are meted out for superior or sub-par performance, the less need there is for the more formal methods.

In such an atmosphere of security—of knowing always precisely where one stands—employees do not burn up energy or waste time with inner anxieties and frustrations. They become free to unleash their full creativity; they are encouraged to take responsibility, to innovate, to risk an occasional mistake in the cause of progress.

This method of supervising is vastly different from that of the soft, democratic good-fellow technique. Indeed, authoritarian supervision, provided it is coupled with consistency of justice, will usually result in higher unit and group output. "He's tough but he's fair, and I know where I stand with him" is a common evaluation of such a supervisor.

THE INDISPENSABLE PERFORMANCE APPRAISAL

Closely allied to consistent praise and censure is consistency in performance appraisal. Each employee wants to know what he is expected to do, how he will be measured, how well he is doing, how he might improve, and how he can qualify for greater responsibilities. Most modern business enterprises today employ some form of performance appraisal or employee rating and urge their supervisors to discuss these appraisals with their employees at least annually.

Unfortunately, this policy is widely circumvented through assumed lack of time or because of distaste for the task. The higher one ascends in the supervisory hierarchy, the more often is the policy breached.

Most executives have an innate distaste for criticizing a subordinate's work. They find it embarrassing and they do it awkwardly. The initial task of appraising a key subordinate's performance is per se a time-consuming job. This is particularly true where no precise measurement standards have been mutually agreed upon or where the nature of the work makes measurement difficult.

Added to this work is the difficulty of finding and scheduling time to discuss the appraisal in a relaxed unhurried interview—especially where the manager's span of control is wide. Accordingly, in the absence of a conscientiously enforced policy on periodic appraisal reporting, the best of executives too often postpone the job indefinitely.

The burning question: "How am I doing?"

So difficult is the policing of this essential and admirable policy that there is no exaggeration in the statement that one of the most consistent weaknesses of current management practice is the failure to answer the employee's burning question, "How am I doing?"

More than once in addressing executive groups across the country, the author has been told by officers of companies that their president has not answered this question to their satisfaction for the past five or more years.

The following incident which occurred in the author's company could have happened in any business enterprise. Mr. X (a top executive) was moderating a conference on human relations with a group of managers. The subject of employee appraisals was raised. Mr. X abruptly asked the group, "How many of you men have had the opportunity of sitting down with your boss and having a heart-to-heart discussion about your job—about how you are doing—not just a casual discussion but a real honest-to-goodness talk about you?" (Only about one hand out of ten was raised.)

"Now, gentlemen, I would like to know how many of you have called in your subordinates and given *them* the benefit of a thoroughgoing discussion about them—about how they are doing—about how their job and performance can be improved? Let's see your hands." (About three times as many hands were raised.) Mr. X observed the group in a moment of silence and then wryly remarked, "Gentlemen, would you each like to be measured by a truth meter?"

Here then is one of those many hidden friction points or impedances in the line that result in incalculable losses in productivity, initiative, sound decisions, innovations, and in constructive self-development. How easily these losses could be eliminated. What do we gain from the soundest financial compensation practices if this greatest of nonfinancial incentives is flagrantly withheld?

Lawrence A. Appley, president, American Management Association, threw down this challenge at a conference of presidents:

If the extent to which individuals are kept informed of their progress, and the skill with which this is done, were to be tripled in every organization in the next twelve months, the resulting impact upon the company, our economy, and society in general would be almost beyond comprehension.

The supervisor's most critical communicating work

General Mills, Inc., in its remarkably fine manual on performance-appraisal discussions, states:

It is generally agreed that nothing is more important or will accomplish more in motivation and development of subordinates than well-planned, regularly scheduled "How Am I Doing Talks."

The General Mills manual, *Discussions of Performances and Progress* represents some of the best current thinking on the techniques of this critical communication work of a supervisor—and credit is given generously by its authors to pioneering work by leading social scientists and by other corporations whose methods were studied.

The guide first explains the purposes of the performance-appraisal discussion. The "How Am I Doing Talks" are not to evaluate or sit in judgment on a man's good or poor performance. The purpose is to help a man get greater satisfaction from his work and each year do a better job.

Ideally [says this company] there should be two such discussions a year. A beginning-of-the-year agreement on targets and an end-of-the-year discussion on how well these targets were met.

[The] discussion should be centered on performance, not personality—improvement, not criticism . . . emphasis is primarily on helping find ways to improve work results, and only secondarily on the man as a person.

The company reviews the following clichés which serve as rationalizations of failure to do this critical work of performance appraisal and discussion:

My door is always open.
I'm constantly talking to my people.
There isn't time.
Let sleeping dogs lie.
These talks are difficult. . . . I can't do them well.

Five key steps in discussing performance

General Mills lists the following steps to follow in holding the year-end discussion:

1. Advance notice—prepare to compare notes.
2. Compare accomplishments with targets.
   a. Give credit for things accomplished and done well.
   b. Review things not accomplished or where improvement is needed. Explore why and how.

NOTE: Emphasis is placed on the necessity for helping the man retain self-respect and pride in his work; of *telling* him what he is doing well but of *asking* him about the things he is not doing well; of finding something to praise before being critical of even a small weakness; of avoiding dwelling on past errors; of avoiding critical words, such as "faults," "mistakes," "weaknesses," and antagonizing words like "reason," "logic," and "common sense," and of avoiding comparison with others.

3. Agree on targets for the year ahead (objectives, standards, self-improvement programs).

NOTE: Appraisers are warned against generalities. They are told to stick to *specific* targets, such as the *amount* of cost reduction or *percentage* of sales increase; likewise *what* books to read, *what* courses to take. They are urged to achieve mutual understanding of the man's responsibilities and accountabilities for the year ahead since job content has a tendency to change.

4. Review what the manager could do to be of greater help.

NOTE: The point is well made that results are the product not just of the man but of the man and his manager together, that the shortcomings of the employee are due in part to his manager's own failure to guide, instruct, or encourage, that the manager must be willing to discuss these things and make a conscientious effort to change where indicated.

5. Cover other things on his mind.
NOTE: A check list of twelve questions is offered to help bring out what's on employees' minds.

This admirable guide to man-manager communication concludes with this sage advice which should be registered indelibly on the minds of all middle-management men. "After you have had 'How Am I Doing Talks' with your men, urge them to do the same with theirs."

Man-to-man discussions with employees are one of the best tools available to managers to aid in developing the organization unit into a better working team (the essence of integration). If such discussions are handled properly, it has been said, 75 per cent of industry's employee communication problems can be overcome.

The author's company, which has been a pioneer in this field of performance appraisals, provides each supervisor with a supply of "Personnel Review Forms" (Figure 2) for distribution to employees *well in advance* of scheduled appraisal discussions. This is an excellent device for enabling prior self-analysis on the part of the employee and helps him to bring up the most important items he wishes to have covered during the interview.

The training of appraisers is essential

The crux of the whole business of appraising is in the training of the appraisers. The form is of secondary importance. With untrained appraisers, the best form in the world will fail; with good appraisers, the poorest form will work. The perfect combination, of course, is good appraisers using good systems and forms.

Appraisers must be familiar with the purposes of appraising, the use of the form, and the techniques of counseling employees on results. Written instructions are not enough. Conference training is a "must."

Confidential

PERSONAL REVIEW FORM

This form has been designed to give you an opportunity to discuss those aspects of your job which are of most interest and importance to you. Please feel free to express how you view your present assignment, and what your immediate and long-range plans are. Thus it is hoped that you can be assisted not only in setting realistic goals but also in attaining them. The value of this information depends on the frankness and care with which you answer the questions.

. . . .

Name

1. Do you feel that you have an adequate understanding of the requirements of your job? On which of your job accountability factors would a clearer understanding be helpful?

2. Do you have a good understanding of the Company's salary compensation plan as it affects you? On what points would you like further information?

3. On most jobs there are some things which we like and others about which we care less. What are some of the things you like best about your job? What are some of the things you like least about your job?

4. What parts of your job do you feel you do best?

5. On what parts of your job do you feel you want more experience or training?

6. Looking at your job as a whole, what would you say you have accomplished in the past year?

7. What changes do you think should be made in your job so as to increase your accomplishments? (Consider such aspects as the cooperation you get from others, the amount of red tape involved, the allocation of assignments, etc.)

8. Do you feel that you have some skill or specific knowledge which could be used to good advantage by GE, which are not being used at present? If so, what are they? Do you have any suggestions as to how they can be used?

9. Do you feel that your job gives you an opportunity to learn things which are useful in preparing you for a better job? If not, what suggestions have you?

10. If you could get any kind of work you wanted, either somewhere else, or here in this Department, what kind of work would you want to do?

11. What are your long-range plans? (For example, what kind of work do you hope to be doing five years from now?) How do you propose to achieve these goals? Specifically: what courses, studies, or reading have you undertaken during the past year? What other studies or programs do you feel you should take in the near future?

12. Have you any suggestions about the ways the Department could help you to broaden your background?

13. Do you have any other comments or suggestions that you wish to make?

Figure 2

Should the work of hourly employees be appraised?

The foregoing has dealt exclusively with appraisal discussions with salaried personnel for the simple reason that such discussions are not generally held with hourly employees. Historically, it has been the consensus that single job-rate structures, rate-progression schedules, or union agreements generally introduce so many roadblocks to good appraisal practice that it is not worth the effort to carry out this function for hourly rated employees.

There fortunately appears to be emerging, however, the concept that good human relations, including "How'm I doing?" discussions, are not reserved for any special groups of employees. The advantages of these effective techniques should be afforded all groups of people, salaried *and hourly*.

Some of the operating departments of the author's company have achieved signal success in appraising hourly people. Their objectives are to let the employee know how he is performing on his present job; to suggest ways in which the employee might improve his present performance and prepare himself for future progress; to create a cumulative record of the employee's job performance; to provide the company with information concerning employees who appear to possess potential for advancement; to provide upward communication.

These objectives are aimed at improving human relations between the foreman and his employees. When a supervisor practices these fundamentals, his relationships with his people are *good* ones. The job-performance appraisal—properly handled—is an important tool for accomplishing this relationship.

In one department, the performance of 2,470 employees on hourly jobs was recently appraised by 135 foremen. A subsequent opinion poll revealed the following evaluation of the worthwhileness of the appraisal.

Ninety-seven per cent of the employees wanted the program continued—at least once each year. Ninety-six per cent felt it was helpful to them. Ninety-two per cent reported receiving helpful suggestions from their foremen in addition to their general rating.

Ninety-nine per cent of the foremen stated the program was worth the time and effort put into it.

The department noted evidence of improved performance. Ninety-three per cent were doing normal or better work, as contrasted with 87 per cent in the previous year. Thirty per cent were doing excellent or better work, as compared with 23 per cent in the previous year. Seven per cent were in the below-normal area, whereas there were 13 per cent in this category the year before.

The department management concluded that the periodic appraisal of production workers is practical, acceptable, and profitable—and that it substantially contributes to better employee relations.

CHAPTER 11

The Foreman's Informative Conference

No single lump of communication work is more effective than a carefully structured, planned, and conducted foreman's informative conference. Although only the foreman meeting will be described, such sharing of information with groups of employees should be carried on by all supervisors at every level. The technique is equally effective whether employed with shop or office personnel.

Stated simply, the purposes of such a meeting are to improve the work of the individual and the teamwork between individuals, to develop better man-manager relations, to give employees greater participation and enhanced job satisfaction.

One company which uses these conferences for a formal sharing of information with employees lists the following goals, which ought to be the goals of every manager:

To encourage individual initiative; to stimulate suggestions; to clear up rumors; to improve teamwork; to relate each employee's work to the over-all work of the group, the department, the company; to impart fundamentals of economics; to establish a climate for full, free, two-way communication; to have available an *accepted* medium for imparting critical information to all parts of the enterprise; to improve productivity and advance the total goals of the enterprise.

In the author's company, much time and attention have been devoted to this critical and productive level of communication which has been painstakingly evolved over a period of fifteen years.

The anatomy of "employee Round Tables"

In many of the decentralized units of this company, it is a requirement that supervisors take their employees off their job for an informative conference quarterly. The term that has been most generally applied for such conferring is "the Round Table." In fact in certain locations, specially designed round or oval tables have been constructed to encourage freer communication.

Attendance is limited to a small group of fifteen to twenty employees. If a foreman supervises twenty-five people, he might choose to include them all in a single meeting. If his span embraces forty to sixty people, he would need to hold two or three meetings every three months.

The meetings are held in a fairly quiet, convenient, and comfortable conference room. Ideally, only the supervisor and all or part of his work group should be present. Yet until supervisors develop proficiency, it may be desirable to have a communication or training specialist audit the meeting. Where this has been tried, it seems not to have inhibited full, natural participation—especially if the outsider remains in the background and performs the role of recording questions and answers.

The content of Round-Table communication

The best conferences seem to be based on an agenda developed through the joint efforts of the supervisor and a staff specialist. In this way, supervisors are free to conduct a meeting in their own unique manner. Yet all employees throughout the plant can be discussing some timely similar topics during a given period.

Written materials can be distributed at the meeting and interpreted where otherwise they might go unread. In fact, such conferences provide the finest possible medium for determining the impact of previously distributed written communication.

One plant which constantly audits such meetings, reports that 85 per cent of the agenda items, and 90 per cent of employee questions for a given year dealt with group-centered problems:

material flow and shortages, faulty work and rework, housekeeping, safety, working conditions, mechanization. Such acute localization of agendas stems from two factors: the employees are most interested in problems of their particular work group, and such an agenda is easiest for a foreman to plan and follow.

In the best interests of the enterprise and the employees, there should be a balance between local and plant or office information.

One plant offers a selection from the following list of subjects to supplement the supervisor's *local* material: employee benefits, employee services (suggestion system, medical, cafeteria, recreation, etc.), business outlook (orders, shipments, competition), self-development opportunities, plant security, labor and management relations, economics.

Some practical do's and don't's

Some supervisors begin their meetings with a presentation, utilizing a blackboard or written materials, and sometimes visual aids, until they cover the agenda; others structure the entire meeting on a discussion basis. The supervisor is trained to observe the following cardinal rules:

Never try to bluff an answer. Say, "I don't know, but I will try to get the answer."

Treat each question with seriousness and dignity to discourage grandstanding.

If unable to answer a question fully at the meeting, see that all employees get a complete answer as soon as possible after the meeting.

Accept all questions except union grievances or intimate personal problems.

Discourage tangents, useless debate, monopoly of conversation, sarcasm.

Refer many local questions to the group first for their opinion.

Notification of the meetings is achieved by posting signed notices which announce the time, place, date, location, and names of participants. Additionally, many supervisors contact each individual personally; in offices, notification is by letter.

If employees are represented by a union, the union steward is notified and included in the *first* meeting. Thereafter, he attends only when his turn comes around. Responsible union officials, genuinely interested in the welfare of their employees, recognize that such meetings fill a genuine need of their members and also that they are popular. Occasionally, a union official will start heckling, but the group will usually silence him or engage him in constructive debate.

The Round Tables are held on company time. Workers on incentive are paid average earnings; day workers and salaried employees present no problem. Budget-harried production officials sometimes balk at the cost. The consensus, however, is that there is very little, if any, loss of real production and that long-range individual and group productivity increases.

Preparing the supervisor

Careful preparation of the foreman is the *sine qua non* of effective Round Tables. Initially, many foremen would rather face a wild bull than meet alone with their own group. One spent a sleepless night before his first meeting worrying what he would do if there were no questions. He pleaded with his general foreman to take up a position outside the conference room door so that he could rush in for an assist if a stillness came over the meeting. He was not called in. After the meeting, the relieved and pleased foreman said: "Man, they started in asking questions and they never did stop! Only covered half my agenda."

Before embarking on this most productive variety of employee communication, the procedure must be started from above. The first-line supervisors must themselves be informed in order to inform their people. The general foreman or superintendent or other middle-management men must hold such meetings with all supervisors reporting to them. In turn, middle-management is owed such treatment by the heads of the business.

Any edict to the effect that "after March 1, all first-line supervisors will schedule informative meetings with their employees" will cause untold damage. Not only must the process start at the top, but supervisors should be given a short course in conference leadership. One of the best of such courses is the "Talking with Groups" training developed by du Pont and now widely used by many companies.

Providing staff aid to the supervisors

Equally important is the provision for providing the required information. This is done in a number of ways. In some plants, a staff specialist assists; in others, a regular "agenda builder," called "Round-Table Tips" or "Informative Meeting Nuggets," is issued regularly to all supervisors to give them the competence that stems from knowledge.

The contents of several of these multigraphed "agenda builders" are revealing: details of the annual in-plant charity drive; highlights of the new union contract; community opinion votes local plant best place to work; new competitor takes big order at low price; tuition refunds for evening study; employee credit union sets up new office; new fire prevention procedures; amount of profits required in last five years to finance local expansion; what is automation; questions and answers about inflation.

The anticipation of the coming Round Table serves to ensure that the supervisor is in fact informed. We read most avidly and carefully that which we must orally re-transmit.

Round Tables should and can be made to serve as a prime means of upward communication. This entails a good reporting system. Good reports can be of enormous help in evaluating and readjusting the total communication program. They provide a means of acquainting the chief executive with just what is on the minds of the majority of his employees, just what *they* consider important. By listening to such upward communication, managers can learn how their policies are accepted, where trouble spots exist, and how trouble spots can be corrected.

The task of writing the report is usually rotated between participating individuals. The reports should record what was discussed, the degree of employee interest in each subject, the specific questions asked, how well employees were satisfied, unanswered questions, and the follow-up action indicated.

BETTER WORK AND TEAMWORK RESULTS

Employee reception of Round Tables is most enthusiastic if the meetings are even reasonably well conducted. The temper of the response is revealed by direct quotations from the participants: "A lot of people said they learned more yesterday about this plant than they have ever known the whole time they've been here." "Meetings like this will cut out a lot of rework. I had no idea that a damaged coil cost fifty bucks!" "It's wonderful to get straight dope right from the horse's mouth." "It's a good thing to bring people together like that. It gets them closer together, a lot closer than at work." "You're not afraid to talk to the boss with the whole gang around you. You get to know him. Before, we didn't get to talk to the foreman from one week to the next."

More meaningful clues as to practical results and employee reactions may be discerned from this summary of answers to an unsigned questionnaire filled out by 406 shop employees in one plant:

What effect does the Round Table Program have on operations?

About 80 per cent felt that people "have fewer accidents," that they "get along better with the foreman," and that they "worry less about the future" as a result of Round Tables.

About 60 per cent felt that people "do higher quality work," that they "get the work out on time," and "get along better with each other." About 55 per cent felt that the people "have fewer complaints" and the "company makes more money."

How does the employee like the Round Table Program?

Seventy per cent like it very much; 20 per cent like it somewhat, and 10 per cent are neutral about it or dislike it.

Eighty-five per cent said they would like to see the Program continued;

5 per cent said it made no difference; 1 per cent said it would be better to stop it, and 9 per cent did not answer.

What portion of the Round Table is most interesting to employees?

Twenty-eight per cent liked the program given by the foreman, including the question-and-answer period.

Eighteen per cent liked free discussion.

Thirty-six per cent liked movies, slides, and other prepared programs.

Ten per cent liked programs given by higher management or outside speakers and specialists.

What is the "atmosphere" at the meeting; that is, what attitudes do employees have concerning the meeting?

Almost 90 per cent said their foreman "does an excellent job of running the meeting," that "they get an opportunity to ask all the questions they have," and that the "foreman really tries to get answers to their questions later if he does not know them at the time of the meeting."

However, 50 per cent believe that the foreman "does not have enough authority to give answers in the Round Table without first checking his boss," and 40 per cent believe "all questions have *not* been answered," that the "foreman avoids certain topics."

What topics would employees like to hear about and discuss at future Round-Table meetings?

There was significant agreement, in the following order, that these topics need *more* discussion:

1. Things customers complain about in our machines.
2. Letting us know ahead of time about changes, new methods, technology, etc.
3. Trying to explain why management higher up does things the way they do.
4. Working conditions.
5. Gripes and complaints.
6. Better and easier ways for us to do our jobs.

Numerous other topics showed the need for more discussion. However, the above were outstanding.

What attitudes toward "management" are prevalent?

About 70 per cent felt that they "may not always like what management does, but feel management is always trying to be fair," and that "management tries to build team spirit."

Despite these impressive results, business and industry is losing millions of dollars annually in untapped employee productivity and idea sharing because of failure to integrate its supervisors into its communication system.

INFORMATION SHARING MUST BE BUILT INTO FOREMAN'S JOB

Walter G. Barlow, vice-president of Opinion Research Corporation, reports these conclusions from a study conducted by his organization.[1]

In talking to foremen about communication, one important fact emerges: foremen are not yet active communicators. As many as 50% do not feel that passing along facts beyond mere routine information is part of their job. For example, 63% of foremen tell us that their company has talked a great deal about competition, but only 25% of manufacturing manual workers say that their company has [passed this information along to them]. We don't have to go far to find the reason because, in general, foremen do not voluntarily share company problems with their men. A total of 81% [of foremen interviewed] tell us that, as they see it, their company faces stiff competition, but only 26% say that "it's part of our job" to talk to the men about meeting competition.

One of the most persistent misconceptions we find among management groups about employee communications is the idea that if you get information to supervision, it will automatically be transferred to the rank and file. Yet we have ample survey evidence to indicate a variety of reasons why foremen do not normally pass on information. For one thing, communicating is an art; and foremen, like most people, don't know very much about it, particularly so far as listening is concerned. Also,

[1] Walter G. Barlow, "Measuring the Effectiveness of Communication," American Management Association, General Management Series, no. 181, New York, 1956.

some foremen keep information to themselves and regard its possession as a prerogative of management, while still others feel that they already have enough to do without having to talk and listen to people. Only when management trains the foreman in how to communicate and then begins to judge the operating foreman partly on the basis of how effectively he does communication, will the supervisor attain his place as an important, if not the most important, link in management's communication apparatus.

A continuing study of supervisory informative meetings, particularly at the foreman level, indicates that some such formalized method of sharing information with employees and tapping their reservoir of ideas is essential for the best interests of the business and will pay off handsomely.

Each business enterprise must find its own unique way of providing the time, the facilities, the skills, and the climate for relating the interests of supervisors and other employees to the interests of the enterprise through formalized, purposeful, face-to-face, give-and-take, two-way communication.

PART FOUR

Principles, Techniques, and Media
of Communication

CHAPTER 12

Principles of Communication

A principle is a generally accepted rule of action. Dr. Herbert I. Abelson, chief psychologist, Opinion Research Corporation, defines a principle as "a partially verified guide . . . in certain situations." He then adds this practical advice: "A true statement of principle should contain within itself some guidance for action."

It has not only been implied but stated that the purpose of this book is to examine the larger role of communication in a business enterprise. In this context, we are concerned not merely with essential administrative communication but with the use of communication to improve productivity, to enhance job satisfactions, to develop mature union relations, to create a receptive climate for innovation, to establish a mutuality of understanding between managers and their employees and community neighbors, and to improve the business climate.

In order to achieve these vital communication goals, the manager is confronted with the complex task of changing stubbornly resistant opinions and attitudes that have been years in the shaping.

Before examining the relatively few principles that are known concerning opinion change, let us inquire briefly into the nature of "opinions" and the process of opinion change.

OPINIONS, ATTITUDES, AND ATTITUDE CHANGE

Some of the most usable guidance in the field of opinion change has been developed through the research of Dr. Carl I. Hovland and his former asociates, Dr. Irving L. Janis and Dr. Harold H. Kelley of the Department of Psychology, Yale University.

In the preface to their provocative report on their findings,[1] they state their purpose as that of "developing scientific propositions which specify the conditions under which the effectiveness of one or another type of persuasive communication is increased or decreased." Early in their reporting, the authors examine the nature of "opinion" and its handmaiden, "attitude," and make this helpful comparison: [2]

Operationally speaking, opinions are viewed as "verbal answers" that an individual gives in response to stimulus situations in which some general "question" is raised. . . .

Both "opinion" and "attitude" refer to implicit responses. . . . The relationship between the two is an intimate one. But while the term "opinion" will be used to designate a broad class of anticipations and expectations, the term "attitude" will be used exclusively for those implicit responses which are oriented toward approaching or avoiding a given object, person, group, or symbol. . . . Opinions are considered to be verbalizable, while attitudes are sometimes unconscious.

The authors point out that attitudes and opinions have a high degree of mutual interaction; that changes in attitudes may affect one's opinions and that, conversely and more importantly, changes in opinion may modify general attitudes: [3]

Opinions [in the view of the authors] like other habits, will tend to persist unless the individual undergoes some new learning experiences. Exposure to a persuasive communication which successfully induces the individual to accept a new opinion constitutes a learning experience in which a new verbal habit is acquired. That is to say, when presented with a given question, the individual now thinks of and prefers the new answer suggested by the communication to the old one held prior to exposure to the communication.

[1] Carl I. Hovland, Irving L. Janis, and Harold H. Kelley, *Communication and Persuasion*, Yale University Press, New Haven, Conn., 1953.
[2] *Ibid.*, pp. 6–7.
[3] *Ibid.*, p. 10.

Another writer observes succinctly that: "opinions require thought —attitudes don't."

Still another gives us this definition, which gets closer to the problem facing the manager who supervises people. "Opinions or attitudes are the inferred basis for observed consistencies in the social behavior of individuals."

What the social scientists are telling us is that we must change opinions if we hope to change attitudes which are inhibiting the full flowering of the business enterprise.

Social scientists are performing an enormously useful role in pushing back the frontiers of knowledge concerning human behavior. Their findings, however, must usually be interpreted and applied to business situations if they are to serve as usable guides for the pragmatic business manager.

In an attempt to convert and condense the findings of Hovland, Janis, Kelley, Lazarsfeld, Schramm, and several score social scientists to a more practical application to business problems, Dr. Abelson has performed an outstanding service to the cause of more resultful communication in business. The following are some of the principles distilled by Dr. Abelson, together with some personal observations by the author based on experience in his own company. Both Dr. Abelson and the author think it appropriate to indicate the tentative nature of these principles. They are, to a large degree, supported by hypotheses rather than conclusively demonstrated matters of fact.

NOTE: The unabridged report entitled *Some Principles of Persuasion: Survey of recent research on how opinions and attitudes are changed* is available through Opinion Research Corporation, Princeton, New Jersey.

SOME PRINCIPLES OF PERSUASION

1. There will probably be more opinion change in the direction you want if you specifically state your conclusion than if you let the audience draw their own.

NOTE: Facts in themselves can lead to false conclusions. Observe how union economists and those representing business arrive at completely different conclusions from the facts in an annual earnings statement:

Fact I. In 195—, the huge _____ company made the exorbitant profit of _____. This proves the need for siphoning off these excessive profits in higher wages.

Fact II. In 195—, total earnings of the _____ company amounted to _____ after taxes. Earnings must somehow be improved or the company will be faced with borrowing to finance the expansion needed to remain competitive and protect job security.

2. Emotional vs. factual appeals. The use of fear.

   Sometimes emotional appeals are more influential, sometimes factual. It all depends on the kind of message and kind of audience. A strong threat is generally *less* effective than a mild threat in inducing the desired opinion change.

NOTE: Readership surveys consistently show that well-edited company house organs are considered more truthful and trustworthy than competing union newspapers or handbills. The latter are usually so emotional and so filled with strong threats as to be self-defeating. This is not to say that fear is always built upon appeals to the emotions. Fear can be built up entirely from a presentation of fact.

3. Sleeper Effect

   More of the desired opinion change may be measurable some time after exposure to the communication than right after the exposure.

NOTE: Many employers who are dedicated to the policy of silence on controversial subjects begin communicating to their employees and neighbors when faced with a strike or other major crisis only to fail because of lack of time to effect opinion change. Dr. Hovland calls attention to another finding that motivates astute managers to communicate continuously on controversial issues. He points out that once a topic has been presented, the audience pays more attention to what is said about it in mass media. This increased awareness leads to more reading and listening and thinking about it, until an opinion has been formed.

4. Credibility of Communicator

   There will be more opinion change in the desired direction if the communicator has high credibility than if he has low credibility.

NOTE: Credibility may be implicit in a previously acquired reputation, as in the case of a new manager who is placed in charge. More often it is a result of employees' observations of character, earnest intent to do right, or demonstrated consistency of right actions. That is why a "do-right-voluntarily" policy consistently implemented is the foundation of any effective employee communication activity.

It must be noted that evidence indicates that a source is quickly forgotten, that after a few weeks, the initial advantage held by the credible source is lost. *Reminding* the audience of the source renews the advantage.

5. Effect of Known Motives
   Suspicion of the motives of the communicator may not work against desired opinion change.

NOTE: Although more evidence is needed, we often note the success of management communication where competing ideological communicators use every persuasive device to cast discredit on the management's motives. Success favors those managers who candidly set about proving to employees that the goals which motivate the managers are good goals for the employees.

6. The people you want most in your audience are least likely to be there.

NOTE: This refers to the principle of "selective exposure", that is, the tendency for people to expose themselves to communication with which they already agree and to avoid opposing material. Democrats, for example, listen mostly to Democratic campaign speeches, avoiding Republican talk, and vice versa. Propaganda material generally is read by supporters, not the opposition.

An analysis of most employee audiences would probably indicate the following orientation: 10 per cent to 20 per cent closely oriented and receptive to management communication, 10 per cent to 20 per cent intransigently opposed, and 60 per cent to 80 per cent neutral. It is the opinions and attitudes of this large shifting independent vote which determine the success of the communication program. Supervisors should be queried to determine which of their group they believe fall into the middle category. Then through nondirective interviewing or other opinion-sampling devices, a determined effort should be made to learn what are the blockades to effective communication with these balance-of-power people and which communication appeals may have the greatest likelihood of affecting desired opinion change.

7. Personal Involvement

Audience participation helps to overcome their resistance [to change].

NOTE: This long-recognized principle underlies the constantly accelerated use of conferences, case studies, role playing, Round Tables, etc., in training and communication.

The heightened involvement that attends participation affords alert managers a continuing opportunity to get higher returns from their communication. The fabulously successful General Motors essay contest of a few years ago involved thousands of employees in constructively thinking as to what they liked best about their job. Another company additionally involves its foremen in the communication process by appointing a foremen's advisory committee on communication to report on the acceptability of important written communication aimed at shop employees and to feed back suggestions for improving group informative meetings.

8. Influence of Groups

A person's opinions and attitudes are strongly influenced by the groups to which he belongs and wants to belong. The person is rewarded for conforming to the standards of the group and punished for deviating from them.

NOTE: These phenomena of human behavior undergird the highly successful community relations programs of many enlightened companies. Sometimes it is necessary to change the norms of groups. This is a difficult task but may be accomplished under certain conditions by proving that the goals of management are goals or values which are also part of the norms of the group. For example, during national emergencies, the influence of patriotism as a group norm usually overrides the influence of the group-imposed work-limitation norm.

In addition to these principles which have been distilled by Dr. Abelson from the research of social scientists, there are others which the professional manager may find useful.

Some additional useful findings

What, for example, do we know about the retention of opinion change? The evidence is conflicting but there is strong evidence of the need for repetition. Unless there is compelling self-interest which led to a high degree of initial learning, the opinion change must be made permanent by reiterating the personal rewards for maintaining the new opinion. Repetition, however, can be self-defeating unless fresh means of emphasis (and often fresh media) are employed.

Of untold value to the manager is the awareness of the principle of primacy. First impressions have great retentivity. Communication which anticipates problem areas or predicted countercommunication is the most effective.

Many trade unions skillfully use this principle of communication, with the result that business is constantly on the defensive, putting out fires and answering charges.

The shorter work week is a typical case in point. Management says nothing about such a subject, secure in the solidly founded economic belief that employees will prefer a more rapidly accelerating standard of living to more leisure time. Instead of explaining this either-or choice when opportunity presents itself, management waits until the union officials make headway in convincing employees that a shorter work week with the same or more pay is the quickest route to better living.

It is perfectly possible for managers to anticipate what its ideological competitors will be telling its employees and community neighbors well in advance of the facts. Progressive managers are now telling their employees what they can *expect* to hear from other sources thus greatly blunting conviction when it is heard.

Too much emphasis cannot be placed on the necessity for business "to get there first" with its opinion-molding or opinion-maintenance communication. The findings of Hovland, Janis, and Kelley indicate that "once a belief is modified by an effective communication, there will be a tendency for the newly acquired opinion responses to interfere with the subsequent acquisition of any incompatible opinion responses." [4]

Various additional principles are cited by Hovland, Abelson, and

[4] *Ibid.*, p. 263.

others, but an exhaustive list is outside the scope of this volume. Readers who wish to delve further into this productive field may refer to Hovland's "Effect of the Mass Media of Communication" in Gardner Lindzey, *Handbook of Social Psychology* (1954) and Joseph T. Klapper, *Effects of Mass Media* (1949).

The need for accelerated communication research

Communication is power. With each passing year, circumstances are placing a higher premium on the ability of the professional manager to compete aggressively in the ideological field; and there is an increasing need for research. A small investment in communication research, as a basis of planning, will pay out richly for even the small business enterprise. Only in this way can managers capitalize the tremendous potential of primacy.

This all too brief review stresses some of the principles which are known about communication. But, in point of fact, the *unknown* far exceeds the known in this complex management work of developing opinions and attitudes which are in the best mutual interests of business enterprises and the people they serve.

Managers are encouraged to keep abreast of new knowledge in the field of persuasive communication either through a staff specialist or by a reading of some good periodic digest of social science findings.

The rewards are high. Each small gain in effectiveness enriches not only the manager's enterprise but the life-giving business system as a whole.

CHAPTER 13

Designing a Communication Structure for the Business

In most large American cities today, one can observe the towering steel frameworks of office buildings creating a new skyline. Almost overnight these unlovely gaunt structures are transformed into shining palaces by the application of aluminum or stainless steel façades.

Contrary to the practice in some businesses, effective communication policies and procedures cannot be applied to the framework of an enterprise as are these modern building materials.

It would be more accurate to describe the process as one of painstakingly erecting a masonry edifice on a solid foundation.

Our foundation should be an earnest intent to do right voluntarily. To convert this intent from the general to the specific, we would do well to express it in terms of a set of "people-centered" goals to supplement our economic goals.

Importance of a published personnel creed

Thomas G. Spates, professor emeritus of personnel administration, Yale University, formerly vice-president, General Foods Corporation, and author of the *American Code of Personnel Administration,* states ". . . employees are entitled to know, in writing, what standards of conduct top management sets for itself and requires of bosses at all levels; and they are equally entitled to know, in writing, what rights they have and what is expected of them."

151

Significantly, those companies which have had the vision and courage to develop a formalized published set of goals for their employees have had a distinguished record of success in their employee relations as well as in the achievement of their economic goals.

An American classic is the statement of the Armco Steel Corporation. The following is excerpted from *Armco Policies*, originally approved by the board of directors in 1919 and revised in 1934:

The following are the main planks in the platform on which the Armco organization has been developed:

1st. A Square Deal: To insist on a square deal always to everyone. There are two kinds of a square deal, the Armco kind is born of the belief that we should do right for right's sake and not simply to secure a desired result.

2nd. Compensation: To provide not only fair remuneration, but the best compensation for service rendered that it is possible to pay under the changing economic, commercial and other competitive conditions that exist from time to time.

3rd. Incentive: To provide every possible and practical sound incentive to best effort, as it is the great mainspring of all human accomplishment.

4th. Opportunity: To provide every possible opportunity for advancement, as it is the ladder on which the individual hopes to reach his ultimate goal—his heart's ambition.

5th. Working Conditions: To create and maintain both good and safe working conditions. Armco believes that good and safe working conditions, in the fullest sense of the expression, are absolutely essential to industrial efficiency and progress.

6th. Living Conditions: To in every possible way encourage good living conditions.

7th. Mutual Interest: To encourage such organization activities as will clarify and enlarge the mutual interests of all who are working with the management of the company.

8th. Cooperation: Through the operation of an Employee Representation Plan a measure of understanding has and always will be developed that will result in real cooperation between management and the organization at large.

9th. Armco Spirit: Through the full and fair application of all Armco Policies, to develop "Armco Spirit" in its broadest interpretation within the organization.

Developing and publishing a people-centered code of conduct is an ideal prerequisite for effective employee communication. The psychological effect of such a code framed and hanging in the office of each supervisor is a most effective incentive for the good deeds which must precede all good communication.

Additional prerequisites

Another prerequisite for successful communication is the difficult task of integrating middle management into the communication chain. This task is a difficult and never-ending one. Important incentives must be offered and rigorous measurements of results applied. Managers quickly learn on what basis they are being measured by their superiors despite what the position guides may state. Only by effectively motivating the management team, by keeping all members of this team well informed, and by measuring each member of the team on his communication effectiveness can the powerful communication potential of the middle-management group be realized to the great profit of the enterprise.

A third prerequisite might well be the issuance of a formal policy on communication similar to, or an improvement on, the following example:

Company policy concerning communication

1. *Need for policy.* The success of this company is greatly dependent on teamwork at all levels, between staff and line, and between all functions. This teamwork will be in direct ratio to the quality of our communication.

By effectively communicating with each employee, we make him feel more secure in his job, more interested in his work, more sure of his assignments, more loyal to the company, and more productive.

By developing better listening habits and freeing the channels of upward communication, the company will be enabled to determine how its policies are accepted, to locate and correct incipient troubles, and to receive valuable information and suggestions for increasing the profitability of the enterprise as well as the earnings of its employees.

2. *Policy.* Each manager and nonmanagerial employee will be kept continuously and fully informed, through the most appropriate channels and techniques, of the objectives, goals, and progress of the company, the department, and particularly of the employee's own work group.

The company will also undertake to share all information of interest and importance with its employees so that they may make their maximum contribution to the enterprise.

Each manager will be expected to develop effective channels of communication with all other appropriate functional managers and specialists to assure the adequate lateral communication so essential to good teamwork.

Each employee will be given the maximum opportunity on all occasions to express his opinions and complaints without prejudice. It is incumbent upon each manager at each level to make sure that communication from employees be facilitated upward in undiluted form to a level satisfactory to the transmitting employee.

In addition, all pertinent information necessary for the development of understanding and support will be purposefully and systematically projected into the community.

3. *Authority for application of policy.* Each operating manager has the responsibility and authority to implement both the spirit and letter of this policy.

4. *Responsibility of the industrial relations officer.* The industrial relations officer is responsibile for counseling line management in the effective methods of applying this policy and of continuously appraising and reporting the results of its application to the president. He is also responsible for the preparation of the detailed procedures necessary for the implementation of this policy.

A final prerequisite should be the appointment of a staff communication manager or specialist to be responsible for the highly skilled and demanding work necessary for the implementation of a thoroughgoing communication policy.

Summary of preliminary design factors

Let us assume that the chief executive of an integrated company or a branch plant has satisfied the prerequisites for successful communication. That is, he has by precept and personal action shown a determination to achieve full, frank, two-way communication. He has developed and published a code of ethics or otherwise convinced

THE CHANNELS OF ORAL COMMUNICATION

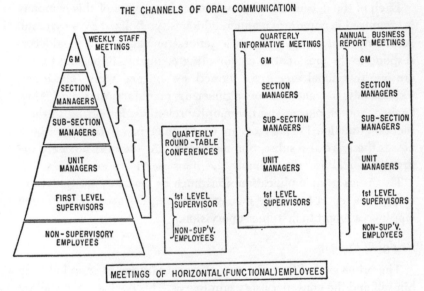

Figure 3

his managers at all levels that they must do right by their associates voluntarily without being dragged unwillingly to do it by the union, politicians, employee uprisings, or community pressure. He has convinced his managers that they will be measured, in part, for their performance in this area and has installed some built-in controls to ensure that they do in fact take their communication work seriously. He has issued a carefully thought-out policy on communication and provided for staff talent to help get along with the job.

He is now ready to set up and put in place a mechanism for satisfying the communication needs of the enterprise.

ESTABLISHING ORAL COMMUNICATION CHANNELS

In designing his structure, he should first look to his channels of oral communication. Figure 3 depicts the channels of oral communication used, with various modifications, by most of the operating departments in the author's company.

Each of the decentralized autonomous businesses of this company is organized in a uniform manner, which is symbolized by a pyramid. At the apex of the pyramid is a general manager who would correspond to the president of a competing company. Reporting to him are five functional executives termed section managers. These are, respectively, the managers of engineering, manufacturing, marketing, finance, and employee and community relations. Reporting to these section (functional) managers are unit managers. (In the larger businesses there are also subsection managers.) At the next level are the first-line supervisors and finally the nonsupervisory employees.

This is an oversimplification, inasmuch as certain nonsupervisory employees report to middle management, but the great bulk of such employees report to first-line supervision.

Bridging the gap

The prime goal of the chief executive is to bridge the gap between himself and the nonsupervisory employees. This he does by installing a pipeline from top to bottom with relay or booster stations.

Origin of the flow of downward communication is the general manager's weekly staff meeting with his five section managers. This should be rigidly scheduled, preferably on an unvarying day and time. Even this group of relatively secure employees needs the reassurance that people feel when they know that each Monday at ten o'clock, for example, they may receive and give the communication so vital to the efficient performance of their jobs.

Nothing breeds inefficiency and frustration faster than the communication void existing where there is no fixed date and time for the essential administrative and planning communication on which decisions are made. Thousands of business executives at this hour are waiting to see their busy boss—have been waiting for days. In lieu of the regular group meeting, the boss calls them individually— when he can get to them—usually at an inefficient time for the subordinate officer.

Where the weekly meeting is a tradition, subordinate officers will store up their give-and-take communication items, except for real emergencies, secure in the knowledge that these can be handled more effectively next Monday morning—and very often with the benefit of group consideration.

Immediately upon completion of the chief executive's staff meeting, or the same afternoon, the section managers meet with their subsection or unit managers to transmit the information essential for *their* efficient performance.

In the smaller businesses, these middle-management men then complete the transmission of information through the management group by conferring with their subordinates—the first-line supervisors. In the larger organizations, this meeting may take place on a Tuesday or Wednesday.

Quarterly—sometimes only semiannually, depending on the size of the organization—the chief executive meets with all supervisors, and the senior professional employees who are normally considered a part of the management team, at an evening meeting away from the plant to review progress in achieving goals, to share essential information of unusual import, and to motivate everyone to step up his performance and teamwork.

Once a quarter, or sometimes every four months, the gap between the first-level supervisors and their employees is bridged through the medium of the quarterly Round-Table conferences which were described in Chapter 11.

The importance of this regularized, formalized sharing and receiving of information with both the white- and blue-collar rank-and-file employees cannot be too heavily emphasized. The saturation of the middle group of managers with essential communication is but a means to the end of satisfying the urgent communication needs of the hundreds and sometimes thousands of workers whose morale is so essential to the success of the enterprise.

Face to face with all employees

Annually, in the author's company, the general manager meets with all employees in a business report meeting. (This is popularly termed "The Boss Talk".) At this meeting, the chief executive individually, or with the help of his five functional officers, gives a report of his stewardship.

If the organization is small, one meeting suffices. If large, he will divide up the employees into groups of between three and five hundred, depending on the size of the meeting place.

Essentially this meeting passes along to the people information as to "how we all made out." Additionally, its purpose is to interpret the goals for the upcoming year. Always there is provision for any and all questions from the floor. Once these meetings become a way of life, there is no dearth of questions.

These meetings provide an excellent opportunity to convey significant, meaningful job-related economic information in a setting in which cause-and-effect economic principles can be more easily grasped and retained.

ACHIEVING LATERAL COMMUNICATION

Often overlooked in a business enterprise is the vital need for better channels of lateral communication. Horizontal communication in most companies is atrocious, despite the great interdependence of the various functions. As a result, employees in the various functions erect elaborate grapevine channels to compensate for the lack of formal lateral channels between functions and between positions at the same level.

Of greater concern to the chief executive should be the misunderstandings, jealousies, jockeying, missed signals, lack of coordination, and wasteful internecine rivalries caused by faulty lateral communication.

Dr. Temple Burling stresses the grave consequences of faulty lateral communication in a typical hospital in this manner: [1]

If coordination is to be achieved, it is important that there be adequate communication *along* the work flow. People whose jobs are related must be able to work out their relationships between themselves and not depend exclusively on orders flowing from some central point above. This is particularly important in the hospital because of crises. Communications "flowing through channels" are too slow to meet emergencies. In some instances the patient might be dead by the time all of the proper channels had been observed.

In the hospitals studies, we found that established provision for vertical communication was much more developed than for horizontal flow. The horizontal channels *get* established because workers want to get their work done and get it done well. They recognize that they can't do it without communicating directly with the people whose work is related to theirs. But these channels of communication often are not official and the employees may even feel guilty about using them; and the administration may be a little guilty if horizontal communication is so effective that much of the time the hospital runs without direction.

These conflicts between horizontal and vertical communication are an ever-present possibility. Information flowing horizontally and decisions made on this basis may at any time disrupt the central planning and coordination. The cure for this is that people involved have enough understanding of the over-all operations and problems of the hospital to know which decisions they can safely make among themselves and which must be referred upward if disruption is not to occur somewhere else.

Many units of the author's company hold formalized monthly meetings with selected representatives of the various functions, engineering, production, purchasing, sales, employee relations, to share information essential for improved teamwork. Very often a portion of the meeting is allotted to one function to explain its role in the over-all business as well as some of its unique problems.

There are many additional methods of oral communication both

[1] Temple Burling, "Aids and Bars to Internal Communication," *Hospitals,* 28:84, November, 1954. See also Chap. 9, "Channels of Contact."

formal and informal, but these, as well as the foregoing, will be discussed in Chapter 14.

Having thus provided for an effective flow of oral communication, let us now examine the much newer area of written mass communication which is yearly assuming greater importance in American business and industry (Figure 4).

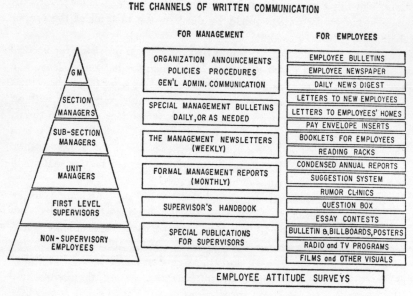

THE CHANNELS OF WRITTEN COMMUNICATION

FOR MANAGEMENT	FOR EMPLOYEES
ORGANIZATION ANNOUNCEMENTS POLICIES PROCEDURES GEN'L ADMIN. COMMUNICATION	EMPLOYEE BULLETINS
	EMPLOYEE NEWSPAPER
	DAILY NEWS DIGEST
SPECIAL MANAGEMENT BULLETINS DAILY, OR AS NEEDED	LETTERS TO NEW EMPLOYEES
	LETTERS TO EMPLOYEES' HOMES
	PAY ENVELOPE INSERTS
THE MANAGEMENT NEWSLETTERS (WEEKLY)	BOOKLETS FOR EMPLOYEES
	READING RACKS
FORMAL MANAGEMENT REPORTS (MONTHLY)	CONDENSED ANNUAL REPORTS
	SUGGESTION SYSTEM
	RUMOR CLINICS
SUPERVISOR'S HANDBOOK	QUESTION BOX
	ESSAY CONTESTS
SPECIAL PUBLICATIONS FOR SUPERVISORS	BULLETIN &, BILLBOARDS, POSTERS
	RADIO and TV PROGRAMS
	FILMS and OTHER VISUALS
EMPLOYEE ATTITUDE SURVEYS	

(Pyramid labels, top to bottom: G M / SECTION MANAGERS / SUB-SECTION MANAGERS / UNIT MANAGERS / FIRST LEVEL SUPERVISORS / NON-SUPERVISORY EMPLOYEES)

Figure 4

Written communication for management personnel

First attention should be given to written communication for management personnel. We will here simply indicate the role of certain written communication devices within the total communication structure—deferring to Chapter 15 a fuller description of these devices. Of prime importance here is provision for distributing and gaining understanding of organization, policy, procedural guides, and general administrative communication. These are the rules of the road. They should be distributed to each employee who needs the information to perform his function adequately.

Spot management news or announcements are handled through the Special Management Bulletin. Usually multilithed, this medium can be placed in the hands of all managers or equivalent personnel within one hour.

The Management Newsletter is distributed to all management personnel weekly, and carries the principal burden of keeping all managers or equivalent informed on a wide variety of subjects.

Formal management reports with varying periodicity are prime tools for the manager in his planning, integrating, and measuring work. They are the basis of any structure of written communication for management and should be appraised and revised regularly to assure that they are strengthening rather than inhibiting the over-all communication system.

To help sell the good features of the job their company provides for its employees, all managers are given a supervisor's handbook describing in considerable detail wage and salary plans, work rules, benefit plans, etc.

If some of the employees are represented by unions, copies of the contracts are placed in the appropriate supervisor's hands; very often interpretive guides to the contracts are also distributed.

To help introduce new technology, new benefit plans, new wage or salary plans, special booklets and conference leader guides are prepared for all supervisors.

WRITTEN COMMUNICATION FOR EMPLOYEES

Although most of the following media are also distributed to management personnel, they are primarily utilized to reach the large nonmanagement group of employees. They will be mentioned here only briefly and covered in more detail in Chapter 15.

Employee bulletins are often used to get spot news to rank-and-file employees. Provision is made to write, reproduce, and place these documents in the hands of all nonsupervisory employees within a time span of several hours.

The employee newspaper is the work horse in the group of printed media utilized for reaching employees. Published weekly or biweekly, it is the most important of the mass media for continuous and effective communication with the majority of employees.

To achieve primacy in news coverage, many operations use a daily news digest distributed each noon to all employees.

Letters to new employees and letters mailed to all employees' homes, signed by the chief executive, are among the most effective of the mass media, as will be shown later.

Pay envelope inserts are another possibility for employee communication but limited experience indicates they should be used sparingly.

Booklets for employees are utilized in introducing all important innovations in job perquisites, technology, and working rules.

Reading racks containing a selection of self-development booklets, "do-it-yourself" pamphlets, etc., provide an additional distribution channel for booklets describing various aspects of company operations and philosophies.

The annual company report, condensed and put into lay language, is highly favored by many managers as significant background information for employees.

The Suggestion System is included in this category of written communication because it is one of the most important channels for upward communication.

Question boxes and essay contests may serve as additional useful channels, and they merit consideration in the design of the integrated structure.

Bulletin boards are perhaps the oldest medium of written communication and far from effective as utilized by most businesses. But they can perform a highly useful role as will be subsequently shown.

Posters, in special locations and periodically renewed, are highly popular, especially in connection with safety-improvement and cost-reduction activities.

The use of billboards to lend emphasis to the other more comprehensive forms of written communication has been widely practiced in national emergencies and can play a useful role in normal times.

Radio and TV programs and films are audio and visual media rather than printed media but are assuming increasing importance in integrated communication programs.

Finally, the employee-attitude survey should be factored into any written communication structure because it answers a basic employee need for freedom of expression and provides one of the few reliable yardsticks for measuring the effectiveness of the total communication effort.

CHAPTER 14

Brief Review of Oral Communication

There is much available literature on the various media employed in internal and external business communication, and it is the primary purpose of this book to consider how a management utilizes communication to achieve the short- and long-range goals of the business.

Nonetheless, it may be helpful to pause briefly to review in more detail the array of communication media listed under "Structural Design" in Chapter 13.

Let us first examine the oral media: we have already covered the basic types of oral communication represented by the weekly, monthly, quarterly, and annual meetings with supervisors and employees, and we discussed in Chapter 9 the common forms of face-to-face communication that the first-level supervisor uses in such routinized activities as interviewing, orientation, performance appraisal, initial job instruction, making assignments (order giving), etc. Additionally, we find the following oral media being used with effectiveness in many businesses (Figure 5).

MEDIA OF ORAL COMMUNICATION

1. The safety meeting

Many companies have found that safety meetings held by a supervisor for his work group are an effective means of promoting employee participation in safety and of developing the competence of the supervisor as a communicator. A good public speaker, a fancy meeting room, elaborate props are not needed to make the safety meeting click. A short meeting held right on the job or in a corner of the plant with packing cases and nail kegs for chairs can produce highly favorable results. Requisites are two in number: something worthwhile to talk about and a supervisor who is conscientious and sincere about keeping his work group free from accidents. In general, the meetings should be held on company time and no less

TECHNIQUES OF ORAL COMMUNICATION

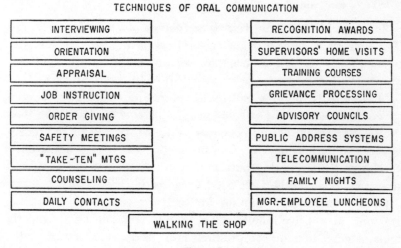

INTERVIEWING	RECOGNITION AWARDS
ORIENTATION	SUPERVISORS' HOME VISITS
APPRAISAL	TRAINING COURSES
JOB INSTRUCTION	GRIEVANCE PROCESSING
ORDER GIVING	ADVISORY COUNCILS
SAFETY MEETINGS	PUBLIC ADDRESS SYSTEMS
"TAKE-TEN" MTGS	TELECOMMUNICATION
COUNSELING	FAMILY NIGHTS
DAILY CONTACTS	MGR.-EMPLOYEE LUNCHEONS

WALKING THE SHOP

Figure 5

frequently than once each month. The important point is to establish some pattern so employees will expect and look forward to the next meeting.

All employees need to be included. This will pose a problem on a continuous production line, but usually with a little ingenuity, a solution can be found. Staggering the attendance at the meeetings so only one-third or one-half of the group is away from the job at any one time might be the answer, or if practical, stopping the line for fifteen or twenty minutes so everybody can attend.

Workers who are stationed in scattered locations can be called together shortly after the beginning of a shift or just before quitting

time. The electric utility companies solved the problem of where
to meet by holding "tail gate" meetings. Line supervisors get their
men together in back of the line trucks for short safety meetings
once each week. Similarly, "tool box" meetings are held for construction workers. As the name implies, workers gather around the tool
shed or tool box for a short, meaningful safety meeting which is
conducted by the crew boss.

2. "Take-ten" meeting

To supplement the more formalized communication of their Round-
Table meetings, some first-line supervisors have utilized a "take-ten"
technique for keeping their employees advised of current significant
events in which a particular work group has a direct interest.

"Take ten" is simply a call for a ten-minute on-the-floor meeting
in which the supervisor calls his people together to share with them
information which has just become available. It may be the receipt
of a new order, or the loss of an order that will have a direct effect
on this particular work group. It may be the imminence of a work
stoppage on which the facts need to be made clear quickly.

Of the planned ten minutes for such a meeting, the supervisor
generally allows five minutes to get his information across and the
remaining five minutes for questions and "feedback." The total interruption in the working time does not exceed fifteen minutes. Supervisors find this a sound investment in fast oral communication and
it saves time in comparison with repeating the message to a number
of individuals. Moreover, if used judiciously, it helps the supervisor
keep ahead of the rumor mill.

3. Counseling

Formalized counseling of employees who are maladjusted to their
work or their supervisor or who carry heavy personal burdens which
are not job connected is, generally speaking, not common in modern
industrial and business enterprises. Certain companies employ specialists with degrees in psychology or psychiatry to perform this
service, and particularly in the South, industrial chaplains are occa-

sionally utilized. Mostly, these professional counselors use the non-directive interview to uncover deep-seated attitudes and their causes without resorting to direct questions. To avoid bypassing the employee's supervisor, the counselor works closely with him, without violating individual privacy. Often they are jointly able to work out a satisfactory solution to the employee's problem. These counselors are generally a part of the employee relations staff although occasionally they may be located elsewhere in the organization.

Formal professional counseling is much more widely discussed than it is used. Many companies believe it interferes with the proper functioning of the man-manager relationship or that it too largely bypasses the supervisor. Accordingly, in the majority of companies we find mostly informal counseling wherein the employee talks over his personal problems with his boss. Where the supervisor feels he cannot cope with the problem, he most generally refers the disturbed employee to a personnel specialist or the plant physician.

4. Informal employee contacts

"Good morning, Joe!" "How is your wife today?" "The big boss was sure pleased with the way you handled that job." "Did you talk to Mary about signing up for the new insurance plan?" "I noticed you weren't wearing your safety glasses this morning, want to borrow a pair?" "Why not try it this way?" These and countless other informal oral communications are used daily by supervisors to motivate, reward, correct, and develop their subordinates. Certain companies, in their supervisory training programs, heavily stress means of improving such informal contacts. They sense that the supervisor is so busy that he may neglect the more demanding types of oral communication—so why not start the improvement program on the medium most used by the supervisor to get out the work?

Studies reveal, however, that supervisors unconsciously overlook certain employees in these daily contacts. As an antidote, one company's foremen's club developed the idea of formalizing the informal contact. Each foreman was given a book with loose-leaf pages, one page being reserved for each employee. Under his photograph were typed certain vital statistics—education and work background, age, continuity of service—names of wife and dependents, hobbies, etc.

The date of each significant informal contact was entered on the proper sheet, together with the subjects discussed and the questions unanswered. Each foreman reviewed his book once a month with his general foreman. These reviews indicated that a certain minority of employees in the group, who were easy to talk to, were the beneficiaries of most of the informal contacts. This emphasized the need for the foreman systematically to direct his attention to the more introverted employees.

5. Recognition and special award meetings

The conferring of suggestion awards, service pins, attendance awards, etc., provides the supervisor with excellent opportunities not only to communicate congratulations to the recipient but to strengthen loyalties and to reemphasize the value of the company's benefits. Everyone likes to be honored in the presence of his associates. Although the employee may appear to be embarrassed, it is a rare one who isn't inwardly pleased with having his achievement called to the attention of his fellow workers.

Such presentations are usually held on the work floor or in the office in the presence of the man's work group. Informality is the rule and several joking remarks unrelated to the award may precede or conclude the serious remarks. If the award is especially significant, it is often extended by top-level management. A news photograph of the presentation is usually taken in order to achieve additional communication in the employee house organ—and, where appropriate, in the city newspaper.

6. Supervisor's home visits

Indelibly imprinted on the author's mind since an early age is the picture of employees paying a social call on his father who was chief engineer of a cement plant. The employees were unskilled laborers, recent immigrants to America. When calling, they invariably brought with them a brace of live chickens from their poultry brood or produce from their little gardens. This presented a serious problem to the author who had to take care of the alarming increase in chicken population; yet, to deny these employees the pleasure of this somewhat feudal custom of their former lands was to offend them deeply.

Nothing more vividly dramatizes the revolution in human relations than today's practice wherein we observe the supervisor calling *on the employee* for a combined social-business chat.

It is the practice in a number of companies, especially in new plants, for the supervisor to pay a periodic call to the home to explain benefit plans to the entire family, to extend sympathy in times of personal trouble, or to convey personally a welcome insurance check. Supervisors who show such interest in their employees in normal times develop an acceptance which serves them in good stead when it is helpful to explain to the family the issues in crises such as labor trouble, temporary layoffs, etc.

Visits to employees who are sick at home or hospitalized are usually deeply welcomed and add the human touch which characterizes the ideal communication climate.

7. Formal training courses

In any listing of oral communication media, training courses have high standing. American business and industry spend a staggering amount of money on adult education to develop higher skills. In the author's company alone, 480 separate training courses were recently listed in a directory of available courses. It is a moot question as to how much of this time and effort is profitable. Company executives suspect that much course content is too superficial, that teaching methods and instructors are deficient, that time and the plant climate do not permit the newly taught employees or supervisors to practice their new-found knowledge, that evaluation of results is crude and unreliable. Despite such doubts, training has the same revered status among business executives as motherhood and Sunday school.

Nevertheless, formalized training can constitute one of the best media of oral communication for the supervisor and the supervised if entrusted to competent professionals who are more interested in measurable improvement in job performance than in the number of courses listed in the annual training report.

8. Grievance processing

Especially high skills in oral communication are required of supervisors whose employees are organized. Particularly is this true in the handling of grievances. William Karpinsky, supervisor of labor relations, organic chemicals division, American Cyanamid Company, suggests a concise seven-step procedure for front-line supervisors [1] for confidence-building handling of grievances. A number of these steps are presented unabridged because of their skilled communication content:

1. *Always listen*
   a. Let the employee talk with a minimum of interruption—getting things off one's chest has a therapeutic value.
   b. Get all the facts.
   c. Two "don'ts" are important: Don't brush off the complainant. Don't argue.
2. *Define the problem*
   a. Make sure that you understand the employee's complaint.
   b. If you are certain of the answer—and if the atmosphere is conducive—explain it immediately. If not, call him back a little later to explain. Whenever possible, avoid legalistic interpretations either of the contract or of a policy statement; dependence upon legalisms induces resentments.
   c. Resolve each grievance on a sound basis before it develops into a serious issue. Avoid hasty or expedient solutions merely to placate employees or to be a "good guy."
   d. A prompt decision is highly desirable but it should not supersede a sound and lasting settlement.
   e. If you are uncertain of the answer, promise to check the details and give an answer within a specified time.

[1] William Karpinsky, "Front-line Contract Administration," *Personnel*, January, 1957, p. 379.

    f. Another important "don't": Don't mislead the employee by promising to do something about the complaint if you are not sure that a remedial action is in order.

3. *Investigate*

4. *Make a decision*

5. *Consult with higher levels* (to assure consistency in contract administration)

6. *Inform the employee*

    a. If an error has been made, admit it and correct the situation immediately.

    b. If the complaint or grievance is to be denied, explain the reasons and attempt to persuade the employee to accept them.

    c. If the employee remains dissatisfied, don't threaten; instead, explain the procedure for appeal. Avoid the curt, "If you don't like it, write up a grievance."

7. *Prepare a written record*

Countless grief, labor strife, and dollars can be saved by properly training supervisors in this highly critical area of oral communication. One of the best programs devised to improve supervisory skills in union-contract administration is that of the Weirton Steel Company, Weirton, Ohio, called HOLCO (How Our Labor Contract Operates).

9. Communication advisory councils

Some companies have formed councils of foremen and other first-line supervisors, whose membership rotates, to advise on the effectiveness of communication designed for their employees. The author has been privileged to sit in on several such meetings and has been invariably impressed with the soundness and practicability of the supervisors' judgment. This is also an excellent evaluation technique and provides one more opportunity for employee participation that does not smack of superficiality.

10. P.A. Systems

Some managers install dual-purpose P.A. Systems in the plant—piping in soft music to buoy morale and utilizing the system when the occasion seems right to broadcast announcements of new procedures, new orders, complaints, labor issues, holiday arrangements, etc.

11. Telecommunication

A unique form of oral communication is in use in certain companies. Each evening significant information of interest to the management is recorded on tape and reproduced continuously during the next day over a special telephone line. Any supervisor can then, simply by dialing a special number, tune in on the message. (Similar to dialing WEather 6-1212 in the New York area for the weather forecast.)

A variation of this technique is a planned telephone relay grid to disseminate high-priority messages from the top management to all exempt employees within one hour and to all nonexempt employees in two hours or less—depending on the size of the plant. The message is telephoned down the chain of command to selected supervisors who relay it quickly to predesignated booster employees.

12. Family night

Gaining in favor in business is the practice of holding an annual family night to bring employees and managers together on common ground and to give members of immediate families in both groups a chance to get acquainted. Along with a program of entertainment and "mixing" common to such occasions, speakers, and sometimes, discussion periods are scheduled to communicate important information to the employees and their families.

A family night program will normally include

1. Welcome by chief executive
2. Entertainment—employee or professional
3. Talks by the manager and key functional members of his staff
4. "Mixing" period, light refreshments, door prizes
5. Special honors or awards which might currently be scheduled for employees

Such get-togethers can be extremely wholesome and enjoyable

affairs. There is no better climate for imparting economic education, interpreting the goals and policies of the business, and selling the outstanding features of the complete company job package. Companies selling to the consumer field can particularly make an impact through a skit showing their salesman striving with a competitor's salesman in winning a typical consumer's favor. The economics of costs, prices, profits, reinvestment to remain competitive, etc., are thus presented in a most meaningful context.

13. General manager's luncheons with selected employees

Some chief executives attempt to keep close to employees many position levels below through an informal weekly luncheon for groups of fifteen or twenty employees selected on a rotating basis. Name tags which designate the individual's operation help the manager identify his guests, and the manager peruses in advance the list of those scheduled to attend.

After a short talk on the progress of the business, the manager throws the meeting open for question. The most purposeful questions and answers are then printed in the next issue of the employee house organ where they are eagerly read. This supplemental communication provides an excellent opportunity to reinterpret important management policies, philosophies, etc.

14. Walking the shop and office

A much employed device to enable top managers to measure the pulse of their operations is the practice of periodic visitations to the shop and offices. Many managers swear by this observing and listening technique for keeping close to their people.

The successful ones, however, observe certain sound precautions. The atmosphere of the "state visit" where the red carpet is rolled out, where aisles and desks are cleaned up in advance, and supervision forewarned of the visit is strictly avoided. If the manager stops to talk with employees, he is careful not to permit these casual contacts to circumvent the established lines of authority. If there are complaints, he will listen sympathetically, then skillfully direct them back into the right channels by suggesting that the employee discuss the matter with his supervisor. If the manager sees some situation that needs correcting, he refers the matter down through the organization so as not to connect it directly with his visit.

In concluding this brief review of the channels of oral communication, one cannot but be impressed and encouraged with the ingenuity of American businessmen in meeting the challenges posed by their rapidly evolving enterprises.

To be sure, a single business enterprise will seldom utilize all the foregoing opportunities available for strengthening oral communication. However, the author knows of one company which uses all but the telecommunicator and P.A. System. The wise manager will select the minimum number necessary to achieve effective three-dimensional oral communication and adopt those media which flourish best in his particular plant climate.

One additional admonition: the foregoing illustrations of oral communication have been primarily factory- or production-oriented. However, these same channels must be established for the benefit of office employees who are all too frequently taken for granted in the communication process.

THE PITFALLS OF ORAL COMMUNICATION

In the foregoing, we have described in some detail how to design an oral communication system for a business and have spread before the reader a rich and varied display of available media.

But now we must warn you that even though you achieve the ultimate in oral pipelines and operate it with a maximum pressure or "head," you may get a disappointing dribble from the end of the line. Or if we liken our system to an electric circuit, we can say that the voltage drop is enormous.

One of the most persistent myths in business is the infallibility of man-to-man, face-to-face (oral) communication.

For example, in a sampling of the communication philosophy of the presidents of the 100 largest corporations, referred to in Chapter

1, the Industrial Communication Research Center of Purdue University found rather general agreement on the tenet that oral communication was the preferred method of transmitting information to employees. Ninety-eight per cent thought that oral communication was at least as important as written communication, and 40 per cent thought it was even more important.

With no attempt to embarrass the intelligent men who direct our largest corporations, or the writers of many standard texts on business communication, we must, nevertheless, state flatly that the business enterprise which relies primarily on oral channels will fail distressingly in accomplishing its communication objectives.

It is granted that no communication is more effective than that which occurs when a well-informed communicator transmits his message face to face to the receiver in an atmosphere of confidence and respect. The process is direct; it is personal. Both the first and the second order, or level, of communication can be employed and there is opportunity to elicit feedback to assure that the correct meaning has been exchanged.

But to take the reverse side of the coin, it may be stated quite generally that the informer is very seldom well informed unless he has a position at the top of the managerial hierarchy where he is an originator of information. To get news "direct from the horse's mouth" is to have gotten it from a very unreliable source if the horse is housed in one of the lower-level stables.

The loss in chain-of-command communication

Several years ago, the late Dr. Irving J. Lee assisted the author in conducting a series of communication seminars for the top officials of the General Electric Company.

One of his most telling contributions was an adaptation of the Allport-Postman [2] demonstration designed to debunk the infallibility of oral communication.

Dr. Lee would select six volunteers from the audience and after

[2] Gordon W. Allport and Lee Postman, *The Psychology of Rumor,* Henry Holt and Company, Inc., New York, 1947, pp. 64–74.

assigning each a number from one to six, would ask five of them to leave the room. The number-one man would then be permitted to look at a slide (Figure 6) projected on a screen for two minutes. The only admonition to the man was that he would be expected to communicate the message on the slide to the number-two man. After

Figure 6

the two-minute period, No. 1 called in No. 2 and communicated his version of the message. Number 2 then called in No. 3 and relayed the message—and so on until No. 5 communicated it to the last man, No. 6. This last man was then asked to write on a blackboard the message as it finally was passed on to him.

The resulting losses (and additions) in detail invariably proved hilarious to the members of the seminar.

In an almost predictable pattern, here is what happened as the information passed through successive layers.

1. Losses in detail began to occur with the first relay man, No. 1.

2. The greatest loss in detail occurred with the second relay man, No. 2.

3. Additions to the message and distortions became quite general in the last three layers.

4. Sharp specifics became more blurred with each handling.

5. Seldom in any experiment was any central idea passed along.

6. Qualified items of information (it seems as if, it appears, I believe) became definite items.

7. Rumors became facts; facts became rumors.

8. Very rarely did the receiver ask if he could take notes; very rarely did he ask questions. Invariably he accepted the message as gospel but passed it along with imaginative refinements.

Dr. Lee would usually give the following tips for achieving more effective oral communication:

Encourage your listener to seek clarification; structure the message so that a central theme is emphasized; don't qualify statements; ask listener to take notes; ask for playback of message to assure that receiver has correct meaning. Never let information go orally through more than three levels. The more important the message, the more media must be used.

Operation of filter effect

The Continental Can Company, in its communication training course for supervisors, dramatically conceptualizes the heavy circuit losses in oral communication as shown in Figure 7.

On the left-hand side of the pyramid is visualized an attempt on the part of the general manager or chief executive to communicate a policy, a decision, an order, etc., down through the supervisory line of authority. Immediately the man-boss relationship, shown in light gray, begins to filter, edit, censor, and distort the original content of the communication until, when it reaches the employees, it becomes propaganda, an unfair request, or a threat to their status or social progress.

The same filtering effect takes place in upward communication, as shown by the two-tone channel arrow in the right-hand section

CIRCUIT LOSSES IN COMMUNICATION

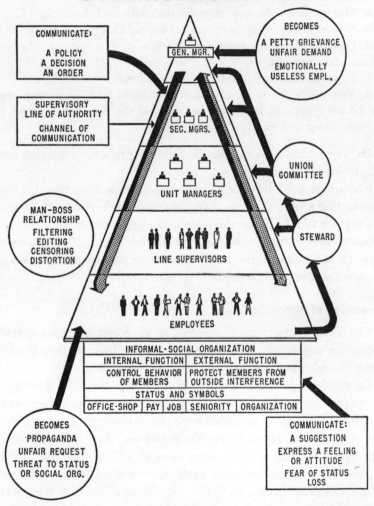

COMMUNICATE:
A POLICY
A DECISION
AN ORDER

BECOMES
A PETTY GRIEVANCE
UNFAIR DEMAND
EMOTIONALLY
USELESS EMPL.,

GEN. MGR.

SUPERVISORY
LINE OF AUTHORITY
CHANNEL OF
COMMUNICATION

SEC. MGRS.

UNION
COMMITTEE

UNIT MANAGERS

MAN–BOSS
RELATIONSHIP
FILTERING
EDITING
CENSORING
DISTORTION

STEWARD

LINE SUPERVISORS

EMPLOYEES

INFORMAL·SOCIAL ORGANIZATION	
INTERNAL FUNCTION	EXTERNAL FUNCTION
CONTROL BEHAVIOR OF MEMBERS	PROTECT MEMBERS FROM OUTSIDE INTERFERENCE
STATUS AND SYMBOLS	

OFFICE·SHOP	PAY	JOB	SENIORITY	ORGANIZATION

BECOMES
PROPAGANDA
UNFAIR REQUEST
THREAT TO STATUS
OR SOCIAL ORG.

COMMUNICATE:
A SUGGESTION
EXPRESS A FEELING
OR ATTITUDE
FEAR OF STATUS
LOSS

Figure 7

of the pyramid. Here the employee's attempt to communicate a suggestion, express a feeling or attitude, or to voice a fear of status loss comes through to the top man as a petty grievance, an unfair demand, etc. In organized plants, the union erects a bypass route in order that the employee's communication may reach the top man in less diluted form. The problem-solving procedure described in Chapter 16 describes how to build a bypass mechanism in nonorganized plants.

ORAL COMMUNICATION MUST BE SUPPLEMENTED

It must be accepted as a hard fact of life that oral communication is too subject to distortion, it is too expensive, it is too slow to serve as the prime carrier of our communication. Too many of the messages transmitted are too complex to pass along through more than one or two relays. The ideological gap between the first-line supervisor and top management is too great. This results in dilution, distortion, and shift of emphasis.

Written communication, on the other hand, is fast, accurate, and much less expensive.

To secure maximum impact, a combination of oral and written communication must be used—with the heaviest reliance being placed on the written media.

One company which uses a combination of both media in superb proportions astutely prescribes the following roles for each:

Primarily, we use oral communication—downward and upward through the chain of command—to integrate the functional work of the organization, although for best results, we must supplement it with written communication (orders, procedures, reports, etc.).

We rely almost entirely on written communication to cover the broader and more complex aspects of the business, economic matters, labor relations, salary, wage, and benefit practices, etc., which are more subject to distortion.

CHAPTER 15

Brief Review of Written Communication

At this point we will examine in a little more detail the wide choice of opportunities available to managers for communicating quickly, accurately, and inexpensively with employees through the printed word. These divide into two broad categories, written communication for management and written communication for all employees (Figure 4, Chapter 13).

WRITTEN COMMUNICATION FOR MANAGEMENT

1. Organization announcements, policies, procedures, general administrative communication

The downward and lateral flow of management communication is heavily laden with administrative or integrative material.

Managers characteristically insist that these be written because of the necessity for transmitting the information to the lowest essential level without distortion. This is sound judgment because it is this type of information which supports the structure and basic workings of the formal organization. Managers interested in improving their administrative communication may find helpful guidance in Charles E. Redfield's *Communication in Management*.

2. Special management bulletins

This is a medium used by some companies to get critical spot news of high perishability or urgency to the entire management team with the greatest possible speed and without distortion. Dictated by the chief executive, it is multigraphed and speeded to the desks of all managers or equivalent personnel within one hour. This is an excellent channel to develop in normal times because it is then priceless in emergencies.

3. The management newsletter

The purpose of this medium is to communicate significant official but less urgent information to management rapidly and in advance of general releases. It is put together and distributed, usually weekly, though sometimes oftener, by the employee relations staff from contributions by the general manager and his functional managers. It is indispensable for informing, integrating, and motivating the management team. It minimizes the spread of rumor and better enables managers, at all levels, by virtue of their possession of full and official information, to represent the company to their employees and to make their leadership felt throughout their sphere of influence.

The newsletter covers such subjects as orders, shipments, complaints, budget realization, employment statistics, progress of planned activities, union negotiations, labor relations, special operating problems, indices of employee performance, the role of managers in specific management programs, community affairs, etc.

These newsletters play a key role in transmitting news to foremen and intermediate management not only for their guidance, but also for the maintenance of their confidence and for the building of their influence.

4. Formal management reports

Great reliance is placed by the chief executive on the upward flow of communication, especially formal reports, as a feedback device to improve his planning, organizing, and integrating work.

Charles E. Redfield wisely observes: [1]

Experience has shown that orders and instructions—like laws—are not

---

[1] Charles E. Redfield, *Communication in Management,* University of Chicago Press, Chicago, 1954, p. 123.

complied with automatically or uniformly. But even in the event of absolute compliance, the results may not be those that were expected. The fault may lie in the underlying decision, in the instruction itself, or in some unforeseeable human frailty. Only as the executive receives information from below can he weigh results, make new decisions, issue new instructions and take whatever other action he sees fit.

But specialization has limited the executive's horizon, as it has all others, so that he has no ready access to information circulating at lower levels.

Reporting is mentioned in all the lists of central control devices, of which there have been many in recent years. Reports are used to measure performance and control costs, to serve the needs for both long-term planning and current scheduling of work, to check conformance with organization policy and procedure, to transmit information of special interest or importance, and to facilitate the coordination of widely separated operations. Reports are also used to establish written records of events that may have future reference value, for anything from the substantiation of a patent to a dismissal.

At lower levels, it is not so necessary, from the standpoint of productive efficiency alone, to have systematic information about the work of other segments of the organization. But at each higher level, information from and about other departments becomes more and more helpful. Efficiency at the top depends to a great extent on the quantity and quality of information flowing from the remote corners of an organization to a glass-topped desk in a spacious office.

5. Supervisor's handbooks

We wouldn't think of sending the salesman of our economic product into the field without a comprehensive handbook. Yet the majority of businesses expect the salesman of their social product to sell the good features of the product and to interpret complex benefit plans, policies, and procedures barehanded. To assist the busy, never well-enough-informed supervisor, the more progressive companies supply him with a loose-leaf handbook.

Such guides normally constitute a succinct summary of legislation, company policies, procedures, job benefits, and related information which a supervisor needs in his day-to-day work. Typical of the subjects covered are provisions of the Fair Labor Standards Act, state and local labor legislation, workmen's and unemployment compensation. Also covered are grievance procedure, duties and privileges of union officers, and highlights of the union contract.

One section is usually devoted to clock-card and payroll routines; another to wage-rate administration. Disciplinary action and such personnel practices as removals, transfers, upgrading, etc., are spelled out in detail. Safety and plant protection are given intensive treatment, as is the entire array of employee benefits and services.

A handbook of this nature needs constantly to be kept up to date through issuance of revised sheets with the latest and most accurate information. The expense involved is a pittance compared to the heavy costs arising when uninformed supervisors must take the time to go up and down through channels to get this basic information needed to perform their job.

Far more important than the time lost is the loss of status the supervisors suffer in the eyes of their employees. Supervisor information is a priceless ingredient of leadership. Managers who expect their supervisors at all levels to be leaders and to be salesmen on the job for the company's social product should give them this salesman's handbook and maintain their confidence in it by keeping it always up to date.

6. Special publications for supervisors

These are such a standard stock item in any company's printed communication as to warrant little consideration here. Supervisors are equipped with them to interpret and sell the benefit plans, the new union contract, new policies, etc. Progressive companies make telling use of them to help administer changing technology better and also in all formalized campaigns to achieve cost reduction and quality improvement, to reduce accidents, to tighten security procedures, and to attain other periodic operating goals.

WRITTEN COMMUNICATION FOR EMPLOYEES [2]

1. The employee bulletin

This is an informal multilithed sheet for conveying urgent spot news or information to all employees within an hour or two. It can be distributed by the supervisors or posted on bulletin boards as conditions indicate.

2. The employee newspaper

The most widely used medium for communicating in writing to employees is the employee publication. The International Council of Industrial Editors estimates that there are nearly 6,000 known employee publications and a possible 5,000 which are not reported in their periodic surveys. The combined cost of the reported publications is believed to exceed 12 million dollars annually. Total monthly circulation exceeds seventy million and total readership is believed to be in excess of one hundred million.

The earliest employee magazine on record is the *Factory News*, a twelve-page journal issued by the National Cash Register Company in 1890. Employee publications grew slowly, receiving considerable impetus during World War I and declining during the twenties and early thirties.

World War II marked the real discovery of communication as a morale builder and the employee publication came into its own. In the postwar years, it has assumed steadily increasing stature as a prime management tool.

The author's company regards the employee news as the backbone of its written communication program.

Most of the company's operating departments issue an employee news on a weekly or a biweekly basis. These periodicals are published in a tabloid newspaper format and generally strive to accomplish four primary objectives:

[2] Although this category of communication is read by *all* employees, it is utilized primarily to reach nonsupervisory personnel.

1. To keep employees informed on company policies, practices, and regulations, and on management's objectives, plans, problems, successes, and failures.

2. To give employees an understanding of the work they are doing, the products they are making, and the reasons for all the various demands made upon them in doing their day-to-day jobs.

3. To keep employees informed on matters in the economic, social, and political fields which affect them and their jobs, so that they will become economically and politically sophisticated and capable of making sound decisions in these areas.

4. To give employees news of themselves and their own activities so that they become better acquainted and feel at home in the organization.

In the handling of news, speed is essential. The newspaper format permits deadlines as late as Thursday for a Friday issue. The more nearly the format resembles the familiar daily newspaper, the more the readership and credibility of the news seems to be enhanced.

The great popularity of pictures as a medium of story telling and news reporting is heavily capitalized and the roving photographer is almost as important as the editor in assuring the success of the publication.

When the employee newspaper is soundly integrated into the complete communication program and when it is edited to achieve its primary objectives, it is invaluable. Unfortunately, too many companies still consider it an employee benefit or an entertainment medium which in some way is supposed to build morale.

This medium is expensive and the return on the investment should be measured as critically as any other facility to ascertain if it is paying its way. In any such measurement, readership statistics are helpful, but there are other more important criteria which are examined in Chapter 17.

3. The monthly house organ

Many companies rely on a monthly publication in the familiar magazine format with a cover—often in color—with large illustrations, and skillfully designed layout. This type of publication has a certain unique appeal to the large audience conditioned to the mass-circulation magazines found in so many homes; it also permits depth treatment of economic subjects and institutional prestige-building articles concerning the company.

One of the classic examples of this type of mass medium is du Pont's *Better Living* which has no peer in its treatment of economic education in lay language.

The author believes that this medium should be used only when a company can afford it as a supplement to the more frequently issued employee newspaper or daily news digest. Speed and primacy of information are essential in today's competitive communication arena, and if the monthly issue, with its long advance deadline, is the only medium for mass communication, the entire communication program is no more flexible than the dinosaurs of a bygone age.

4. The daily news digest

The argument against the sole use of a monthly mass medium is more telling when it is realized that even the weekly employee newspaper is thought not to be fast enough for some intensive users of the mass media.

The author's company is one of a number where plant managers issue a daily news digest.

An arrangement is made whereby the local radio station, usually at no charge other than to require a courtesy line, permits the company to receive the headline news, local and national, at 10 A.M. daily. These short news items are typed on a mat by the editor of the employee newspaper. Between these news flashes are interspersed appropriate management messages. This type of publication is quickly produced in the desired quantities and stacked up at the entrance to the plant cafeteria and at outlaying snack bars.

Very few hourly employees read a morning newspaper; indeed in many small communities, none is published. As a result, the news digest is picked up and read during lunch by practically all employees.

In one week's output of one such daily news digest, the following representative array of management messages was observed:

Because of a rise in cost of living, a pay boost of ½ per cent will be effective next Monday. Plant will be closed on Good Friday. First-quarter earnings report. Another eye saved by safety glasses. Employee-attitude survey to start next Monday. Employees troop back to work in neighboring plant, having gained nothing after a two weeks' strike. Our employees enjoy best health insurance plan in area, etc.

This medium is unexcelled to refute untrue charges that may have been incorporated in union handbills passed out at the plant entrances that very morning.

Here is a fast, flexible, extremely low-cost medium of printed communication which is winning rapid acceptance.

5. Letters to new employees

A friendly human touch is the sending of a letter of welcome to each new employee. In view of the limited number of employees added to the payroll in normal times, such letters can be personally signed by the chief executive, thus adding an effective touch to the customary orientation program.

6. Letters to employees' homes

Here is one of the most effective of all mass media. Monthly, bimonthly, or quarterly, the chief executive writes a letter addressed to the homes of all employees.

Such letters can be produced quickly and at moderate cost, can be sent at any time with no fixed or periodic schedule, and can be sent to a selected group, when necessary. The content of the letter receives special attention; a very high percentage of employees and their families read it, and the message is read in the privacy and relaxed atmosphere of the home where it is more likely to get calm and thoughtful consideration. The personal touch is effective even though the employees realize the letter is going to others. Such letters establish closer liaison between the manager and his employees than any other printed medium.

These letters are an excellent integrative device. They cover a wide range of subjects: increase in compensation, new benefit plans, introduction of new technology, progress reports, the competitive situation, the outlook for job security, economic background material, and the issues in labor disputes.

In emergency situations, letters have proved particularly effective in keeping employees and their families informed in the face of the great volume of misinformation which is so often circulated by union newspapers and other community media on such occasions as negotiations, strike threats, strikes, representation elections, disasters, etc.

Many letters to employees are designed solely to convey information, and no reply is invited or anticipated. In other cases, however, the value of the letter is enhanced by including some such invitation. The invitation must, of course, be sincere—the comments of employees must be genuinely desired and provision made for their consideration.

On occasion, the manager will include an invitation to write him personally, and may even enclose a special form and a self-addressed, stamped envelope which the employee can use for this purpose. If he is soliciting questions, the letter should state that the answers will be given promptly in the employee newspaper so that the employee will not expect—and the manager will not be committing himself to—the writing of a personal reply to each employee who responds.

In most cases, however, the invitation takes other forms, such as the statement, "I hope you will discuss this matter with your supervisor."

It is particularly important that first-line supervisors be briefed in advance and therefore be put in a position to follow up the letter in their own personal communication with employees. They should always receive advance copies of any letter to be sent, often with a more detailed explanation and answers to questions which employees may ask, and alerted to the opportunity, which the letter may provide, for fruitful discussion with individual employees.

Managers desirous of using this medium should especially consider the obvious advantage of beginning with a letter to all new employees.

The use of letters to the home should be inaugurated and maintained in normal times. Some companies, unfortunately, resort to this medium *only* when they are in trouble. In such cases, their newly evidenced interest in their employees and families is likely to backfire badly.

7. Payroll envelope inserts

This medium, used by some companies, has no great following. If the insert deals with changes in pay or is closely related to compensation, well and good; otherwise, the material may engender resentment.

8. Booklets for employees

Most popular in this category is the orientation booklet given to each employee added to the payroll.

A typical welcoming booklet will usually include a letter of welcome from the chief executive, a promotional presentation of the job package, a description of the products or services which the plant produces; policies, procedures, work rules, training and self-development opportunities.

Other popular booklets are *A History of the Enterprise, The Company's Code of Ethics, Descriptions of Benefit Plans, Company Recreational Facilities, Interpretation of Union Contract.*

9. Reading racks

Reading racks are based on the assumption that the sight of water will make one thirsty and that then he will drink. Attractive racks are located at convenient locations throughout the plant and filled with twenty-five to fifty copies of perhaps a dozen booklets covering a wide range of interests from *Tips on Picnic Lunches,*

Home Gardening, Stamp Collecting, Hints on Preparing Income Tax, Home Workshops, etc. Along with these are included booklets which management would like its employees to read in order to work more smartly or to develop greater understanding and appreciation of company goals and problems.

As fast as booklets are taken, new quantities are inserted. This practice is by no means inexpensive and results are hard to prove; nonetheless, hundreds of companies utilize this medium and a number of publishing houses do a large business catering to them.

The Opinion Research Corporation, in a study of readership of this free-choice reading medium, reports the following findings: [3]

Our most recent survey work regarding reading racks has aimed at helping answer the question: Once having picked up a booklet, does the employee read it, get anything out of it, take away any lasting ideas? Furthermore, will employees read the more serious, informational type of booklet as well as the ones on fishing, home and health, and the like?

The three separate readership studies of the intensive, probing type we have made suggest some preliminary answers. In the case of a large utility (Company A), we found that 51% of a cross-section of employees could prove, with no chance to look at the booklet or in any other way being prompted, that they had read the pamphlet, "All About Meat." This was, perhaps, to be expected. A total of 31%, or nearly one in four, could prove they had read the informational booklet, "Putting Your Money to Work," and 12% could prove they had read a thoughtful, scholarly document entitled, "The Personal Practice of Freedom."

An intensive analysis of the detailed probing involved in each of the above examples shows that the two serious documents, while read by fewer employees, nevertheless made an attitude-affecting impression on a significant proportion of the cases. Readers not only read; they absorbed as well.

In the case of a large eastern manufacturing (Company B) 56% could prove they had read a booklet entitled, "How To Be An Expert Driver," which was perhaps also what one might expect. However, 51% or half of all those tested, could prove they had read one called, "It's Your Future,"

[3] *Public Opinion Index for Industry Archives,* Opinion Research Corporation, Princeton, N.J.

a detailed study of the company's benefit program for employees. Even more significant, detailed probing revealed that editors of the pamphlet had impressively accomplished certain attitude objectives regarding the company's fairness and generosity that they wanted to reach in the employee's thinking.

The research so far suggests that if care is taken in the selection of materials for the reading rack, and it is effectively employed, it can achieve a high carry-over of ideas.

10. The annual financial report

Nothing dramatizes so vividly the increasing social consciousness of business as does the evolution of the annual report. From a dry, esoteric maze of figures and strange words, such as nonconsolidated affiliates, sinking funds, contra, etc., distributed only to stockholders and financial establishments, it has metamorphosed into a Cinderella of four-color covers with beautiful illustrations, simplified figures, and easily understandable summaries. In many companies it is mailed to all employees; in still others, management meets with groups of employees for a dramatized presentation of the report followed by a question-and-answer period. Some companies also distribute it to their community mailing list. Regardless of the method, astute managements recognize the annual report as one of their top opportunities for explaining the problems of the business and interpreting the beneficial contributions of business to employees and public. Indeed, many companies prepare special condensed versions of the annual report written in lay language for distribution to employees.

11. Individualized benefits report to employees

The author's company has developed a written communication medium which has proved spectacularly successful—and rightly so. Biennially a personalized four-page letter is sent to each employee at his home address reporting his current equity in each of the benefit plans provided by the company.

The report indicates how much he has contributed to date toward his pension plan and how much the company has contributed. It then shows him how to calculate his ultimate retirement income, including Social Security, based on a fixed income level. The hope is expressed, however, that the income will not be static and that the annual pension will increase steadily.

The report shows how many shares of stock and how many government bonds are credited to the employee if he is a participant in the savings and security program.

The report itemizes the amount of life insurance coverage the employee enjoys under the group insurance plan. It itemizes the amount of weekly payments for which he is eligible if he becomes sick. It lists the physician's charges, hospital bills, expenses, and surgical fees which are reimbursable under the company's comprehensive medical plan. Finally, it concludes with a brief review of all other benefit plans that constitute the total job package.

Here, indeed, is a dramatic device, loaded with self-interest for the reader and his entire family. It performs a valuable verification service for the employee and helps the company to reap extra dividends of good will from its ever-mounting investment in extra job benefits.

12. Bulletin boards

Plant and office bulletin boards are one of the oldest, cheapest, and in general, most poorly used media for written communication with employees. Properly used, they can be integrated into the complete communication structure with telling effect. Improperly used, they become a vertical morgue for a hodgepodge of stale announcements, state laws, and cartoons posted by employees.

The apocryphal story is told of a plant management group in Trenton, New Jersey, which decided to renovate its bulletin boards by stripping off all old announcements. When next to the last layer was removed, the following announcement in print reminiscent of Ben Franklin's press was revealed: "All able-bodied men will report at 3 A.M. tomorrow for the crossing of the Delaware. Signed, G. Washington."

When a company has a properly designed and integrated communication program in effect, the bulletin boards are used primarily to lend emphasis and repetition to appeals which have been covered in greater depth in more effective media.

One of management's perplexing dilemmas in the utilization of this medium concerns the value of syndicated poster series. For a fixed fee per board, a company can purchase a series of multicolored posters which smile at the employees, point at them, and exhort them on a wide variety of subjects ranging from greater productivity, less waste, more teamwork, etc. The employees are reminded of the glories of the American way of life, free enterprise, and the fact that everyone is a capitalist.

Such syndicated material may well have been effective during the war years, but hard-hitting locally prepared materials are often less expensive and probably much more effective. Bulletin boards [4] should be used as supplements to the over-all communication program, just as billboards and car cards are used by many national advertisers to supplement magazine advertising and radio and TV messages.

13. Audio-visual media

Most companies utilize various visual and audio-visual techniques to supplement their written communication. Among these are throw-over charts, slides, flannel boards, sound slide films, and sound motion pictures. Such devices, employed at group meetings, are usually very effective in aiding management to tell its story to employees.

[4] For a sensible and very complete overview of the use of bulletin boards, see Robert Newcomb and Mary Sammons, *Speak up, Management!* Funk & Wagnalls Company, New York, 1951, "Let Your Bulletin Boards Talk," pp. 74–92.

CHAPTER 16

Upward Communication

The good "time-users" among managers spend many more hours on their communications up than on their communications down.[1]

Management's unilateral approach to employee communication has long been obvious to objective observers. One such observation will suffice because of its cogency: [2]

Communication tends to be regarded as the process of getting information across from one group, the management, to another group, the employees. There is even a tendency to concentrate on one employee group, the manual workers, with little attention being given to other employee groups—office workers, sales staff, etc. It is true that increasing attention is being given to communicating to supervisory groups, but sometimes this is due not to a recognition of the need of this for its own sake, but to the realization that those in supervisory positions are important links in the chain of communication from top management to employees.

The fact that formalized communication has been so largely a one-way street should not occasion so much surprise on the part of critics peering through a window into business enterprises.

If it be true that the longest journey begins with a single step,

---

[1] Peter F. Drucker, *The Practice of Management*, Harper & Brothers, New York, 1954, p. 347.

[2] P. H. Cook, "An Examination of the Notion of Communication in Industry," *Occupational Psychology*, January, 1951.

there is some comfort in knowing that many businesses have only recently taken the first step of communicating downward intensively to their employees. As Cook further points out, ". . . it is not being denied that passing on information can contribute to better industrial relations; although when this happens, it is probably due not to the facts that are communicated, but to the attitudes behind the act of communicating which are also communicated. The fact that management is willing to give information is most important."

To be sure, it would have been wiser to have first bulldozed and paved an uphill street from employees to top management, but that is a much more complex and time-consuming task and most of us are not quite sure that we, as yet, know how to do it.

There is, however, now developing in business an awareness of the need to convert employee communication into a dynamic and effective two-way process.

Some persistent road blocks

Most of the obstacles to upward communication have been covered in earlier chapters—faulty organization with too many levels; the filter effect so graphically illustrated in Continental Can's diagram (Figure 7); the tendency of associates to surround the head man with a brass curtain; an unfavorable climate for upward communication established by the head man; failure to act on receipt of bad news from below, especially when such upward communication is initiated by first-line supervisors; regarding critical comment by employees as a healthy blowing off of steam which can largely be ignored; lack of confidence by employees in the motives and integrity of their top management; lack of understanding from the top of the true objectives or needs of the employees; poor listening habits at every level of supervision; and lack of a formalized mechanism for getting employee's reactions, questions, ideas.

The president or manager who is determined to obtain good upward communication must first clear out the foregoing underbrush through approaches described in Chapter 13. Immediately, his upward communication will improve markedly. This is true because good two-way communication is not so much a *cause* of high morale as it is a *result* of such a condition.

This improvement will not long continue, however, unless some formalized mechanism is put into place—some means of constantly getting and evaluating employee reactions, questions, and ideas.

Let us examine some of the elements in such a mechanism that have proved workable in many companies. Many of these have already been covered in earlier chapters because, in the context of this book, two-way communication has been implicit in all our discussions. A check list, immediately below, is followed by discussion of each of the items.

CHECK LIST OF UPWARD COMMUNICATION TECHNIQUES

Good organization structure

Making each successive level of management responsible and accountable for effective two-way communication

Motivating each manager to accept and discharge his upward communication responsibility through the process of performance appraisals in connection with merit increases

Installation of problem-solving procedure for all employees not represented by a union

Counseling

Teaching supervisors good listening habits

Rumor clinics

Question boxes

The plant panel

Employee Round Tables

Manager's luncheon with selected groups of employees

A suggestion system

Performance appraisals

Postemployment interviews

Exit interviews

Planned floor contacts

Employee attitude surveys and department interviewing

The following observations concerning these elements of an employee feedback mechanism may be helpful:

1. *The organization structure.* It is not within the scope of this book to discuss the principles of scientific organization design. Fortunately, management is devoting increasing attention to this prime fundamental of the process of managing. Suffice it that a clean organization structure with a minimum of levels and with responsibilities and accountabilities precisely defined through position guides is a prime prerequisite for effective upward communication.

One of the most constructive steps taken by the author's company in organization design has been the elimination of those arch inhibitors of upward communication, namely, the assistant manager, the assistant to the manager, the administrative assistant, the coordinator, and the "committee."

The executive who is having upward communication headaches should first look at these information blockade points; if he still believes these positions to be necessary, he may wish to install information bypass pipes to assure that he will get the information he so urgently needs for the soundest decision making.

2. *Making each manager responsible and accountable for two-way communication.* The position guide of each manager and supervisor should specifically spell out the position's responsibility and accountability for effective two-way communication and, particularly, for the necessity of transmitting upward, and promptly, the unfiltered, uncensored ideas, reactions, problems, and questions of all subordinates.

3. *Gaining voluntary acceptance and discharge of the responsibility.* Few facts of business life are more obvious and more ignored than this one. Subordinate managers have a well-developed sixth sense in knowing which elements of their responsibility their boss considers important. The responsibility for two-way communication can be printed in specially colored type in the position guide but will never motivate the incumbent unless his boss, by his questions, his sincere interest, his performance appraisals, and his merit increases and promotions lets it be known that this responsibility is indeed an important one.

NOTE: The executive head of the business can accomplish more in the cause of effective upward (and downward) communication through these three management actions than through the use of any auxiliary mechanisms. Yet because there will always be breaches of policies and intent as long as they are administered by human beings, the following supplemental devices have proved helpful.

4. *Problem-solving procedures.* One of the employee's basic needs is for the correction of personal injustice, whether real or fancied. Smart managers are working overtime to train supervisors to look for real or alleged defects in the employees' jobs and rectify them before they become deep-seated grievances.

Recognizing the justice of a court of appeals, many companies have installed a formalized problem-solving procedure.

The following is an example of such a procedure including a question-and-answer box, written grievance, and procedure in operation in a Middle Western plant of the General Electric Company:

EMPLOYEE AND MANAGEMENT COOPERATION PLAN

We have long recognized that the responsibility for good employee relations (our day-to-day dealings with one another) is an *individual* problem. It is a problem none of us can dodge by criticizing one another or making excuses for ourselves.

If there is something about your job, working conditions, health and safety or anything else for that matter that's bothering you, *bring it out in the open.* Use the Question and Answer Box or the following three-step procedure.

Step 1

Your Foreman—Talk the problem over with him, honestly and sincerely. He's your friend. Part of the reason for his selection as a foreman was based on his ability to treat employees' problems with respect and dignity. Furthermore, he has the authority to take corrective action right on the floor.

Remember to feel free to put your problem squarely before him. Tell him thoroughly every detail so there can be no misunderstanding.

As an aggrieved employee, you will be notified promptly of the foreman's decision. In some instances, where over-all policy decisions are involved, it may be necessary for the foreman to go to a higher level of supervision before the complaint can be settled. Your foreman does not profess to know all the "answers," nor does he profess to be right all the time, so we've provided for a next step.

Step 2

Review Council—This group is made up of the Manager-Shop Operations, your immediate Supervisor, and the Personnel Practices Specialist. Their job is to study the problem, question or complaint, and work out a fair solution. This step and its outcome will be recorded in writing by the foreman on appropriate forms for this purpose. The Company expects these men to make or get a prompt and fair decision to you within two working days or tell you within that period of the approximate date when the matter can be corrected. You, or if more than one is concerned—those involved—may be invited to attend the discussion with your foreman for a review of the problem or an explanation of Company policy in the matter concerned.

If you want to discuss the problem with our Personnel Section, prior to taking it to the Review Council, you should feel free to do so. Notify your foreman of your decision so that he will know your preference—in fact, he will be glad to arrange for a time and place to meet and discuss the problem.

Step 3

Manager-Employee Relations—As a final step, your problem will be referred to Manager-Employee Relations. If necessary, the Manager-Employee Relations will arrange an appointment with appropriate department personnel, including Department General Manager, if necessary. You can have trust in his judgment and fairness for he is interested, sympathetic and understanding. He, like the rest of us, is anxious to have you feel satisfied that every consideration is given to your problem.

Remember that we have no way of knowing what's bothering you unless you either put your complaint in the Question and Answer Box or let us know in accordance with the procedure described above. This is a sure way we can carry out our pledge of making and keeping our Company a good place to work and of treating you fairly.

There is no unanimity of agreement among managers as to the

need for such plans. Failures exceed success in their use. Their success depends entirely upon the climate for full, free communication within the plant. Obviously, the better the climate, the less the need for a formalized procedure—yet many industrial relations managers in nonorganized plants work hard to make them effective even in the presence of a good climate. They understand the psychological value of a policy that ensures the right of higher appeal.

5. *Counseling.* We discussed in Chapter 14 the pros and cons of formalized counseling and observed the widely held conviction, among industrial concerns, at least, that counseling is a responsibility of the employee's immediate supervisor except in the handling of the most difficult cases.

Nonetheless, formalized counseling is apparently practiced successfully in some companies, especially where personnel is predominantly female. Here is a capsule of one such counseling procedure in one operating department of the author's company as described by the employee relations manager to whom the counselor reports.

1. *Prevention of Complaints*

Prior to any contemplated action or change involving employees as individuals or groups (e.g., new construction, ventilation, setting new rates, etc.), the matter is discussed carefully by Mrs. _____ [the counselor] and other members of management. Discussions revolve around the method and the timing of the proposed action, the best means of communication and the probable employee reaction. Advance planning such as this is most helpful in preventing unfavorable employee reaction. It requires, of course, that the counselor be thoroughly familiar with Company policy and procedure, and that she know, as individuals, the people to be affected.

2. *Discovery of Complaints*

As we know, not all employee complaints or problems are expressed. Many are "bottled up" with subsequent ill effects on the employee's attitude, behavior and productivity. Thus, it becomes important to get at the root of the employee's difficulty to draw him out and "clear the air." This may be accomplished in a variety of ways.

a. By touring the plants and discussing with employees their jobs, benefits, families, outside activities, etc. "Walking the shop" in this manner often develops openings leading to employees revealing possible problem areas *before* trouble develops.

b. Attendance at employee activities, such as bowling nights, Christmas parties, outings, etc.

c. Visits to employees' homes for parties, showers, weddings, christenings, etc. Association *off the job,* especially in the informal atmosphere of the employee's home, develops a spirit of friendship, trust and confidence between employee and counselor.

3. *Adjustment of Complaints*

If management is to take reasonable action in the human relations area, it must have access to as much information as possible. And very often the foreman does not or cannot supply adequate information.

Thus, it becomes necessary to tap a source other than the foreman—logically, the employee himself. The employee will "get it off his chest" if he believes he will be heard fully and will get the management action his situation deserves. Mrs. ———— has been successful in getting the employee to communicate upward. She has acquired the reputation of being "in the employee's corner," inasmuch as she actually represents the people to higher management when their problems and complaints are real and constitute potential friction areas. An aggrieved or troubled employee occasionally needs a representative, other than the foreman, who has stature and who will battle for the employee's rights.

6. *Teaching supervisors good listening habits.* The following editorial comment, appearing in the magazine *Personnel* (July, 1955), pretty much sums up the gap that presently exists in all business between the appreciation of listening as an important element in managing and the attention devoted to the improvement of listening skills by managers.

AMA [American Management Association] has been looking at listening. In preparing a forthcoming handbook on the art of face-to-face communication, AMA researchers found a wealth of studies and training materials on how to get a point across—in other words, how to make other people listen. They found also many praiseworthy statements on the virtues and benefits of listening. But surprisingly little was found—and that little came chiefly from the field of education rather than industry—about how to listen intelligently and understandingly to another person.

This omission in training is hard to explain from a dollars-and-cents point of view. Listening is part of the job of every executive; studies show that it enters into almost everything he does, and that he spends several hours a day in the physical attitude of listening. One would expect business to try harder to get its money's worth from these high-paid hours. . . .

More and more, industry is beginning to make the effort. Though few companies give listening training, a fair number stress it as part of the training for counselling, interviewing, and general communication. In a poll by the Bureau of National Affairs a few years ago, the overwhelming majority of top executives agreed that "the fine art of listening remains one of the most overlooked tools of management." Eventually, it may be hoped, this "got to listen" will be transformed into "how to listen" as the special techniques which have been developed in schools and universities begin to be applied by industry.

Managers who perceive the value of listening will need to clarify their concept of what is meant by "listening." Merely learning to "keep quiet" or "pay attention" is one thing—getting the employee to have such confidence in the listener that he will take him into his confidence on matters about which he feels deeply is something else again. This presupposes that we will "open up" to the employee to the same extent that we want him to "open up" to us.

American Telephone and Telegraph, and the author's company, are in the vanguard of the business enterprises which are conducting formalized training in listening to improve grievance detection and prevention, performance appraisals, and feedback reception necessary to sounder managerial decisions. This is an encouraging trend. Effective listening is a discipline involving a considerable degree of humility. There is a great need for more humility in our entire approach to the art of human relations.

7. *The rumor clinic.* A supplemental device to aid upward communication, used by certain operating departments of the author's company is the rumor clinic. Employees are invited and periodically urged by the plant manager to write him concerning rumors that

have come to their attention. The inquiring employee is given a straightforward answer in writing and those rumors which seem to be of greatest plant-wide interest are reprinted in the employee newspaper together with the manager's answer.

Surveys show that the rumor clinic is one of the most popular features of the paper. Employees read it avidly because here the manager is answering *their* questions—not trying to force information on them. It will be recognized by many readers that this is a well-nigh perfect medium for getting widespread understanding of management's policies, practices, and intent. Certain policies can be restated over and over in answer to various rumors concerning the breaching of these policies.

Some departments take an advertisement in the plant-city newspaper once a month in which the rumor clinic is reproduced for the benefit of the community neighbors. A readership survey showed that it enjoyed wider readership than any other advertising in the newspaper.

The Line Material Company, well-known manufacturer of electrical equipment, carries a somewhat similar feature in its employee house organ, *Inside Line;* entitled "What's Your Question?" it carries this highly motivating byline, "W. D. Kyle, Jr., answers employees' questions." (Mr. Kyle was the president.)

8. *Question boxes.* "Get it off your mind and into the box" is a catch phrase that describes the objective of the "question box." These boxes are located conveniently throughout the plant and contain a pocket with a supply of forms on which the employee may write his question and speed it on its way to the manager's office. Managers utilizing this aid to upward communication report very satisfactory usage. Here again, the reporting in the plant newspaper of replies of general interest results in additional coverage.

9. *The plant panel.* Here is a courageous device used by one plant in the author's company. Each week four employees, selected by supervisors, are asked for their opinions on a controversial and timely question. Participants are given two days to return their written answer. An editorial presenting management's opinion on the ques-

tion is written and this along with the employees' answers is printed in the employee newspaper. The objectives of the device are several: to provide recognition for the point of view of the employee, to flush out misinformation, to show management's willingness to present conflicting opinions on controversial matters, to provide management with another ear for upward communication, to bring life to the editorial page.

The sponsoring manager of this device astutely remarks: "The value of this technique is limited to the extent that we are willing to take a chance of having our employees openly challenge our point of view and use our newspaper to do it. It is also limited to the extent that we are willing and able to defend our position openly."

10. *Employee Round Tables* (see Chapter 11). The employee Round Table as utilized in the author's company is held once a quarter, or oftener, by the supervisor for all employees in his work group. Of ninety minutes' duration, the last forty-five minutes is customarily allotted for employees' questions and suggestions. It will be recalled that a list of questions asked and answers given (or not given) is sent up the line following the meeting. The following employee quotes were extracted from a report by a firm of outside consultants which conducted depth interviews with a random sampling of employees. They indicate the valuable role these meetings can serve in facilitating upward communication when they are properly conducted:

We have informative meetings . . . every few months . . . that's good. We get a lot of information on the orders we are getting and how business is. It's the only way we can get through to the foreman—when he's away from the pressure of his job. We can usually get something done at these meetings. We should have more.

11. *Manager's luncheon with selected employees* (see Chapter 14). This device is used quite broadly by managers in an attempt to get closer to employees many position levels below. By far the largest portion of the time is devoted to questions from the attending employees. Here again, the reporting of the questions and replies

in the employee house organ results in an eagerly read reaffirmation or interpretation of policies and intent.

12. *The suggestion system.* One of the oldest and most widely used of the formalized devices for upward communication is the Suggestion System. Central features of most systems are: monetary awards ranging from 10 to 15 per cent of the first year's net saving resulting from the adoption of an employee suggestion; ineligibility of supervisors to participate; suitable forms and conveniently located suggestion boxes to facilitate employee participation; a suggestion committee to review the value of the suggestion and to determine the size of the monetary award; vigorous promotion of the system through a wide variety of communication media.

The Suggestion System was originally conceived to tap the rich latent reservoir of ideas for improving the product or the service produced by the business enterprise as well as to develop employee interest in finding a "better way." It expanded quite naturally into a medium whereby employees could also get a hearing on what they conceived to be better working conditions.

Of late years, it has been looked at with fresh interest by management as an important listening station in the upward communication system. In many instances, dissatisfaction or even irritation becomes the basis for complaining, usually registered in the form of a grievance. On the other hand, by encouraging the complainant to develop a possible solution, the system induces the employee to become a suggester, interested in promoting improvements, rather than one merely bewailing tough luck or unhappiness with a situation. By encouraging the submission of suggestions, and by consistently considering the ideas presented as possibly being worthy of adoption, upward communication through the medium of a well-functioning suggestion plan can operate in a most constructive manner.

Many examples will come to mind whereby the circumstances described in the suggestion might just as well have been the basis for a justifiable complaint, but by applying constructive thinking to the problem, the employee enhances his value to the organization and receives merited reward for his constructive approach in helping to solve a difficulty.

Some of the significant feedback the Suggestion System can provide is illustrated by the following two examples taken from our files:

1. The plant mail carrier noticed a steady increase in the volume and the weight of the load he was being called upon to carry. His pack was becoming more burdensome, he was becoming irritable, and it was becoming more difficult for him to maintain a satisfactory delivery schedule. Here were seeds of discontent which could well fester a grievance.

However, as he reflected upon the problem, he developed the idea that an adaptation of the light golf-club cart, with a basket which could be used in advance to sort his mail for easy delivery, would enable him to give better service despite the larger volume of mail he was handling. Consequently, a suggestion describing his solution was submitted, its merit quickly recognized, and a suitable award given to the mail carrier; additionally, the conditions which had begun to cause him concern were corrected.

2. An employee working near an entrance doorway was unable to convince the jitney drivers using it to close it promptly in cold shivering weather. Noticing that the means for opening and closing the door were difficult and inconvenient, he suggested the installation of an electrically operated door, with a switch so located that the jitney driver could open or close the door without leaving his jitney. Thus a grievance was converted to a money-making suggestion, with resulting job satisfaction for both employee and drivers.

Not all suggestions, of course, are particularly outstanding examples of improving irritating conditions. (For instance, there was the stenographer who disliked the taste of postage stamps. Instead of griping, she suggested that other secretaries do as she did—which was to lick the corner of the envelope instead.) But from our own experience, we know there is real value in the suggestion plan as an effective means of upward communication, which encourages constructive thinking in a positive way and becomes a means to develop and improve employee morale. Both suggestions and grievances should be reviewed regularly for clues as to what employees are attempting to tell us.

13. *The performance appraisal.* The key role played by performance appraisals in integrating the enterprise and the astonishing difficulty in ensuring that everyone is periodically informed as to how he is doing was examined in Chapter 10.

The performance-appraisal discussion, if properly conducted, represents the full flowering of upward communication. Here, of all times, the manager should listen intently and unhurriedly. Here he should exercise his keenest powers of perception to assure static-free reception of both the first and second levels of communication.

There is a rather poignant anecdote of the mother who noticed her young son laboring over a crayon drawing of a man's face. "What are you doing, Sonny?" she inquired indulgently. "I'm drawing a picture of God," said the boy. "But Sonny, no one has ever seen God," said the startled mother. "I know, Mummy, but they will when I get through here!" The impulse to play God in the appraisal discussion is a temptation few appraisers can resist. Yet, nothing will so inhibit the therapeutic upward-communication values of the discussion.

Appraisal time is a time for listening, of helping the appraisee evaluate his accomplishments, of helping him to relieve the pent-up anxieties for which his superior may be so largely responsible.

General Motors Corporation, in its *Handbook for the Performance Record for Production Employees,* has this to say to its supervisors. "Evaluation is a way of getting a record of the actual performance of each employee in terms of his job requirements. Its purpose is not to blame or condemn employees for limitations and deficiencies—thus lowering morale. Its purpose is to provide factual starting-points for individual employee development leading to more effective productivity with less strain and greater satisfaction—thus raising morale."

14. *Postemployment and exit interviews.* Certain companies make a practice of conducting a planned nondirective interview with each employee three to six months after coming on the payroll. The purposes of this interview are manifold. Importantly, it shows management's regard for the employee as an individual rather than a clock

card; it indicates more than any words in the official "relations hand-book" that people are important. It offers an excellent measure of the effectiveness of the company's orientation program, and it often serves to detect misfit employees before they acquire too much seniority.

The interviewing is normally performed by a member of the employee relations staff who has been trained in interview skills; some success, however, has been experienced in using the plant nurse, part time, to do the interviewing with female personnel.

The exit interview is an old-established practice in personnel administration. It ensures that the departing employee receives accurate terminating information particularly as to benefit plans; it uncovers, in most cases, the true reasons for leaving; it promotes good relations with departing employees; most importantly, it often provides some of management's most valuable upward communication inasmuch as the departing employee normally is freed from all inhibitions.

The exit interview is normally conducted by one of the regular interviewers in the employment office. Care must be exercised not to violate the confidence of the employee. A well-conducted exit interview program can provide a continuing source of current information regarding the employees' view of the operation and of management practices. An excellent vehicle for upward communication, it should be a permanent part of any sound communication program. It is worthless, however, unless the feedback is used as another helpful measure for continual adjustment of personnel practices.

15. *Planned shop contacts.* Reference was made in Chapter 14 to the formalizing of foremen's contacts with employees through the use of a pocket-size booklet containing the names, pictures, and vital statistics of all reporting employees. Such mechanical aids to upward communication are almost impossible to maintain on a continuing effective basis. In this particular example, the idea emanated from the foremen's association and was one of their principal activities, which no doubt accounts for its success.

16. *Employee-attitude surveys.* Here is one of the most widely used management tools for obtaining a wealth of upward communication simultaneously from all employees. Because of its importance and because of its value as a measure of employee relations effectiveness, it will be treated separately in Chapter 17.

In concluding this brief review of the enormously complex problem of attaining the highly sought goal of trustworthy upward communication as a basis for better managerial decision making, we feel constrained to offer these admonitions: no one technique can be relied upon. What is needed is a planned, integrated system employing those techniques which, on an empirical basis, produce the most reliable results in the context of a specific plant climate.

CHAPTER 17

Measuring the Effectiveness of Employee Communication

We approach this important subject with humility. The things we do not know far outnumber the things we think we know.

The present tools used by business to measure the effectiveness of its communication are crude. One of the prime obstacles is the confusion that exists as to just what we are attempting to measure.

The temptation is strong to measure the readership of various media (a *relatively* simple task) rather than to measure the change in attitudes and resulting behavior which should be the purpose of utilizing the communication being measured.

An obstacle of greater magnitude is presented by the complex characteristics of "good" employee morale and "acceptable" employee behavior which are the end results we should be trying to measure. Then, too, no two definitions of employee morale are the same; and we are further confounded by the question raised in certain experiments as to whether high morale necessarily results in high productivity.

These complexities should not deter us. Far better to measure with the crudest instruments than not to measure at all.

The following simple pragmatic approach to this measurement problem may prove helpful. This approach may be described as *tailoring the measurement to the objective.*

Our formalized communication programs can be divided into two broad categories: (1) specific limited-objective communication and

(2) long-term integrated communication programing to advance the objectives of the business.

1. *Specific limited-objective communication.* Much of our employee communication effort is directed toward achieving specific limited objectives. The list is long and familiar: increase participation in the benefit programs; "sell in" a new pension plan; revitalize the Suggestion System; prevent a walkout or strike; reduce the number of grievances; introduce a new machine or new technology; change the parking rules; lower the accident frequency rate; change over from cash payment of employees to check payment.

Here we are in a relatively simple area of measurement. We establish as part of our yearly programing the attainment of one or more of the foregoing goals and we measure our success quantitatively by observation. To be sure, we do not usually know how much of our success we owe to the persuasiveness of the communication. Perhaps our supervisors were primarily responsible. But our experience indicates a substantial correlation between the intensive use of intelligently planned communication and successful attainment of limited-objective goals.

2. *Long-term integrated communication programing to advance the objectives of the business.* Presumably in a business where formalized employee communication is used intensively to achieve over-all business objectives, management hopes to improve job satisfaction in the belief that this will increase productivity and quality, lower costs and increase profits, and facilitate the achievement of other goals of the enterprise.

But because of the many variables that affect these results—improved technology, good management planning and decisions, idiosyncrasies of customers, cyclical changes in the economy, etc.—the quantitative measurement of end results, such as unit costs, profits, etc., tells us all too little about the effectiveness of the communication input.

Accordingly, managers must back up and content themselves with the measurement of employee opinions and attitudes and of observable job performance. They must be content, in other words, with measuring those things which our communications are directed at affecting. When these variables are found to be at a desirable level—when employee morale, for example, is found to be high—then we may hypothesize that our communication, among other forces, has been effective. Measurement of the *precise* influence of communication, as distinct from those other forces, must await the development of new and more refined research techniques.

The following six approaches to this type of measurement seem most promising:

1. The feedback from upward communication

All the techniques listed in Chapter 16 can be helpful, if studied and analyzed collectively, in telling us much about the effectiveness of our communication efforts.

2. Employee-attitude surveys

The most economical method of measuring the effectiveness of employee communication is the periodic employee-attitude survey. Enlightened managers use this tool to achieve three key objectives:

1. To measure the quantity and quality of communication getting through to the employee

2. To measure the impact of the full range of employee relations activities designed to satisfy the basic needs of their employees at their work place

3. To increase their understanding of their operations in order to do a better job of managing

If managers are effectively to discharge their responsibilities in this area of business performance, namely, to take the kinds of actions that will result in good employee attitudes, they need to have information concerning the kinds of attitudes that do exist and the changes that occur, so that the resulting knowledge can be used to improve performance in the future.

Attitude surveys provide a means for systematically collecting the consciously expressed opinions, likes, and dislikes of individuals under controlled conditions. These can be recorded either by questionnaire or interview. The author's company primarily utilizes the questionnaire method because it provides an economical way of obtaining broad coverage of subject matter from all employees with not too much sacrifice of penetration. However, the more penetrating depth-interview method may be strongly indicated in certain situations and hence will be discussed shortly.

The attitude survey reflects the *perception* of employees. We must bear in mind that the attitudes and opinions of employees, as recorded in a survey, may not reflect actual conditions—but they do reflect what employees believe to be the actual conditions. These beliefs, founded on fact or fancy, prejudice or misinformation, are the realities with which the manager must deal.

The attitude survey not only provides a type of measurement of morale, but is a morale-building device per se. Employees are eager to express their opinions. The great majority express a high interest in the outcome and treat the survey most seriously. Morale noticeably increases during the making of the survey and before any remedial action, based on the findings, is initiated.

The survey, although measuring among other factors the impact of communication, is in itself one of the best communication techniques. It communicates to the employees the warming, rewarding knowledge that managers need and earnestly seek the ideas of their employees in order to manage the business more effectively. Thus in one more way—and a very effective way—the common interests and mutual interdependence of employees and managers are dramatized.

There is growing and heartening evidence that a positive relationship exists between good employee attitudes and good performance by employees. Employees rated by their supervisor as good performers respond considerably more favorably to the questionnaire than do low-performance respondees.

Constructing an employee-attitude survey

Most of the operating units of the author's company utilize a standardized questionnaire calling for an "agree" or disagree" response to forty questions in eight broad attitude areas or categories. Each of the categories is relatively independent of the others, and each contributes added new information about the total array of categories.

Every effort is made to use questions which have a high degree of surface validity. That is, each question covers a topic about which there is a generally accepted favorable or unfavorable response. For example, in attempting to determine attitudes toward pay, this statement is made: "All in all, I am satisfied with the pay I get." Agreement with this statement is considered a favorable response and disagreement is considered unfavorable.

Here are the eight broad categories normally used in the employee-attitude survey and a brief description of each:

1. *Working conditions:* these items cover employees' reactions to their physical working conditions, including space and facilities.

2. *Compensation:* the items in this category are concerned with employees' attitudes on pay.

3. *Operating efficiency:* this category covers employees' impressions regarding how well things "go" on the job, including regularity of work schedules, smoothness of procedures, and changes in job methods.

4. *Group harmony:* this category covers the feelings that employees have toward others in the work group and gives an indication of team spirit within the group.

5. *Future opportunity:* the items in this category measure employees' feelings regarding their chances for better jobs in the future.

6. *Communication:* this category indicates how well employees are satisfied with the methods by which, and extent to which, they are kept informed about what goes on in the plant.

7. *Supervision:* the items in this category are concerned with how employees react to their immediate supervisors and the ways in which their supervisors do things.

8. *General management:* this category covers the extent to which employees feel that management is fair and considerate in its treatment of them.

Operating management often includes a few additional categories of particular interest locally.

Since one of our big objectives is to measure the quality and quantity of the communication transmitted to employees, the reader may be interested in the following statements which are included in the *communication category* (the employee is asked, in regard to each, whether he agrees or disagrees):

1. The company's Suggestion System works well.

2. When management talks or writes to employees, it sidesteps or evades the things which usually bother people on the job.

3. I am not satisfied with the amount of information we get about policies and decisions that affect us.

4. There seem to be good reasons whenever changes are made here.

5. When new methods of doing the work are installed, we get a satisfactory explanation of the expected benefits.

Tips on administering the survey

Before administering a survey, an announcement of the intent, objectives, mechanics of administration, and timing is made to employees in all the familiar media. At this time also a promise is made to report back the findings to the employees and to remedy unsatisfactory conditions to the degree practicable.

The survey is administered on company premises on company time to groups of employees who gather in a conference room or cafeteria or some specially equipped area to fill out the questionnaires after a short briefing by the administrator of the survey. The questionnaires provide opportunity for free-response "write-ins." Employees are requested not to sign them unless they specifically desire to do so. The filled-in forms are deposited in a sealed box and the boxes shipped to the company's headquarters for scoring and analysis. The entire opinion-gathering process requires approximately thirty minutes of the employee's time.

The follow-up to the remedial action

When the completed survey report is delivered to top management, the remedial action usually follows this sequence:

1. Feedback to employees (and sometimes community neighbors). As

rapidly as feasible, arrangements are made to feed back a summary report of findings to employees through mass communication media. Usually the general manager sends a special booklet summarizing the findings to the homes of employees with a personal letter of transmittal which comments on the findings and indicates remedial action planned. In some plants, summary findings are published in the plant news. In others, the general manager meets with all employees in groups to deliver the feedback orally. There is no standard pattern for feedback by individual supervisors to employees reporting directly to them. In some components there is *no* communication of the survey report by individual supervisors as it affects their groups. This is believed to be a mistake. Where such communicating *is* done, the supervisors often prefer to discuss the composite plant findings and thereby stimulate revealing questions from their group rather than to discuss the specific attitudes revealed by their group.

2. Planning the remedial action: there are two broad types of remedial action (*a*) tangible observable action by top management and (*b*) corrective action by individual supervisors in their manager-man relationships.

Nature of the remedial action

Remedial action by top management usually consists of correction in the material or tangible areas of job satisfaction, for example, the paving of a parking lot, the renovation of a cafeteria, the reduction in irritating red tape and elapsed time in benefit payments, etc.

Some recent findings indicate that management can achieve fabulous increases in morale overnight by quick correction of such tangible areas of dissatisfaction. Such correction, of course, should be quickly and widely communicated as evidence that management meant business with its survey and that management does care about the things that seem important to employees. Even where managers are unable to correct the situation at once, much good will can be obtained by communicating that they recognize the problem, that they do *care* about it, and that they are *planning* to correct it.

The second type of remedial action is by far the most difficult—but the most effective and the most enduring. This is the action taken by managers (or supervisors) at all levels in the component to improve their relationships with the people reporting to them, using the survey findings as a guide. Managers can perform no greater service in manpower development than to help those supervisors reporting to them to understand the true nature of their supervisory weaknesses as revealed by the attitude survey, then to motivate them to correct their weaknesses, and finally, if necessary, to coach them as to how to do it.

Thus it may be seen that the employee attitude survey is a multipurpose tool which provides significant feedback to management not only as to the effectiveness of its communication but of most of its other activities designed to fulfill basic employee needs. It is also, in itself, a morale builder and a prime communication device. It is normally administered once a year or every eighteen months. Through standardization, the manager is able not only to compare intraplant group satisfaction, but also to compare the percentage of satisfaction in his plant with norms established for a composite of company plants.

Finally, it is unsurpassed as a method for providing the framework for the next year's industrial relations programing.

3. The nondirective depth interview

This is a more costly, time-consuming method of measuring the impact of communication and other relations-improving practices of management.

After appropriate announcement by the managers, skilled interviewers conduct depth interviews with employees selected by a scientific random-sampling formula. The interviews are held on company premises and company time and normally require a minimum of sixty minutes per employee. Offsetting the greatly increased cost, which at times may be justifiable, this method has two significant advantages in its favor. It permits attitudes to be probed in much greater depth, and it provides clues as to the underlying reasons for the specific attitudes of employees.

4. The employee relations index

Another indirect method of measuring the effect of employee communication and other managerial practices in the employee relations area is through a study of employee behavior at the work place.

The author and his associates, particularly Dr. William C. Schwarzbek, L. G. Gilmore, J. T. Fontaine, and Joseph M. Bertotti, in cooperation with the consulting firm of Richardson, Bellows, and Henry, have for the past several years been developing a method which has been designated as "ERI," or the Employee Relations Index. The following description is abstracted from several published articles by the author.[1]

In an attempt to develop a better yardstick for measuring the effectiveness of our employee relations activity, we first had to isolate and define the end result we were attempting to obtain from our employee relations policies, practices, and implementation. We decided that the end result that we would try to measure was this: The extent to which groups of employees accept, and perform in accordance with, the objectives and policies of the company.

In the past, we have used the following different methods of evaluating the effectiveness of our employee relations among employees. All of them are probably familiar to you:

1. *Ratings* of status of employee relations
2. *Audits* of policies, practices, and conditions affecting employee performance
3. *Surveys* of employee and management attitudes
4. *Production* and financial data recording conditions affected by employee relations
5. *Personnel statistics* on various employee activities

Each of these, of course, has its merits. As a matter of fact, *no complete evaluation* of the effectiveness of an organization's em-

---

[1] American Management Association, fall Personnel Conference, New York, 1956; cf. Willard V. Merrihue and Raymond A. Katzell, "ERI: Yardstick of Employee Relations," *Harvard Business Review,* November–December, 1955.

ployee relations would be *possible* without applying most or all these methods in combination, for they do complement each other. But the need for an over-all yardstick, one which can be applied frequently and routinely with a minimum of cost and dislocation, has long been recognized. To fill it, the method based on personnel statistics has seemed to hold out the greatest promise, since it has the desirable features of being reliable, objective, and most important, since it is based on kinds of employee statistics that have been gathered for years in most plants as a matter of routine.

The Employee Relations Index is essentially a variation of the personnel statistics method, with some important differences.

Symptoms of good or bad employee relations

Our pilot research led us to believe that the following kinds of records of employee behavior might reflect the state of employee relations in a plant:

Absenteeism	Grievances
Safety	Work stoppages
Turnover	Disciplinary suspensions
Suggestions	Benefit plan participation

There were many others, of course, but *these* records of employee behavior seemed to satisfy our two basic criteria: (1) they were the ones that seemed most likely to be routinely available at our plants; (2) they seemed to represent well-defined individual symptoms of good or bad employee relations in the plant. Each one was termed an "indicator" of the state of employee relations.

We started with the generally accepted notion that, all other things being equal, work groups having high absence rates have *poorer* employee relations than those having low rates, those with *much* turnover have *poorer* employee relations than those with little turnover, and so on. However, a major issue in the above concept is the phrase—"all other things being equal." In practice, all other things are *not* equal. Some work groups may have a rash of genuine illness that pushes *up* their absence rates. Also, some work groups may be composed of workers with job skills that are much in demand, which would tend to increase their turnover rate. And so on for the other indicators.

This means that no one of the indicators alone could be expected to serve as a valid measure of employee relations.

So here is where we parted company with the analysis of individual personnel statistics.

Isolating the common factor

We realized that absenteeism, safety, turnover, and the other indicators were, in many respects, as different as apples and oranges. However, apples and oranges do have something in common—sugar!—and this might be called their *common* factor.

We believed that although all of these indicators could and did vary independently, some *common factor* existed which caused them to vary together. The question naturally arose as to the nature of this common factor. The answer is necessarily a matter of inference. However, we did know that a group's absences, dispensary visits, turnover, suggestions, work stoppages, grievances, actions requiring disciplinary suspensions, and insurance plan participation are all patterns of behavior that seemed to depend on how much individuals in the work group tie in with management's objectives.

If an employee is inclined to reject his job and management's objectives, he is more likely to *withdraw from the job* by absences, by dispensary visits, or by quitting, to a greater degree than a better-motivated employee.

Or he may try to *change his job* through strikes, grievances, or suggestions.

He may *break rules* thereby incurring disciplinary suspensions, or he may fail to affiliate by failing to participate in benefit plans.

The idea that our eight indicators contained a common factor caused us to consider the possibility of a single index of employee relations. To develop it, we knew that two hurdles would have to be crossed. First, we would have to *establish*, statistically, the presence of a *common factor* in our separate employee relations indicators. Secondly, we would have to *devise a single, composite index* based on the combined influence of the separate indicators. Such an index, we hoped, would be relatively immune to the specific things that may cause absence rates or dispensary visits or turnover rates, alone, to give a misleading picture of employee attitudes.

Initially, we collected data on thirty-three types of employee behavior.

After we had collected data from six plants, we analyzed the thirty-three sets of data, by work groups, and then, using a mathematical method known as factor analysis, discovered that the thirty-three kinds of data were all, as we had hoped, variants of these eight basic indicators:

1. Periods of absence
2. Initial dispensary visits for occupational reasons
3. Separations from payroll
4. Grievances
5. Work stoppages
6. Number of suggestions
7. Disciplinary suspensions
8. Participation in insurance plan

Even more important, we found that these eight different indicators were, themselves, correlated. Thus, we confirmed our hypothesis that *each* of the eight kinds of indicators was strongly influenced by the *same cause* or *factor* as the others.

Significance of the common factor

The factor analysis also enabled us to state the *degree* to which a *common factor* underlies each of the eight indicators. For example, if we think of the work groups as *varying* from one another in, say, absence rate, we know from the analysis (Figure 8) that about 25 per cent of this *variation* is due to the common factor. Note that the common factor is exerting the highest influence in absenteeism (this is the easiest way to record disapproval). Similarly, about 10 per cent of the intergroup variation in turnover and in grievances can be ascribed to this factor and between 10 per cent and 20 per cent of the variation in the remaining indicators.

It should be noted that the remaining 75 per cent to 90 per cent of variations in absence rate and the other indicators are *not due to this common factor.* These represent the bona fide illnesses, changes

ERI INDICATORS—VARIATIONS DUE TO COMMON FACTOR

0	25	50	75	100
25%	PERIODS OF ABSENCE			
20%	INITIAL DISPENSARY VISITS			
7%	SEPARATIONS FROM PAYROLL			
11%	GRIEVANCES			
10%	WORK STOPPAGES			
14%	DISCIPLINARY SUSPENSIONS			
15%	NUMBER OF SUGGESTIONS			
12%	PARTICIPATION IN INSURANCE			
0	25	50	75	100

Figure 8

in jobs for reasons other than dissatisfaction, suggestions due to helpful motives, and so on.

Constructing a significant single index

Having established a common factor, we now had to come up with a single gauge of the state of employee relations in a work group. Again mathematics came to the rescue by providing a means by which the eight indicator measurements could be *added together* so that they formed a composite index representing the common factor. This was done by means of a *multiple-regression* formula in which the eight indicator scores of any work group can be entered, and a composite index computed for that group.

The ERI formula (Figure 9) may be considered as a statistical method of adding apples and oranges through the device of adding their sugar content. The formula is such that each of the indicators gets a weight proportional to the degree it is influenced by the general factor.

ERI Formula

$$ERI = B_1 K_1 X_1 + B_2 K_2 X_2 + B_3 K_3 X_3 + B_4 K_4 X_4$$
$$+ B_5 K_5 X_5 + B_6 K_6 X_6 + B_7 K_7 X_7 + B_8 K_8 X_8 + C,$$

where $X_1 . X_2 . X_3$ . . . etc., are the scores on the 8 ERI elements; B_1, B_2, B_3 . . . etc., are weights for each of the elements; K_1, K_2, K_3 . . . etc., are constants depending on the level of the element in the plant; and C is an over-all constant for the plant.

Figure 9

These eight weighted indicators are then combined to give the group's over-all index, which we have termed the *Employee Relations Index,* or ERI. The formula is set up in such a way that the *average work group* gets an ERI of 100. *Higher ERI's represent better employee relations,* that is, fewer absences, less turnover, and so on; lower ERI's indicate poorer employee relations.

Once the indices for all of the plant's work groups have been calculated, they can be reported to management (Figure 10) in a summary form by work groups.

In addition to each group's ERI, the summary report shows individual scores for each of the eight indicators, and also various background data that may be helpful to interpretation.

Figure 10. Quarterly Summary Form

Work group	No. emp.	ERI	Absentees°	Disciplin. suspens.°°	Work stoppages°°	Plant separations°°	In. occup. disp. visits°	Grievances°°	Suggestions°°	Insurance, %	Overtime	Average rate of pay	Continuous service	No. of dependents	% Male	Average age	Union dues checkoff	Shift
Test	43	107	11	0	0	13	3	0	2	93	51	$1.86	5.0	1.1	95.5	30	71.5	2 & 3
Insp. & Q.C.	21	96	6	0	0	4	2	4	73	100	115	2.19	18.2	1.5	100.0	45	66.7	1 & 2
Maint.	28	90	7	0	19	11	4	6	0	100	66	1.96	14.4	1.8	80.0	50	76.1	All
Maint.	28	101	8	0	27	11	3	1	3	100	126	2.04	8.3	2.3	96.0	46	100.0	1 & 2
Loading	17	105	17	0	0	9	3	2	0	100	182	1.74	9.5	2.7	100.0	45	81.4	1 & 2
Panel & packing	30	117	5	0	0	3	5	0	3	100	177	1.85	17.0	1.8	93.5	47	63.3	1 & 2
Supply	30	111	10	0	0	10	5	0	0	100	91	1.74	11.1	1.8	93.5	42	63.3	1 & 2
Mach. shop	35	82	24	0	41	24	6	4	0	100	22	2.40	13.1	1.9	100.0	40	100.0	Day
Mach. shop	27	101	12	0	25	3	3	0	6	100	300	2.19	13.4	1.7	100.0	38	96.5	1
Mach. shop	31	55	25	1	0	35	7	2	5	96	13	2.02	5.3	1.8	100.0	37	87.6	2
Fabrication	47	94	9	0	0	15	3	0	3	100	17	2.45	14.9	2.0	100.0	42	90.8	1
Fabrication	53	103	11	0	0	15	4	1	0	96	2	2.45	10.2	1.8	100.0	38	89.2	2
Fabrication	29	90	18	0	24	3	7	3	5	100	7	2.81	15.0	2.5	100.0	38	96.6	1
Assem.-Wire	48	112	12	1	0	8	3	0	2	98	72	2.42	11.3	1.9	91.5	36	89.4	1
Assem.-Wire	66	100	11	1	0	5	4	0	2	98	63	2.17	12.0	1.4	100.0	39	92.4	1
Assem.-Wire	51	115	6	0	0	3	5	0	9	100	3	2.18	13.2	2.1	100.0	40	99.7	1
Assem.-Wire & paint	65	78	9	1	0	33	4	1	6	95	39	2.04	6.8	1.6	100.0	33	79.0	2
Supv. & panel.	44	100	9	0	31	12	3	1	0	100	13	2.22	12.3	1.7	97.1	35	100.0	1 & 2
Stockroom	38	102	10	0	0	20	4	0	2	95	76	1.67	6.1	1.3	100.0	34	89.5	1
Fab.	36	94	19	0	1	19	5	1	0	94	275	2.45	11.8	1.9	100.0	37	88.7	1
Fab.	18	92	15	0	20	21	5	0	0	95	58	1.96	5.4	1.4	100.0	32	94.5	2
Assembly	49	111	10	0	0	2	2	0	46	100	130	2.31	12.7	2.3	100.0	37	91.9	1
Assembly	10	115	8	0	0	0	4	0	23	100	145	2.36	9.0	2.3	100.0	36	91.0	2
Herkolite	18	104	13	0	0	12	5	0	8	95	112	2.44	16.3	1.7	100.0	45	89.5	1
Herkolite	8	97	19	0	0	20	1	0	0	88	24	1.85	6.9	1.9	100.0	36	100.0	2
Mean			13.0	.1	6.7	11.8	3.6	1.3	8.8	98.2	126.5	2.17	10.9	1.45	96.7	38.8	87.7	
Standard deviation			8.0	.3	11.3	9.0	1.6	1.7	17.4	2.9	141.8	.3	3.7	.6	3.8	4.6	10.2	

° Expressed as per 100 employees per week. °° Expressed as per 1,000 employees per week.

ERI diagnoses the illness—not the cause

ERI, like a clinical thermometer, is also a first step in diagnosis. After taking a patient's temperature, a physician will normally question him, in a systematic way, to get all the information that may throw light on the *cause* of illness. In the same way, managers will bring to bear any other information at hand to tell them more about why an ERI is high or low—and thus enlarge their understanding of what is going on in that work group.

One of the systematic ways of obtaining more information about a work group is the employee-attitude survey. Such surveys provide us with valuable information about areas that are most likely to affect employee morale. Some of these areas, for example, are *working conditions, compensation,* and *future opportunity.* We have reason to believe that, in the future, a two-step diagnosis employing first, ERI and second, the employee-attitude survey, may bring us closer than ever before to whatever factors cause poor employee relations.

It is beginning to appear evident, on the basis of the work done today, that we have developed a measure better than anything we have seen to date; this measure reflects the degree to which management has succeeded in gaining simple acceptance of, and performance in accord with, company objectives and policies, and I hope (we) can agree that this is a pretty fair definition of the ultimate objective of the employee relations activities into which we are pouring so much time and money, and at which we are working so earnestly. Much work remains to be done to obtain further validation and to make it more effective. However, the needs of management can never await certainty; management decisions have to be made daily on the basis of the best available evidence. For example, the accounting measures, with which we have had the longest experience in industry, are nowhere near as precise a set of measuring tools as the novice would expect. Accordingly, we are moving ahead cautiously with the application of the measurement to the area of employee relations, and it is hoped that other companies will want to move ahead along similar lines.

It can be expected that the sharing of results and experiences among the various experimenting companies will then vastly accelerate the acquisition of understanding and work in this complex but vital area of evaluating human motivation and behavior.

5. Surveys by outside organizations

A review of the literature of communication reveals a distressing dearth of activity in measuring the effects of communication within business enterprises.

The National Industrial Conference Board conducted one of the few surveys of communication effectiveness some years ago.[2] The Board questioned in detail two groups of employees about job matters and company matters. One group in plant B had been subjected to rather full and intelligent communication by its management. The other in plant A had not been exposed to any similar program. Both plants were operated by the same company but in adjoining states.

The scores on all the categories of questions discriminated sharply in favor of plant B employees. The answers to the three final questions, as recorded in the conclusion of the report, indicate the results that may be expected from an investment in a soundly planned employee communication program:

Three final questions looked into the workers' reactions to communication in terms of its success and values in their respective plants. The first asked directly:

Question—Does your company do a good job of telling you what's going on and what's being planned?

Answers	Plant A	Plant B
It does a very good job......................	18%	55%
It does a fairly good job.....................	60	31
It doesn't do much of this at all...............	22	14

[2] "Communicating With Employees," National Industrial Conference Board, Studies in Personnel Policy, no. 129, New York, 1952.

The extra attention that Plant B has given to communications seems to have paid off, according to these scores.

The two remaining questions may be thought of as pertaining to overall morale. A chief goal of communication is to build a team spirit—to develop positive feelings and attitudes toward the organization. Compare the figures in the following tables:

*Question—*Do you feel a part of your company?

Answers	Plant A	Plant B
I feel I really belong........................	29%	62%
I feel I just work here......................	42	14
Sometimes I feel one way and sometimes the other	29	24

*Question—*Generally speaking, how does your company compare as a company to work for compared with other companies that you know about or have worked for?

Answers	Plant A	Plant B
One of the very worst.......................	1%	0%
Worse than average.........................	4	3
Just average.................................	35	19
Better than average.........................	40	33
One of the very best........................	20	45

Differences of these magnitudes don't just happen! Something causes them. It cannot be proved that communication is *the* answer, but it would be illogical to think that communication did not contribute to the differences. Lacking a laboratory setup and laboratory conditions, it is possible only to make reasonable guesses. A reasonable guess here is that communication is a powerful factor affecting the ideas and attitudes of the employees in the two plants.

6. Testing how well communication is assimilated

A method based on well-established test principles, for measuring objectively how well management is getting its messages across and identifying specific areas of confusion or misinformation, was reported in the November, 1952, issue of *Personnel.*[3]

The experimenters, Harry B. Funk and Robert C. Becker, studied the policy manuals, memoranda, letters to supervisors and rank-and-

[3] "Measuring the Effectiveness of Industrial Communication," *Personnel,* November, 1952, p. 237.

file employees as well as all verbal instructions in a given organization—then constructed a test to reveal the degree of assimilation of the communications.

The test was found to discriminate sharply between staff employees and their supervisors in a technical office and a special control group.

The authors concluded their report with this admonition that might well be printed and displayed in the offices of all who have responsibility for employee communication:

The writers venture the prediction that the development and application of similar communication knowledge tests in a variety of business and industrial organizations will lead to much needed improvements in current communication programs. Without some such techniques of evaluation, it is probable that waste and ineffectiveness will continue to characterize communication programs in business and industry.

PART FIVE

Specific Management Uses of Communication

CHAPTER 18

Use of Communication in Achieving
Employee Participation

Communication is not an end in itself. There is no profit in communicating just for the sake of communicating. Communication is a means—and a very effective means—for the solution of managerial problems and for the attainment of managerial objectives.

Many of the most perplexing and frustrating daily problems confronting a manager are people-centered. They have their roots in a lack of understanding, or outright misunderstanding, causing apathetic, negative, and hostile attitudes and resultant actions or inactions of individuals at all levels in the enterprise. Where the root cause is as stated, these attitudes and actions may be modified and reconciled through effective communication.

Communication concentrates the attention of the organization on the goals to be reached, gives employees the information they need to do their part, motivates them to overcome the obstacles, seeks and channels their participation.

Many companies today are working hard to achieve employee participation, primarily through communication.

Esso Standard Oil Company lucidly describes the participative process for the benefit of its supervisors. The foreword [1] cuts right to the core of the process as follows:

---

[1] *What Is Employee Participation?* Esso Standard Oil Company, New York.

Participation isn't selling ideas under a disguise. And it isn't going through the motion of letting others talk while not wanting or using their reactions.

It is a seeking for ideas, reactions and feelings.

It is acting in a way that each employee gets a feeling of recognition of his importance as an individual.

It is a sharing of information, ideas, plans and problems with those affected, giving an opportunity for their comments to influence the decisions to be taken.

We believe that better results come about through seeking a balance of viewpoints and through mutual sharing and solving of problems by the people affected.

(We believe) that employees should be invited to discuss matters affecting them.

That they should have an opportunity to share the problems in their group.

That their views are important in working out problems of their group.

That better solutions to problems come this way.

Robert C. Hood, president of Ansul Chemical Company, Marinette, Wisconsin, whose company practices participative management, defines his philosophy thus: [2]

Participative management is a way of managing a business enterprise aimed at unleashing the full creative power of people through participation. Two broad supporting principles underlie this definition:

1. People, not products, are the real competitive difference between companies.

2. People support what they help create. Participative management is more than a set of academic principles. It is a practical approach to managing a business. . . . [It] develops mutual confidence, stimulates better individual work and teamwork, and taps the vast latent personal resources of a business.

[2] *Effective Employee and Community Relations: A Report on Ansul Chemical Company*, Chamber of Commerce of the United States, Business Relations Department, Washington, D.C., 1956.

Widely varying degrees of so-called participative management are utilized by business enterprises in this country. There is some question whether the term itself is not misleading since basic decisions of any great economic import must, of necessity, be unilateral because responsibility and accountability cannot be discharged through group action. However, the final decision can often be influenced by, and benefit from, this dynamic process of upward communication which we term participative management. The semantics are unimportant and should not becloud the goal which is this: to obtain the benefits of employees' reactions and suggestions before the fact instead of after the fact.

The key to the successful functioning of resultful employee participation is skill in communication to develop maximum understanding of the problem and to motivate employees by expressing goals in terms of the common interests of the employees of the enterprise.

The following examples are case studies in participation achieved through the intelligent and intensive use of communication.

1. Cost reduction—Ansul Chemical Company

With costs increasing at a faster rate than sales (a familiar periodic phenomenon in many businesses), Ansul reasoned that costs were more a problem of people's attitudes than of methods. If employee attitudes could be changed so as to create a *concern for cost*, then cost reduction would quickly follow.

Through intensive communication, both oral and written, employees were motivated to be concerned about costs. Supervisors solicited suggestions on how costs could be reduced. They never told employees what to do—or when, where, or how to cut costs. In the beginning stages, cost *concern* was paramount to specific methods of cost reduction. The program took more time than if an authoritarian approach had been used, but the results (40 per cent increase in profits on only a 3 per cent increase in sales) were more spectacular and, of greater importance, longer lasting.

2. Developing increased business—The Steel Improvement and Forge Company

One of the most skilled practitioners of managing by communication is Charles H. Smith, Jr., president, the Steel Improvement and Forge Company, Cleveland, Ohio. Over the past ten years, he has won national recognition for his success in achieving integrated employee participation through intelligent planned communication. A case in point:

Faced with surplus capacity, he took his problem directly to the employees in a beautifully planned thirty-minute film-slide presentation entitled, "Here's Our Problem." To attack the problem participatively, President Smith devised a customer's service committee where foremen, top managers, and employees (on a rotating basis) could pool their ideas on each incoming order or bid.

Bulletins reporting on each meeting were mailed to employees' homes; the house organ likewise reported progress; question and suggestion boxes were installed widely to encourage other than committee members to participate. The bogey was achieved and, more importantly, a priceless mutuality of interest was ingrained in the organization as a continuing dividend.

3. Developing competition-minded employees—Johns-Manville Corporation

No doubt a majority of progressive companies attempt periodically to bring home to their employees the intensely competitive nature of their enterprises and the effect of competition on individual job security. But few tasks are more difficult than to cut through the apathy and misunderstanding of the work force and effectively to explain to employees in understandable terms, "What's in It for Them?" Johns-Manville Corporation, New York, succeeded by virtue of perceptive planning, continuing intensive communication programing, and a theme, "Let's *All* Work Smarter," which appeals to the craftsman's pride latent in all employees. Key features of the plan, instituted in all plants, were

1. Regular hourly meetings at periodic intervals between supervisors and employees to solicit ideas on problems of increasing efficiency, cutting costs, and improving quality.

2. Display panels showing good features of competitive products. Panels illustrating J-M products that had slipped past the quality-control specialists, had been shipped, and had resulted in complaint.

3. A monthly newsletter on the competitive story to supplement the regular company magazine; colorful illustrated posters changed weekly covering competition, waste, quality, etc.

4. Specific results attested to by plant and mine managers were impressive and are reported in their words: [3]

"A greater awareness of delivery problems," "fewer foreign materials in the products," "better over-all quality," "more efficient and less costly methods from ideas developed at meetings," "maintenance costs reduced," "less work contracted for outside," "a dramatic drop in petty grievances."

The following key result is the dream of any manager or entrepreneur producing products or services on a volume basis in a highly competitive business:

Our local managers have noted an entirely different attitude toward our quality control inspectors, our industrial engineers and our research people. Whereas formerly, shipping something past the inspector was more or less of a game, we now find production workers calling the attention of the inspector to goods that are coming through that are not up to standard and asking him to check further back on the production line to find out what's wrong.

4. Participative planning of new work stations—Pitney Bowes, Stamford, Connecticut

Here is a rather unorthodox approach to a participation and communication problem. In designing workbenches for a new meter line, no standard provision was made for tools, sections for small screws, pins, and parts. Employees to be assigned to the stations were invited to offer suggestions about the placement of the individual items. The resulting output and morale were significantly

[3] *The Communicator*, Employers Labor Relations Information Committee, Inc., New York, March, 1955.

higher than where methods engineers had previously made unilateral decisions on such placement.

NOTE: Methods men and planners throughout industry are continually amazed at the resourcefulness of employees in developing short cuts to make work easier or to increase earnings.

5. Reducing losses on a railroad—New York Central System

Through intensive communication, it was possible to develop an individual awareness and concern among employees in shipping areas over the revenue lost by careless checking of weights.

Employees were motivated to double check the weights. The appeal to employees was so successful that many employees found errors totaling more than 2,000 pounds. Subsequently, a Tonners Club was formed and employees were invited to qualify. In a single year, the railroad received an additional income of three-quarter million pounds of freight.

6. Waste and spoilage reduction

No specific case study will be offered. American business and industry conduct a ceaseless attack on this ubiquitous problem. The plan of attack is familiar—an intensive tracking down of hundreds of items of waste and spoilage and corrective measures applied as fast as they are found. Supervisors are given courses in job-methods analysis; audits are made of every operation which hasn't changed in two years; employees are motivated and rewarded for resourceful ideas; prizes and victory dinners are awarded to work groups. Time after time, the results are little short of phenomenal.

The communication program is the motivator, inspiring individual employees voluntarily to find a better way in the area within their control.

7. Alleviating congestion in parking lots—General Electric Company, Evendale, Ohio

Our free-enterprise system shares the rewards of production so well that it creates a distinctively American problem, the overcrowding of industrial parking lots. In a defense plant faced with a big build-up of employment, the congestion in the vast parking lot was inhibiting recruitment of new employees.

The following plan, skillfully communicated, solved the problem. Four new express bus runs to the defense plant, excitingly termed "Jet Arrows," were negotiated for by the plant management. Likewise, an office was established for the purpose of facilitating "car pools." A well-planned communication program was launched to stress the advantages of the car pools and "Jet Arrows."

Management newsletters, Round-Table meetings with supervisors, and poster ads in the city press were so effectively integrated that the overcrowding ceased to be a problem within a few months after the plan was launched.

One of the most effective devices utilized was a series of "Before and After" picture pages showing how typical employees relaxed going to and from work vis-à-vis the harrowing experiences suffered while driving their personal cars.

8. Improving product quality—General Electric Company, Lynn, Massachusetts

This case may perhaps differ from its counterpart in thousands of enterprises only in its intensiveness. After weeks of careful planning, the program was initiated with a six-session training program for first-line supervisors on the techniques for correcting faulty employee attitudes which were at the root of the problem. After the training, the supervisors' detailed attack was supported by full-scale mass communication—including articles in the employee house organ, Round-Table meetings, a special *Quality Progress* newsletter, and a series of twenty-six posters and individual 40 × 60-inch progress charts for each foreman's work area which measured progress on a weekly basis. The theme selected was "Keep the U in Quality." Because this was a defense plant where employees were acutely aware of security measures, a special "security" badge was worn by employees to dramatize the close relationship between quality and employment security.

Despite the fact that this was an orthodox approach to a familiar business problem, there was a measurable improvement in quality in excess of 25 per cent or a total saving that ran into seven figures.

9. Participating in the selection of a holiday—General Electric Company, Pittsfield, Massachusetts

This particular year, Christmas fell on a Tuesday and upward communication channels revealed a wishful hope that the manager might shut down on Monday to provide for a long weekend.

It was decided to conduct an employee referendum so that each could record his vote for swapping the Monday before Christmas for the following Saturday—without premium pay for work performed Saturday.

All media of communication were enlisted to develop complete employee understanding of the problem and the procedure by which they could participatively resolve it. Approval was unanimous.

10. Attaining cooperation for a new waste-treatment process—General Electric Company, Erie, Pennsylvania

In an attempt to be a good corporate citizen, a new system for waste treatment for acids, soluble oils, and cyanide was installed at a cost of $750,000. However, to prevent stream and lake pollution, it was essential to attain and maintain the cooperation of all employees using contaminants. A series of meetings was held for full explanation of the new waste-treatment system. The basic appeal used to gain cooperation was that employees, as well as everyone in the community, would benefit from the antipollution program.

Three specific media were used at these meetings:

1. A movie, "Clean Waters," was shown to promote understanding of the problem, and to point out that the company was being a good "citizen" by installing these new facilities.

2. A specially prepared slide presentation was shown. The narrator, a person familiar with the new facilities, explained how to use them.

3. Every person was given a pamphlet which summarized, in photographs and text, what was presented in the slide program.

This series of meetings was handled by two men over a period of two to three months. The change to full usage of the new facilities was made with a minimum of difficulty and with strikingly successful results.

"People support," as Robert Hood has stated, "what they help to create." Accordingly, the list of successes in employee participation is endless. But always the prime *modus operandi* is effective employee communication. Managers interested in the use of communication to achieve stretching goals through employee participation will attain best results through following these three essential steps:

1. *Get the attention and interest of the employees involved.* This must never be taken for granted. Even when income security is threatened, as in the case of a strike vote, apathy, other interests, and a perennial hope that nothing will come of the action, combine to keep a majority away from the union hall. Hence, the generation of widespread personal interest and concern in the problem is vital.

The oral channels of communication are most helpful in this step since the manager's feeling of deep concern is best conveyed in face-to-face situations. Letters to homes are also useful to convey a feeling of importance of the subject and the manager's concern with it.

2. *Achieve full understanding of the goal or problem.* The second step, of course, is to give employees the information and understanding they need in order to become convinced of the soundness and wisdom of the course the manager is advocating and to *understand exactly what it is they can do to help achieve the ends desired.*

3. *Motivate employees to act in their own best interests.* And finally, of course, there must be motivation. Employees will not be motivated unless they are convinced that what their manager is asking them to do is in their own best interests. If management's goals will benefit the employees, this benefit must be translated into employees' needs, and employees can be shown how they can satisfy one or more of their basic needs at their work place by helping to achieve the goals of the enterprise.

The attitudes of employees toward their jobs, and toward the operating problems and goals of management, are not set in concrete.

They can be modified, so that employees will become willing and eager to help solve these problems and reach these goals.

Mainly, this is a problem in interpretation. Attitude surveys and depth interviews reveal that managers do a universally poor job of interpreting the goals, programing, budgets, deadlines, etc., much below the second level in the organizational hierarchy. Yet employees are eager to help if they know the goals and the specific action *within their area of control* that is indicated.

Indeed, you will find the majority will derive their greatest job satisfaction through purposeful goal-oriented work—through understanding their part in the total picture—through being convinced that their full resources are needed—through the creative thrill of purposeful participation.

CHAPTER 19

Use of Communication in Administering Change

Paradoxically, the only constant in today's dynamic business complex is change. Change, or its highbrow synonym, innovation, is an offspring of the prime mover of our business system which is competition. In our intensely competitive system of working for each other, change is absolutely essential. No business can remain static. It must go forward on the vehicle of change or it will fall backward.

Change is implicit in the term enterprise. It makes an enterprise out of a business.

Peter Drucker, in *The Practice of Management*, dramatically describes the importance of change or innovation. He asserts that every business enterprise has two basic functions: marketing and innovation.[1]

It is not necessary for a business to grow bigger [he states] but it is necessary that it constantly grow better.

Innovation [he continues] may take the form of a lower price—the form with which the economist has been most concerned, for the simple reason that it is the only one that can be handled by his quantitative tools. But it may also be a new and better product (even at a higher price), a new convenience, or the creation of a new want. It may be finding new uses for old products. . . .

Innovation goes right through all phases of business. It may be innovation in design, in product, in marketing techniques. It may be innovation in price or in service to the customer. It may be innovation in

[1] Peter F. Drucker, *The Practice of Management*, Harper & Brothers, New York, 1954, pp. 39-40.

management organization or in management methods. Or it may be a new insurance policy that makes it possible for a businessman to assume new risks. The most effective innovations in American industry in the last few years were probably not the much publicized new electronic or chemical products and processes, but innovations in materials handling and in manager development.

Innovation extends through all forms of business. It is as important to a bank, an insurance company or a retail store, as it is to a manufacturing or engineering business.

Employees understand the need for change

Most employees, when they can view the process objectively, will concede the necessity for change in the business enterprise; indeed, when asked their opinions in employee opinion polls or in training courses, they readily admit that change is probably largely responsible for their ever-rising standard of living.

Unfortunately, change in the established routine of doing work inevitably produces change in employees' work habits and often disturbs their position both in the formal and the informal organization structure. As Peter Drucker observes, "Change is not only an intellectual process, but a psychological one as well."

"The key to the problem," says Paul R. Lawrence,[2] "is to understand the true nature of resistance. Actually, what employees resist is usually not technical change, but social change—the change in their human relationships that generally accompanies technical change."

In the highly important informal social organization of workers, the social change that new technology brings may diminish their prestige and disrupt highly prized relationships with fellow workers. In addition, it may sometimes reduce their earnings or exact greater effort for the same earnings. In such cases, it is always labeled by the union, and often by the employees, as the hated "speed-up."

F. J. Roethlisberger, professor of human relations at Harvard, neatly poses the problem for the administrator in this way: "How can

[2] Paul R. Lawrence, "How to Deal with Resistance to Change," *Harvard Business Review*, May–June, 1954, p. 49.

the external changes required for the survival of a social system be initiated, administered, and assimilated by this system so that the internal needs for stability, i.e., for well-understood and accepted relationships in the system, be also maintained?" [3]

RESISTANCE TO CHANGE—A COUNTERVAILING FORCE

Needless to say, this problem is very real and largely unsolved, as a current investigation of any business enterprise would reveal. Almost every introduced change sets up a countervailing force familiarly termed "resistance to change," which is initiated by the employees whose job security or habits or relationships the proposed change threatens, or even appears to threaten.

The resistance takes many forms: anxious queries, wild rumors of impending disaster, union grievances, noncooperation with the specialists who are planning the change, panic at the sight of a stop watch, slowdowns, sitdowns, walkouts, strikes, refusal to meet new output goals, or subtle group behavior to discredit the new system.

Resistance to change has a myriad of manifestations and is universal. It is costing American business a multibillion-dollar loss every year; it is a serious drain on our standard of living; most importantly, perhaps, it arouses suspicion and distrust of management on the part of the workers which could be the seeds that will eventually destroy the system—unless management fairly shares the progress which the change makes possible, unless it convincingly communicates to the employees that it is fairly sharing such progress, and unless it administers change with due regard for the human considerations.

Despite the complexity of the problem, certain segments of American management are making encouraging progress along three lines. First, in understanding the reasons for the resistance, second, in more carefully planning and timing the changes, third, in more skillfully communicating any proposed change before, during, and after the actual change is made.

[3] Harriet O. Ronkin and Paul R. Lawrence, *Administering Changes: A Case Study of Human Relations in a Factory*, foreword by F. J. Roethlisberger, Harvard University Bureau of Business Research, Boston, 1952, p. viii.

The more perceptive managers first decided to challenge the concept that resistance to change was as inevitable as death and taxes. Leo B. Moore, assistant professor of management, MIT, verbalizes a concept that is being adopted by astute managers in their solution of the problem. He states: [4]

I question, however, whether this is resistance to change as much as it is resentment or anxiety over the way change is introduced. Trying to convince someone of the advantages of the new method often results in sounding like criticism of the old—which the person likes because he is accustomed to it, or which he may even be proud of because he sponsored it originally. More than one foreman has flatly rejected a new machine by saying, either in anger or in hurt, that there is nothing wrong with the performance of his department. Also, sometimes the change is introduced in such a way that it appears to threaten established work habits and relationships; it never gets a chance to be accepted in its own right. Many a supervisor has made a new process turn out to be just as impractical as he predicted it would be.

Once we understand that the key to the problem is "the way the change is introduced," we are well on the way to the solution.

Suggested methods of introducing change

Experienced managers strive for the maximum lead time in introducing new machinery, new technology, new methods of work or incentives, or rearrangements or relocation of work groups. If the proposed change will require fewer employees, every effort is made to introduce it in upswings in the business. As early as practicable, the rate of new hires in the employment office is sharply decelerated, and openings elsewhere in the plant are filled by transferring some of the employees to be displaced by the change.

Whenever practicable, it is wise to move slowly, to make one change at a time, and to communicate with the employees before, during, and after the change.

In a recent trip to the plant of a Southern textile fabricator, the

[4] Leo B. Moore, "Too Much Management, Too Little Change," *Harvard Business Review*, January–February, 1956, p. 41.

author was shown a new machine which, when installed, would displace twelve of the present female operators on a subassembly line. The machine under development was located in a small air-conditioned development laboratory in a remote section of the plant. "Are the persons to be displaced aware of this machine?" "Oh yes," said the manager, "we brought them in when we reached the first mockup stage. We explained the competitive reasons why this new machine was vital to their continued job security. We reminded them that we had been constantly mechanizing and that none of them had lost a day's work over the past five years because of this automation. We assured them that our careful planning called for them being transferred to other work in an orderly fashion when it came time to install the machine. Now when I walk the floor, the girls kid me about our slow progress and quip that the 'Z Mill' (our chief competitor) will beat us yet."

Another company which purchased a giant boring mill designed to turn out more with one operator than the previous one did with five, placed the machine in a temporary location on a balcony and staged inspection tours with a question-and-answer period for all employees in the shop. By giving the employees an opportunity to express their fears and to ask questions about their own personal security, the manager wisely relieved tensions and resistance. This personalized communication was carried on against a backdrop of frequent articles in the employee newspaper describing the machine, the competitive reasons for its purchase, and the insurance it provided for future job security.

Administration of change in an insurance office. An interesting example of the careful planning being exercised by some managers is contained in a case study by Professor Harold F. Craig, Graduate School of Business Administration, Harvard University, which describes the conversion to electronic accounting in a large insurance office.[5]

The particular conversion was skillfully administered and proved

[5] Harold F. Craig, *Administering a Conversion to Electronic Accounting,* Harvard University Bureau of Business Research.

to be very successful. But note the depth of understanding of the social implication of change as evidenced by the following questions taken from a list which served as a basis of planning:

1. In order to provide for the economic utilization of the new machinery, what changes will be required in the formal organizational structure?

2. What degree of displacement of people and machines is involved in the new procedures?

3. Does the rate of conversion allow sufficient time for the training of existing personnel on the new jobs or will the organization need to hire people trained elsewhere?

4. What changes in the existing jobs of clerks and in the traditional promotional avenues throughout the organization will the new system cause?

5. What effect will the displacement of people, the changes in promotional avenues, and the hiring of people trained elsewhere have upon the traditions and codes of the organization regarding security of employment and opportunities for promotion?

6. What effect will all these changes have upon the social groups within the organization?

A communication plan is often the missing link

A basic understanding of the psychological factors involved in any change and the proper planning and timing of the change will not prevent serious repercussions if the communication plan is slighted or mishandled.

How often have we witnessed the following dilemma in our shops and offices? A special group of planners is given the assignment to introduce new technology or automated equipment. For eighteen months they labor secretly with their own development engineers or outside vendors. Comes the time for the introduction of the new equipment and a wave of fear and resentment, fed by fantastic rumors, spreads through the organization. Mass meetings are called, walkouts are scheduled, or at a minimum, management is faced with a determination on the part of the affected employees to limit output from the new equipment.

A hurry-up call is made to the employee or public relations department, which, if it has little influence, may not even have been aware of the impending change, or at least its timing. A communication plan is hastily drawn up, approved, and materials are released. Too often, however, the situation has deteriorated so badly that a senseless strike ensues or morale is so shaken that the full beneficial effects of the change may not be realized for several years.

Any manager seeking to put an end to these tragic disruptions will do well to ask one simple, highly motivating question when the first preliminary technical plans for the change are presented to him by his technicians for review. It is this: "Where is your plan for ameliorating the effect of the change on the personnel involved, and where is the plan for communicating the change to them?"

Essentials of a successful communication plan. The communication plan will normally include some or all of the following steps:

Group meetings will be held with all employees. In these meetings, the reasons for the change are explained in detail. The employees are shown the potential savings anticipated and why these savings are needed to cut costs, to meet competition, to protect jobs. And, of course, the change itself is thoroughly explained so that each employee can see exactly what the impact will be on his own particular job. All employees' questions are answered and every effort is made to explain how the benefits to them and to the department far outweigh the resultant temporary dislocation. These group meetings are followed up with smaller meetings between the employees and their individual supervisors, exploring individual problems and other aspects of the change. Questions are answered and suggestions for improving the plan solicited. And, of course, the story is put into the hands of employees in written form for further reflection and study. The written media may include articles in the employee house organs, progress posters, exhibits of the new equipment, scale models of the rearrangement, letters to homes, question-and-answer columns in the house organ, etc.

It is amazing how much resistance can be avoided by properly informing those to be affected so that they understand the need for the change, how it will affect them, and how they can cooperate to effectuate it.

Every advance in technology, in operating procedures, in physical rearrangements, or any major change in established routines, should be looked upon as a three-stage job. First, there is the technical development or physical planning. Second, and at least equally important to the success of the technical plan, is the planning for the personnel involved in the change. Third is the early and continuously modified communication planning to explain to employees the need for the change and to obtain their active cooperation in making it work.

Space will permit recording only a few of the many cases in the author's file of encouraging examples of cooperation when introduction of change is administered intelligently and with full use of communication before, during, and after the change.

Examples of intelligent administration of change

In company A, one department had been carrying on finishing, inspecting, and packing as three separate operations for almost fifteen years. Through technical innovation, the manager was able to change the method so that a single operator performed all three operations at one station with ease. Naturally, the union opposed the move, but because the problem had been explained to employees through an effective communication program well ahead of time, they refused to back up the union officers in their protest. The manager of this department testified that this communication program was the chief factor in effecting a methods change which resulted in a sorely needed 10 per cent cost saving. (And yet, the entire first year's saving, and more, could have been lost if uninformed employees had struck as they often had done in the past!)

Company B planned a 4.5-million-dollar expansion and rearrangement program involving the purchase of new equipment, machine tools, and a major physical relocation of existing equipment and tools which threatened to be quite disruptive of long-established work groups within the plant. The chief executive wisely insisted that all affected employees be brought along step by step as the program planning developed. Meetings were held six to nine months in advance of any actual change in equipment or relocation of any work group. These meetings resulted in two major benefits to the department. First, there was noted a marked difference in the people's acceptance of this major change as compared to their resistance to more minor changes in the past; and second, in reviewing the relocation and purchase of new equipment, suggestions were made by the individual workers for major and minor changes in the plans that resulted in considerable savings for the company.

Follow-up meetings were held just prior to the time the actual work or rearrangement began. Meetings were conducted by the immediate supervisors of the groups involved in cooperation with the manufacturing engineer responsible for the layout and rearrangement. The changes went in without a hitch and the operators came up to estimated output much sooner than had been expected.

Equally effective was the role of communication in administering a major change in company C, but let the industrial relations officer describe it:

Three years ago, we started work on a major automation program in Section "K" at an estimated cost in excess of one million dollars. It was planned initially, and still is forecast, that a full installation of this automated equipment would permit doubling our productivity with the same floor space and with a slightly reduced number of direct workers.

One year ago, when we were about to install equipment, our top manufacturing people in the section discussed with all production and maintenance people the advantages of the changes, both to the company and to the employees in the plant. During these meetings, the competitive advantages as well as the benefits to the employees in future job security, and many other points, were carefully outlined. Since that time, as we have continued to install equipment, the foremen have had their groups together and repeated the explanation as to what the new equipment was expected to achieve to the mutual advantage of everyone concerned.

We have repeated at appropriate intervals in our daily Newsletter the progress of this installation and further repetition of advantages. Within the next month we plan a feature story in our *Employee News* on the progress of this installation along with repetition of the advantages. At no time in the course of more than two years have we had any recognizable resistance, whether at the foreman-steward level or at the second step level. The latter point is one where we certainly would expect a more or less violent reaction. We realize that we must not relax our communicating efforts, but feel that the employee communications carefully carried on over this long period of time will result in a minimum of resistance when the line is fully in operation three months hence.

Communication is key in changing incentive system. In another plant, the industrial relations section was given a well-nigh impossible task—to gain acceptance and full cooperation for a major change in an incentive system which would result in temporarily lower take-home pay for many employees. The change was decided upon as the only alternative to remaining competitive in this particular business. The following is the sequence of oral and written communication utilized.

A month before the scheduled introduction date of the new incentive plan, all affected foremen were given intensive training in the fundamentals of the plan, its equitable administration, and anticipated problems.

One week before "I-Day," a letter announcing the new plan, the underlying need for survival of the enterprise which prompted it, and the date set for its introduction was sent to the homes of all affected employees by the general manager.

Immediately after the receipt of the letter, affected employees were invited to an informative meeting by their foremen. At this time, a 35-millimeter film-slide presentation clearly describing the new incentive plan was shown, followed by a question-and-answer period. At the close of the meeting, each employee was presented with a booklet describing the plan in simple illustrated fashion.

On the following day, a second informative meeting was held to cover additional aspects of the change. The meeting was then followed by on-the-job instruction as a further aid to the employees in achieving expected output.

As a backdrop to this intensive oral communication, all regular printed media were used to present the full story to employees in authentic, unfiltered form.

The following comments by the general manager, who was noted for his conservative method of expression, provide a significant summation of the results:

In spite of a difficult union situation, we believe our employees have more confidence in management because of a program which made them participating members.

Both employees and their union have been cooperative and complimentary. The communication plan was fundamentally responsible for the acceptance and cooperation received in handling a well-organized critical change.

TRAINING SUPERVISORS TO ADMINISTER CHANGE

In certain companies, intensive supervisory training is carried on to develop an awareness of the many problems implicit in all types of plant and office changes and to develop expertness in minimizing resistance to change. Lectures, films, role playing, and the case study method are employed.

Readers who are interested in the more difficult but extremely effective case study method of developing expertness may wish to refer to Glover and Hower, *The Administrator* [6] which includes many excellent case studies in "Administering Change."

[6] John Desmond Glover and Ralph M. Hower, *The Administrator: Cases in Human Relations in Business,* Richard D. Irwin, Inc., Homewood, Ill., 1949.

CHAPTER 20

Use of Communication in Crises

Thus far we have dealt almost entirely with positive communication. We have discussed the use of communication to upgrade the effectiveness of management and advance the best interests of all concerned with the enterprise; to satisfy the employee's basic right to know and to be heard in order to increase his job satisfaction; to enable the employee to participate in decisions that affect his job security and his opportunities for advancement; to tell him how he is doing; to help him know where he stands; to get work done through persuasion rather than by command. Additionally, we have observed how communication is used to help manage a positive program of employee, community, and union relations and business-climate development.

But every business, no matter how well managed, has its quota of disruptive emergencies: floods, fires, and explosions may occur; epidemics may strike; sudden slowdowns of buying by customers build up inventories which necessitate adjustments in the work force; poor decisions or poorly communicated good decisions of managers breed suspicion and feed emotions resulting in slowdowns, walkouts, or strike threats; legislators at local, state, and national level seek to win votes through antibusiness legislation and discriminatory taxes. The list is legion—culminating, in the intensity of its tragic consequences, in the strike, which will be discussed in Chapter 21.

It is almost axiomatic that the majority of business crises are controllable by the manager and that lack of communication or break-downs in communication are contributory to a very high degree.

When crises strike, the manager discovers that communication is a stout ally indeed. Obviously, fire-fighting communication is most effective when full, free communication has been a way of life with the business and when media, and credibility for them, have been painstakingly built in times of normal operation. But even in the absence of a prior history of effective communication, remarkable results have been achieved when the manager perceptively and intensively applied the power of communication to the emergency at hand. Communication, of course, can only bring understanding of underlying facts, remove misunderstanding or correct misinterpretation. Any attempt to use communication as a fog or smoke-screen will be ill-advised, short-lived, and costly.

We can do adequate justice to the principles involved by examining the application of communication to some typical crises that afflict business enterprises.

WHEN THE ELEMENTS STRIKE

When Hurricane Diane brought devastation to six Northeastern states, it provided a stern test for the disaster-communication plans of the stricken plants. The following is a capsule of how one company, noted for its skill in communication, met the crisis.[1]

Five of U.S. Rubber's New England plants were affected by the flood, but the major, and most pressing problems centered around the plants located at Naugatuck, Connecticut. These three properties—a footwear plant, a chemical plant and a unit producing synthetic rubber—provide employment for 7,400 persons. Damage was severe at the footwear and chemical plants, but only slight at the synthetic rubber unit.

The problem was acute and twofold:

First, rumors were in circulation that the situation in the area was much more serious than it actually was, and perhaps inevitably, reflection of them colored early unofficial news dispatches on the flood situation. One such rumor said flatly that the chemical plant "is gone," implying

[1] Condensed from *The Communicator*, October, 1955.

that the flood actually had washed away the complete plant. Another had it that damage at the footwear plant was so serious that U.S. Rubber would never reopen the unit.

The second complicating factor was that newspapers in Naugatuck and nearby Waterbury, the publications normally read for Naugatuck news, also were put out of business by the flood. Although they were able to print emergency editions on printing equipment located in nearby towns, immediate distribution was impossible and often took place 24 hours after the newspapers had obtained news to communicate with its readers.

As soon as it was possible to talk with any degree of accuracy, the company issued a news release estimating the true damage and making it clear that it was taking immediate steps to return the affected plants to full operating capacity as early as possible. This action was designed to assure the company's stockholders that despite a serious situation, the effects of the flood would be temporary.

This news release was placed in New York outlets, the most important of which were the newspaper wire services able to get dispatches in the approximate area of Naugatuck. Damaged telephone and telegraph services, however, prevented it from being published in Naugatuck and Waterbury newspapers until two days later.

Company officials found, however, that some Connecticut radio stations were obtaining dispatches over their newspaper wire services, and this ultimately proved to be the quickest means of getting information to employees in the flooded area.

A New York newspaper then precipitated a new crisis by publishing a lead article to the effect that industrial promoters from some southern states planned to meet promptly with executives of companies, including rubber companies, affected by the flood. These promoters, the article said, would try to persuade the companies concerned to move part or all of their production capacities to southern plants. Despite the fact that this story lacked foundation, its publication again churned up the rumor mills of New England communities affected by the flood.

U.S. Rubber moved swiftly to counteract the story. "We are giving no thought to closing any New England plants or moving any production out of New England as the result of the recent flood," H. Gordon Smith, Executive Vice President, said in an official statement. "We are making good progress in our efforts to get flood-damaged plants in Connecticut and Rhode Island back into full production." This release again went over the actual situation, discussing conditions at each of the affected plants and outlining corrective measures being taken.

To acquaint management people with the significance of the flood, the company's internal publication, *News Digest,* discussed the effect the multi-million dollar loss would have on 1955 income. A similar story was told in a special letter to stockholders.

As the flood waters receded, U.S. Rubber commenced preparations to tell the full story to its more than 60,000 employees. An extensive article, illustrated with photographs, was prepared for the company's employee magazine. Although many employees probably would not read this account until the plants were again in full production, the company felt that it should provide a complete record of how it and they fought their way out of difficult times.

Some principles of press relations in crises

The following sound admonition to managers in the author's company is designed to teach them, before the fact, how to communicate in emergencies such as disasters, fires, electrocutions, injuries, etc. It is excerpted from a manual entitled *You and the News About General Electric.*

a. Verify the basic facts as to what has actually happened and make these facts immediately available to the press. Tell them what has happened, what personnel and facilities are involved to what degree, and all circumstances immediately known.

b. Follow up this initial information with a full explanation of the circumstances as soon as subsequent facts are available, and correct any misunderstandings that have appeared.

c. Remember that bad news cannot and should not be hidden, and those who have tried have invariably regretted such attempts. You will find that cooperation with the press, offering to help them, being honest, is the only course of action.

d. It is important that several steps be taken beyond the basic facts, in order to tell the full story so that the best possible interpretation will follow.

e. Put the event in perspective by showing how it is an exception to the rule, and prove this by citing the past good record of the operation.

f. Make clear the steps being taken to care for the interests of the employees, the community and any others involved, to confine or eliminate the happening, to resume or maintain operations, to prevent recurrence through additional safeguards. We have, and our statements must reflect, a sincere, warm, human interest and concern for those affected by the event.

g. We must have an earned and known record of having previously developed safety to the highest point possible, and we must always be trying to do better. If we deserve such a reputation of safety, tragic and regrettable happenings will be viewed in proper perspective and recognized as rare exceptions to the rule of our success at safety.

LAYOFFS

Industry is making encouraging progress in employment stabilization, but periodic adjustments in the work force create emergencies in even the best-managed companies.

Although our society attempts to insure itself against this seemingly inevitable risk in a free economy through unemployment compensation laws, layoffs can be devastating to the morale of the entire plant and community unless handled with full consideration of the human factors concerned and in a climate of full, frank communication.

Sound planning for this crisis is based on three principles:

1. The manager must show by deeds as well as by words that he is deeply concerned over the impending layoff of employees no matter how few are involved. That old cliché, "a minimum number of employees is involved," is cold comfort if you happen to be one of that minimum.

2. The earliest possible notification should be given to those employees affected as well as to all the remaining employees and to the community.

3. The company should explain what it has done to prevent the layoff, why this effort was not quite good enough, and what is being done to help find other jobs for or to reemploy those affected as soon as possible. If the company has had a good record, this should be reported so as to give proper perspective in which to view the temporary crisis.

The following examples are illustrative:

Cost of one layoff rumor—30,000 man-hours

In company A, an aircraft plant, where job security was uppermost in employees' minds, word got around that the Air Force had just canceled a huge order for bombers. Workers ceased work and gathered in anxious groups. The telephone switchboard was jammed with incoming calls from wives and merchants who had heard the news on a local radio station.

A plant official immediately refuted the rumor on the P.A. System. He made a tape recording of his talk and played it on each of the three shifts. A factual newsletter was sent to all supervision. A reassuring letter was mailed to the home of each employee. Next morning a complete statement of the facts was carried on the front page of the local newspaper. Within twenty-four hours, plant production was back to normal, but this single rumor had cost the company an estimated 30,000 man-hours of production.

This case study dramatically illustrates the explosive disruptiveness of layoff rumors and the pressing need for well-developed channels of crisis communication.

Considerate treatment—early and full communication

In company B, a falling rate of orders made it necessary to reduce direct labor by approximately 10 per cent. Fifteen days before the effective date of the reduction, a statement explaining the situation was read by the supervisors to all employees. Union officials had been notified on the same date. One week before the layoff, each affected employee was notified. Simultaneously, a letter was sent to the homes of *all* employees, indicating which employees were affected and reassuring those unaffected. Plans for increasing the business to provide for the early return of those laid off were discussed with candor.

On the date of the layoffs, supervisors met with all remaining employees to explain the necessary rearrangement of the work force to maintain efficient operations.

At the same time all outgoing employees and all remaining employees who were transferring to new jobs were given individual interviews.

Because of this considerate individual treatment and the full, free communication of all the facts, most of the employees released expressed the opinion that the plant was a fine place to work and voiced the hope that they would soon be able to come back.

Advertising to place displaced workers

Shortly after the Korean War, company C faced with a layoff of only 3 per cent of its employees (and a minute portion of total community labor force) met the problem with the enlightened action and full communication that typifies management's maturing social consciousness.

The president utilized all of the company's many communication channels to detail the reasons behind the layoff, explained the company's severance pay benefits, promised that those laid off would be recalled as soon as business picked up, and outlined his plan to place the displaced workers in other companies. He then placed advertising in nine area newspapers to announce the availability and qualifications of these competent workers. At the same time, publicity releases fully explained the company's efforts to avoid the layoff, its deep concern for those affected, and expressed the hope that all would find satisfying work even though this might mean their permanent loss to the company.

The added sense of confidence and security of employees unaffected, the good will of the community, and, it is hoped, the respect of those that have to be displaced will build substantial and continuing deposits of good will for any company which handles these distressing but temporary economic crises *considerately*, and communicates fully.

ILLEGAL WORK STOPPAGES

The illegal work stoppage is a familiar and costly phenomenon of the American industrial scene. Although most union contracts contain a no-strike agreement, the clause is consistently violated because too many managers are fearful of greater production losses to adopt a firm policy of enforcement of their legal rights.

Illegal work stoppages, no matter how long-standing the practice, can be drastically minimized through the application of the following forthright managerial action:

Step 1. The formulation of a clear, concise, unequivocal policy that tolerates no contract breaches of this nature and that spells out the disciplinary measures to be enforced whenever the contract is thus breached.

Step 2. Communication of the policy to union officials.

Step 3. Saturation communication of the policy to all managers, supervisors, nonsupervisory employees, and to the community sufficiently in advance of the application of the policy.

Step 4. The courage to meet the first breach with full firm application of the announced disciplinary procedures and a previous and clearly announced willingness to invest in a strike, if necessary, should the disciplinary measures provide such a reaction.

The following case study illustrates how one management group dramatically ended a chaotic succession of work stoppages through the application of these principles:

Step 1: the policy. The essence of the policy is as follows:

"In the future, appropriate disciplinary action will be taken in the case of employees who participate in or instigate any stoppage in violation of our union contracts. This may be in the form of time off, suspension, discharge or other suitable action, depending on the circumstances."

Step 2: communication to the union. A letter was sent to the local union officials detailing the history of the illegal disruptions and graphically describing the final massive stoppage and its adverse effects on the security of the employees, the community, and the business. The new policy was spelled out and the local officials were put on warning that the next illegal stoppage would necessarily bring implementation of one or more of the appropriate disciplinary measures listed.

Step 3: communication to employees. Finally, the policy was incorporated in a letter sent to all employees and with appropriate variations, to community neighbors. This letter expressed the conviction that it was wrong that so many should lose so much because of the actions of a few. It explained the provisions of the contract which had been expressly negotiated for the peaceful settlement of disputes—expressed the hope that disciplinary action would never have to be taken—and invited all to give their full support to the new policy in the common interest.

Step 4: application of policy. The local union officials waited for several months before testing the application of the new policy by calling an illegal stoppage. After a thorough investigation by the management, the policy was implemented promptly but moderately (loss of a half day's pay) in connection with more than 100 employees.

It was observed that the formulation and use of this four-step plan—compounded of firmness, simplicity, understandability, and forthright communication—resulted in an almost total cessation of the disruptions to stabilized production, work, and earnings.

REPRESENTATION ELECTIONS

The final situation we will consider is now a familiar phenomenon in American business—the representation election. The national labor law guarantees employees the right freely to choose to be represented by a union or to choose not to be so represented. Although the law is crystal clear on this freedom of choice, a communication crisis is sometimes precipitated when professional organizers decide to attempt to organize an employee group that hitherto has felt it needed no outside representation to assure it of a fair deal.

A surprising percentage of employees, although prizing their privilege of inviting union representation, if and when they feel they need it, more dearly prize their freedom of choice. Today, even some of the most reputable unions seem determined not to permit such free choice, or grossly to distort the facts in seeking the right to represent employees.

Dr. Sylvester Petro, professor of law at the New York University

School of Law, a genuine though objective friend of labor, graphically illustrates the lack of free choice in many of today's organizing drives.

Writing in the *Labor Law Journal*, he states: [2]

In the organizational stage, union conduct is characterized to a considerable extent by coercion, both physical and economic. Union organizers sometimes sell unionism to workers, but with great frequency union membership is forced, not sold. Most often, the coercion is of the economic type. Organizational picketing, hot-cargo contracts, blacklisting, secondary strikes and other kinds of boycotts, and compulsory unionism agreements—these are the most usual methods of forcing unionization upon unwilling employees and employers. Outright violence is used when economic coercion fails. Those who doubt this simply are unaware of what is going on. Moreover, it must be understood that such conduct is not used only by unions which have felt the wrath of the Ethical Practices Committee of the AFL-CIO. There is scarcely a large union in this country which has not used and is not using one or more such methods today.

In the context of this new determination of many unions to force their services on employees and the legal right of employees guaranteeing freedom of choice between union representation or no union representation, what is the obligation of managers of such enterprises when union organizers show up at their gates or business entrances? Many managers feel they have a responsibility to discuss frankly the advantages and disadvantages of union representation, and correct the record of any untruths issued in the organizing campaign, so that the employee choice will be made in the light of hearing both viewpoints.

Many successful managers, when faced with a union petition for an election, take an immediate attitude survey to see what dissatisfaction, if any, is at the root of employee sentiment. Others conduct depth interviews. In either case, the results are promptly published.

[2] Sylvester Petro, "Compulsory Unionism and Responsible Unionism," *Labor Law Journal*, December, 1957, pp. 868–873.

Supervisory meetings are held with employees to discuss each group's problems. In one company studied, the following statement made by the chief executive was widely and favorably received:

We thought we were doing pretty well but we take this petition for an election as your way of telling us that we must manage still better. You have told us in what ways we must improve. We would like you to give us a vote of confidence for another year and measure our performance. Remember union representation does not come on a thirty-day free-trial basis. Once you vote to be represented, it will be most difficult to de-certify. On the other hand, you can always bring in the union a year later, which is the usual minimum period in which NLRB can be peti-tioned for another election. The union may appear to be a solution to your real needs, but too often it is not. It shall be our job to discover the needs that some of you believe unionization can solve and then resolutely set about to fulfill those needs.

As this study proceeded, it was observed that those companies which had had in place long-established and respected channels of communication now found it appropriate to discuss frankly the new issues raised in the minds of employees as the union organizers sought to develop real or fancied issues where emotional content could be built up in their campaign. The most effective media were, to judge by frequency of use, daily newscasts, letters to homes, supervisory meetings with employees, an early morning radio news program, and the regular company house organ.

The content of communication in organizing drives

The content of the communication depended on local conditions and the strategy of the organizers. In general, however, the or-ganizers seemed to concentrate on certain familiar themes which could invariably be anticipated by studying the campaign drives in neighboring plants or in prior years.

It was observed, with some surprise, that the organizers seldom used more than a half-dozen general themes although there were varying local themes. Each allegation or claim, no matter how flimsy or distorted, was dealt with promptly, fully, forthrightly. Management's communication was relatively far more calm, factual, and objective. There was evidence of careful intent to ensure that no promises were made that could not be fulfilled, and all statements appear to have been checked carefully with legal counsel.

In addition to the prompt answering of standardized claims and allegations of local injustices, many managers went on to point out the high unnecessary cost of belonging to a union, the resulting loss of individual decision, the possible loss of wages in wildcat strikes, stoppages, etc., the likely control of one's destiny by a small cadre of entrenched officials, etc.

Choice of media utilized

Generally speaking, in the cases studied the unions relied most heavily on oral communication—in the shop, at mass meetings around town, and in evening visitations to the home. Their main medium of written communication appeared to be the handbill, although occasionally they ran advertisements in the city press and bought local radio time.

Management seemed to rely much more heavily on a combination of oral and written communication. Although written communication carried the major share of the load, particular emphasis was placed on supervisors' informative meetings with employees. This, of course, placed a high premium on the proper and continuous briefing of supervisors.

The most effective communication was often the personal discussion by the top executive in an appearance before all employees, or to groups of employees if the plant was large. If the manager was widely respected and had a good prior record of performance, a summing up of the pros and cons and a sincere man-to-man appeal for a vote of confidence seemed to carry great weight with the employees.

CHAPTER 21

Use of Communication in Strikes

Assume that all efforts to prevent a strike have failed and that the plant or business is closed down by an effective picket line or by general employee adherence to the strike call.

Whether the strike is legal or not, the employer may have received no formal advance notification of the timing of the strike. However, most experienced employers have developed an awareness of the types of grievances and union behavior that are likely to presage a strike.

Accordingly, these employers, while doing everything possible to head off the strike threat, simultaneously develop a mature and complete strike-termination plan in case the strike occurs. A cardinal principle, of course, is making sure that the company offer or the company position is such that there is no valid reason for the strike, looked at in the light of all the pertinent considerations. It is also essential that the company be willing to make public disclosure and to welcome public scrutiny of such position.

All successful strike-termination plans are based on two cardinal principles:

1. The recognition that the best way to end a strike is for employees to return to work voluntarily;

2. The use of flexible, intensive communication to all affected audiences.

There are, of course, other ways of ending a strike. The employer can capitulate to the union demand or relinquish the responsibility for settlement to mediators or arbitrators. However, employers who resort to such tactics might as well have utilized them to prevent the strike initially.

Another method which unfortunately is often employed is to sit out the strike passively to the bitter end—until the employees, the community, and the employer are emotionally exhausted and virtually bankrupt.

Strikes must be viewed objectively and not emotionally. A strike is economic warfare, and union leadership is candid about treating strikes, strike tactics, and strike communication as "war" to gain their ends. No employer should permit himself to be jockeyed or surprised into one unless he is prepared to make the investment necessary to bring it to a sound conclusion. Such a program requires courageous leadership, projected overtly through sincere and forthright communication.

BLUEPRINT FOR A STRIKE-TERMINATION PLAN

In developing a strike-termination plan, before the fact, the chief executive usually sets up a strike task force to handle the hundreds of details which have to be considered before and after the strike becomes effective.

Such a strategic planning group will depend on the company involved, but in a typical business enterprise might consist of the chief executive, the industrial relations manager, the union relations manager, the manager of manufacturing, the marketing manager, the legal counsel, the communication and community relations manager, etc.

This group is charged with the responsibility of keeping in touch with all aspects of the situation, foreseeing all contingencies, proposing and analyzing alternative courses of action, and making all policy and strategy decisions.

The manager of marketing should give prior notification to distributors and customers and urge them to build up their inventories. He has to get the maximum inventory out of the plant and into customer stocks and warehouses. He must also keep in touch with all his customers and try to keep them supplied by shifting stocks, by borrowing from Peter to pay Paul.

The manager of manufacturing must decide when to cut off the incoming flood of materials and parts from suppliers, and he must consider the pros and cons of working overtime to accelerate the shipment of finished goods to customers, distributors, or warehouses. He should make advance decisions as to disposition of tools, dies, fixtures. He must have a plan for protecting the plant and maintaining the equipment and goods in process. Since the plant must be kept open for those who wish to work, he must make all advance arrangements to permit key supervisors to live in the plant until the strike is settled.

The legal counsel refreshes his knowledge of local and state laws and ordinances pertaining to right of access to property, blocking of public roads, rights and restrictions on picketing, requirements for labor injunctions, secondary boycotts, hot cargoes, assault, libel, unfair labor practices, etc. He, of course, must handle the seeking of an injunction against any illegal picketing or acts of violence.

He should be prepared to conduct investigations of violence, intimidation, and illegal picketing. He must especially review and counsel with regard to any plan for testing the picket lines. Finally, he must review all proposed plans and all printed and formal mass communication to make sure that they observe both the letter and the spirit of the law.

The manager of finance, or comptroller, must work out advance planning for paying any back wages to employees on strike as well as for paying nonstrikers on the job. He must arrange to keep track of all costs, losses, and damages resulting from the strike, since these may have to be reviewed in court later. He usually gets saddled with the job of providing office space and facilities outside the plant for office employees who may be denied access to the plant; he must also prepare to house the necessary records and record-keeping equipment.

The personnel practices manager must be prepared to pay health insurance claims to strikers and nonstrikers.

The union relations manager must be prepared to handle all contacts with the union, with Federal and state mediation services, the National Labor Relations Board, and the like.

The community relations manager must make advance contacts with city, community, and state officials, with law enforcement officials, with local news agencies, with merchants, clergy, and all public groups who will be affected and whose understanding and support are so vital.

An important figure in this planning complex is, of course, the communication manager, inasmuch as each member of the team needs help on the communication aspects of his particular assignment. In addition, there must be available a master communication plan designed to meet the exigencies of all aspects of a full-scale strike.

The best method of ensuring that the strike plan need not be used is to have the courage to invest in a strike, *provided the company has voluntarily offered all that is right under the particular circumstances,* rather than be forced to submit to appeasement that will do greater harm to all in the long run. The decision to take the strike under these circumstances should be announced calmly and with unmistakable conviction to the union, employees, community, and government officials and mediators. This helps to ensure that employees will not be led into a needless strike through customary claims by union officials that: (1) the strike threat will be used only as a bargaining club, and (2) a short strike is all that is needed to force management to capitulate.

As the strike deadline nears

As the strike deadline nears, all effort must be concentrated on keeping the plant open for those who wish to work. The final outcome may be determined right here. Once a plant is tightly closed down, it is all the more difficult to get it open again.

The more people that can be kept working, the more eager others are to return to work. So no matter how hopeless the situation may seem, positive steps must be taken to keep the plant from closing down completely.

The following steps are essential:

1. Frequent and complete instructions to all supervisors.
2. Notification of all office people, if they are not members of the striking union, that they will be expected to work. They should, however, be counseled not to risk bodily harm if massed picketing develops and there is uncertainty over effective law enforcement.
3. Notification of employees of other unions not involved in the dispute that they will be expected to honor their contracts and keep working.
4. Notification of employees of the striking union that the plant will be kept open for all who wish to work.
5. Instructions as to the rights and obligations of pickets.
6. Instructions to all employees as to their right to cross picket lines.
7. Obtaining formal published assurances by local police or county sheriff of protection for all who wish to gain access to the plant.
8. Absolute refusal to negotiate with the union officials on admittance of "key" employees on passes issued by unions.
9. If the strike is illegal, notification of employees of possible penalties to which strikers are subjecting themselves.
10. Instruction of employees called out on an illegal strike as to steps they can take to disassociate from the strike.

A ten-day strike that might have lasted three months

To observe the functioning of a wisely conceived strike-termination plan and the key role played by communication when creatively utilized by a management which has previously won credibility with its employees and community, let us examine the chronological steps in an actual strike situation.

This particular case study illustrates what an energetic management did to combat a full-blown and deadly serious strike at a large plant. Note the emphasis on communication of the facts and issues to the employees and to the people of the community. This is a sound principle so long as the management believes it has been doing the right thing voluntarily for its employees and is, therefore, able to speak up vigorously in support of the position it has taken and the basic principles for which it stands.

1. *Tuesday, April 2.* This moderately large plant which manufactured a defense product was in normal operation. During the night shift, three members of a craft union, which we will designate as union A, refused to wear their safety glasses and were sent home for the rest of the shift as a disciplinary measure. Next morning, most of the employees in union A (approximately 1,000) did not report to work. The bulk of the production workers (4,000), represented by union B, reported to work, however.

2. *Wednesday afternoon, April 3.* Union A pickets appeared at all plant gates. Signs announced that union A was on strike, not because of the "safety glasses incident," but because no contract agreement had been reached. A quick check with local A officials elicited the statement that they were unable to get their people back to work. The picket lines were effective. The production employees would not—or could not—enter the plant. Production slowed to a trickle. The strike of union A was on. Meanwhile, the company ran an advertisement in both morning and evening newspapers, clearly setting forth the issues.

3. *Thursday, April 4.* The strike continued. The plant was completely shut down. All production was halted.

On Thursday evening, the company filed application for an injunction against the strike on the basis that union A was violating its contract which contained a no-strike clause. A hearing was set by the courts for the next day (Friday).

Meanwhile, union B, representing most of the production workers, announced they were actively joining the strike—also for failure to reach agreement with the company on the contract. The company thereupon made application for an injunction against union B on the same basis that it did against union A, and a hearing was set for Saturday. But meanwhile, the strike—now full blown—continued.

4. *Friday, April 5.* The court granted a temporary injunction against union A, enjoining further strike action as a violation of the no-strike clause in the contract.

But there still remained the more serious strike of the much larger union B.

A second advertisement, a straight reporting of the facts with regrets and hopes, was placed in the city press.

5. *Saturday, April 6.* The court held hearings on the union B injunction and announced it would issue its decision on Monday at 2 P.M. The judge, however, appealed to both sides to end the strike to speed the defense effort.

The company immediately prepared a statement for radio, TV, and the press emphasizing the illegality of the strike, but offering to meet with the union Sunday.

6. *Sunday, April 7.* A full-page company advertisement invited the union to call off the strike so that defense products could again start rolling. It concluded as follows:

We want to start production Monday morning. We want to resume collective bargaining right away. We hope the union calls off the strike— and that we can do both. We sincerely believe that such an arrangement will be in the balanced best interests of all, and a significant example of free people working together in the defense of a free world.

The company and the union met all day Sunday. Various minor concessions were made, but both sides were firm on the basic issue of a new noncommunity wage-rate pattern. The company immediately reported on the meeting in full detail to all members of the press, radio, and TV.

7. *Monday, April 8.* Early Monday afternoon, the court announced its decision. A temporary injunction against union B was granted on the basis of the union's obligation under the contract not to strike.

The injunction prohibited continuance of the strike, encouraging strike action, picketing, or any interference whatsoever with normal production.

The company announced immediately—by every medium possible—that the plant would resume normal operations on Tuesday morning. The "official" strike was now ended.

To tell its story, the company purchased all available television spot announcement time for Monday evening and Tuesday morning.

Hand-printed cards, hastily prepared, served as visuals. The announcements were varied to fit the time; none ran longer than thirty seconds. All urged employees to report to work Tuesday at the first shift.

Employees are requested to report for work at the plant tomorrow morning at the start of the first shift. The court has directed both Union "A" and Union "B" to call off their strikes and remove their picket lines immediately. It is our understanding that both unions have agreed to respect the court's decision.

In any case, our employees are entirely free to come to work starting first shift Tuesday. We are anxious to continue negotiations with both unions regardless of the court's decision—for we definitely want to reach an early solution to differences that will be satisfactory to all.

8. *Tuesday, April 9.* A full-page advertisement announced the absence of pickets and urged all employees to resume work while the issues were resolved peacefully.

About 50 per cent of the first shift came to work Tuesday morning—but by noon, over half of them had walked out.

On the second shift, the story was the same—only worse. Less than half came in, and only half of them stayed on the job. Production was disrupted. Morale was down.

There were no pickets—officially—but there were milling crowds at the plant gates. There was no strike "officially," but certain union people were actively discouraging attendance. Even inside the plant, walkouts were apparently being encouraged, first in one section, then in another. The plant was obviously pretty well disorganized, and production was oozing rather than flowing. The "unofficial" strike was now on.

Union B sent the company a telegram proposing "round-the-clock" negotiating to get the plant back to full production—and released the telegram to all community news outlets. The company immediately answered the telegram in a newspaper advertisement, offering to resume negotiations when production was fully restored.

It was obvious, however, that the plant was pretty close to being shut down. Energetic and immediate action was clearly necessary.

Late Tuesday, therefore, the plant management decided it was imperative to make it *crystal clear* to the employees:

That the plant was back in operation and would continue to operate;
That the strikes were illegal, and that any strike action was punishable by law;
That it was perfectly safe to come back to work.

9. *Wednesday, April 10.* It was decided to communicate directly to employees on each major point. Letters to the home, long used in times of peaceful operation, were considered not fast enough. Accordingly, starting midday Wednesday and carrying through Thursday, spot announcements were carried over the radio repeatedly asserting that the strike was over, that the plant was back in operation, and that it was safe and sensible to come to work.

Because the strike had been declared illegal by the courts, the company now decided to use one of the key elements in its strike-termination plan—a telephone pyramid campaign to tell its story directly to each employee.

Each member of management was given a card which briefly stated:

1. The strike is illegal.
2. Both unions have announced they would obey the court order.
3. Violations of the court order are punishable by fine or jail sentence.
4. Employees are thus guaranteed the full protection of the law.
5. Your country needs our defense products. Let's get full production rolling at the next shift.

Each manager then telephoned the people who reported directly to him. Each manager gave each person he telephoned the message listed above, and asked them all to pass the information on to the people who reported, in turn, to them.

This "telephone pyramid" campaign started Wednesday afternoon and was believed to have been extremely helpful in getting the necessary information to employees. But one more obstacle, and a serious one, threatened to inhibit a full return to work.

Crowds of unofficial pickets at the plant gates had an obviously frightening effect on employees. There were no signs and no real picket lines, but the effect was almost the same. Employees didn't like to walk through a sullen group of even a few people who looked as though they might be about ready to erupt—even though an eruption would have been illegal.

The company, therefore, made the following arrangements:

FIRST: It asked the police department to provide uniformed officers of the law at each plant gate all day Thursday. Previously, there had been none. The effect of their sudden presence was described as very sobering.

SECOND: It arranged for a member of top management to be at each gate at each change of shifts. He was to do nothing—other than be a visual symbol of responsibility. This, too, had a sobering effect on the employees gathered at the gates for the seeming purpose of discouraging attendance.

10. Thursday, April 11. An advertisement in the morning press blazoned the headline that production was rolling.

The results were heartening. At the first shift on Thursday, about 65 per cent showed up and *stayed on the job.* On the afternoon shift, between 85 per cent and 90 per cent reported for work and stayed. When the night shift reported, attendance and production were back to normal.

On Thursday afternoon, union B told the court it would agree to get all employees back to work if the company would agree to vacate the injunction. The company stated it would agree to have the effectiveness of the court order stayed *for so long* as the union made every "good faith" effort to keep its members on the job. The union agreed. The "unofficial" strike was now over, too.

The foregoing is no isolated phenomenon. Based on a study of strikes in a number of companies, the author advances the following conclusion: in the majority of cases where management has had a good issue on which to stand, where it previously had won respect and credibility among its employees for its deeds and forthright communication, where it had a mature strike-termination strategy and communication plan, and where it carried out its plan vigorously and flexibly, it successfully terminated the strike in a reasonably short period of time and with no tragically late concessions—even in the absence of an injunction.

Unfortunately, too many companies foolishly take a strike as ill prepared as the new-shorn lamb in January. Their plight, as described in the following requiem to a long and tragic strike in the textile industry is a poignant reminder of the penalty of unplanned or poorly planned communication or of communication stunted by a hostile climate of distrust:

The strike lasted 68 weeks. It was tragically needless. The strikers gained nothing. The strike might possibly have been averted—or at least shortened—if communication among company, employees, and community had been more effective in preventing distrust of the company's announced intentions. When the company finally despaired of telling its story to the striking employees and the community through usual channels, and adopted a different strategy of communication, the strike ended in relatively short order.

It is most heartening, on the other hand, to note the increasing tendency of American businessmen to abandon the abject appeasement and habitual silence so common in the past decade in the face of strike threats or strikes.

One example will suffice to illustrate the trend. It is quoted from the January, 1956, issue of *The Communicator* and bears the candid title, "On How to Talk about Strikes."

As 1955 ended, Line Material Company of Milwaukee, Wisconsin (a division of McGraw Electric Company), was demonstrating anew its ability to talk things over with 3,800 employees around ten plants and eighty sales locations.

"To Strike or Not to Strike?" asked a headline in its employee magazine, *Inside Line*. "A company that admits it does not know all the answers tells why it hates strikes and describes the length it will go to avoid them or meet them. . . ."

What the company was doing made sense. Management knew that a strike by 150 employees in its Birmingham plant had been discussed at its other plants, but it wanted to discuss it and relate it to the entire corporate "family." Its goals were simple:

(1) to discuss the strike fairly and frankly;

(2) to heal any remaining wounds, and to re-emphasize the bonds between the company and all its employees;

(3) to use the Birmingham strike as a peg on which to discuss use of the strike weapon to secure short-term gains.

Communications at Line Material constitute an essential function, and because of communications continuity, management was now able to talk with friendly assurance.

The article set forth in readable terms the problems of competition. The Birmingham plant, one of three filling Line Material's hardware needs, was in a fiercely competitive business and for some months had been operating in the red. Despite price cutting by its hardware competitors, the operation was nearing a point where profits were a possibility when the CIO Steelworkers insisted that the company follow the Big Steel wage pattern. When it could not, the plant was closed by strike action.

In discussing the case, *Inside Line* talked in terms employees could understand:

"The company itself must take some of the responsibility for what happened at Birmingham. In that light, perhaps this article is long overdue. The company probably goofed when it assumed the people knew these facts. Had they known them, they might not have left their jobs. It is certainly not the fault of the Birmingham employees that Southern Plant has been unprofitable. They're as hard working, cooperative and imaginative as any group of Line Material employees anywhere. But you can't beat economics. There are times, in a cutthroat market which hardware now is, when even the most efficient production is not enough to combat selling on price alone.

"Since the company has been asked about its attitude and position toward strikes, this appears to be a ripe time to explore its feelings on the matter.

"In a word: It hates them.

"It hates them because everybody involved gets hurt: the employee, the company and the customer. Strikes are bad public relations.

"This is not to say that some strikes in some companies are not justified. This is not the best of all possible worlds: management is human, too, and can't be right all the time."

Getting down to specifics, *Inside Line* then discussed in detail what had happened during the bargaining at Birmingham. Then in frank and friendly terms, it reverted again to management's concern for the well-being of all its employees.

"Line Material has always tried to air and resolve these issues before they boil over into anything like a strike," the article said. "It has always regarded its people as individual human beings, not clock numbers. It has always encouraged its people to speak up when they have something on their minds. . . .

"Because the company doesn't like strikes doesn't mean, however, that it won't take strikes. Sure the company loses money, because part of the overhead expense is there anyway whether employees are working or not. The company's main consideration in deciding whether to take a strike or not is illustrated again in the Birmingham example.

"Bargaining agents for the plant claimed Line Material could afford the few cents above the company's final offer that they went on strike for. They were right! They said Line Material was having a good year profit-wise. Right again! They said Line Material's association with McGraw Electric Company puts it in still sounder financial position. Righto! There is no question that Line Material could go on and on financing a losing operation until it had to cut back on costs (such as wages, or even jobs) in its profitable plants to support operations that weren't turning a profit.

"But wouldn't it be economic folly for the company to allow this sort of thing to continue?

"Plainly, the line has to be drawn when the welfare of *all* people in the company is at stake. To do otherwise would be to fail the majority to favor a few."

This is the sort of talk Line Material employees appreciate, and probably is responsible for the *Milwaukee Sentinel* saying in November that it is a firm "where every worker, from management level to shop level, knows that the company's first and main concern is with him as an individual human being." It is talk based on mutual respect resulting from careful and continuous communication within the company.

CHAPTER 22

Management Philosophy and Practice in the Area of Risk-taking Communication

> *An essential quality of leadership is courage; a moral boldness which readily assumes the burden and risks of decision, together with the courage to stand on what may be an unpopular and lonely spot, once the decision has been made. Moral conviction supplies moral courage. It is a special sort of quality; it entails the courage to say, when the chips are down, "I did it; I was responsible."* [1]

> HAROLD W. DODDS
> *President Emeritus*
> *Princeton University*

Dodds was probably not thinking of risk-taking communication when he enunciated this truth. However, it is basic to this discussion.

One of the prime essentials of business leadership would seem to be the courage to take a public stand on any issue which vitally affects the welfare of the business, the willingness to rebut any unfounded attack on the enterprise, its leaders, or the people being led.

Nevertheless, there are widely varying management philosophies as to the wisdom of utilizing communication of a controversial or risk-taking nature.

Probably the majority of business leaders today avoid communi-

---

[1] *The Journal of Communication*, 7:2, summer, 1957, p. 73.

cating on controversial subjects unless their backs are to the wall. They question management's responsibility to inform employees on economic issues where there are differences of opinion; they doubt that such communication will be successful. They avoid taking a public position if, by so doing, there is some possibility of arousing the displeasure of some employees, customers, share owners—and particularly of union officials.

A growing minority contends that the communication of subjects of active interest to employees, the public, and union officials is a necessity, that employee understanding of the economic facts of life has a particularly constructive influence on the policies and aims of union representatives.

This management minority believes that what the great mass of employees and their families think and want will be a major factor in establishing the social, political, and economic climate in which business will operate in future years—and that responsibility of business leaders is to prove to them, by both deeds and words, that private management working in the climate of a free economy has satisfied and will continue to satisfy their wants to a greater extent than can be satisfied under any other system the world has known.

It is fervently to be hoped that the minority protagonists of courage will convert the apprehensive majority who put their faith in silence, appeasement, and retreat. Quite possibly the type of climate in which business will operate tomorrow will largely depend upon which management philosophy, courage or appeasement, gains the ascendancy.

An appraisal of current management philosophies

In order to appraise the present thinking in management circles as regards this vital question of operating philosophy, Fred Rudge, Inc., of New Canaan, Connecticut, a highly respected firm of consultants to management, particularly in the field of labor relations, and strong advocate of speaking up, is conducting a continuing survey to determine the extent to which management is utilizing risk-taking communication and the results that have accrued.

The following is an abstract of their findings.

As an initial exploration, fifty-six companies were canvassed to inquire into the following areas of communication where clearly identified differences of viewpoint exist:

1. Issues involved when negotiations bog down or during a strike
2. Economics and other collective-bargaining factors prior to and during negotiations
3. Union representation elections
4. National labor policy and the Taft-Hartley Act

Forty-eight of the personal interviews were with management executives vested with the industrial relations responsibilities, and eight were with other executives in industrial relations work.

More than half of those interviewed represented corporations with sales upward of 100 million dollars. In terms of size or nature of enterprise, the companies are not representative of their industry or business generally. Furthermore, what was learned was necessarily subjective in nature, for it represented management impressions rather than the result of surveys among the groups management had addressed.

Certain trends were indicated that are of interest not alone to personnel and industrial relations administrators, but to the chief executive officer responsible, in the final analysis, for labor costs. As to trends:

1. Virtually *all* the companies interviewed speak up when negotiations bog down badly or where there is a strike. There is no hesitancy at this point to talk directly and with conviction to the employees and often to members of the community.

2. Before negotiations, only a very few express management views about, or give an appraisal of, the factors that influence management's position at the bargaining table. Only infrequently is an effort made to communicate management's position to employees during negotiations.

3. Just prior to representation elections, virtually all companies, not now fully organized, discuss the management viewpoint on unionization with their employees. Except in one instance, those who took a position in favor of "no unions" report that the outcome favored their position.

4. Only one in ten discusses national labor policy or the Taft-Hartley Act with employees.

It was concluded that management in the companies interviewed, by and large, was willing to communicate if there was little or nothing to be lost and much to be gained (that is, in strike situations or in representation elections). It was equally clear that most of the managements concerned kept away from controversial areas, if they were not of the crisis variety—and if communication of the management point of view risked upsetting already established union relationships (that is, in prenegotiation or negotiation communications or in communications about Taft-Hartley).

The contrast between union and management publications

These findings are indeed discouraging; and they were earlier highlighted by a study by Fred C. Foy, president of Koppers Company, of management's use of its employee house organs as contrasted with the unions' use of their publications. According to Mr. Foy: [2]

Only the unions are vigorously and effectively driving home to their members their arguments and their point of view. Week after week they pour out a flood of carefully planned and well-written articles which—irrespective of geographic area or union identity—advocate more government participation in the economy and reflect a solid front on almost every major policy question. This conclusion is based on a careful study of such union publications as The CIO News, AFL News Reporter, The American Federationist, The Machinist, United Rubber Worker, and District Fifty News, circulated to millions of union members.

In contrast, the management publications regularly reaching the same union members fail—with only a few exceptions—to present any point of view about what management feels is good for America. Usually well-written and often beautifully printed, they cover mainly employee social news, company sport activities, and brief news reports about the company. For the most part, they are conspicuously silent on such basic sub-

[2] Fred C. Foy and Robert Harper, "Round One: Union vs. Company Publications," Harvard Business Review, May–June, 1955, p. 59.

jects as the profit system or on key current issues before the legislatures. This conclusion is based on an intensive study of some 700 company magazines published for employee consumption.

Additional conclusions gleaned from the Foy-Harper report warrant the most careful consideration in any management group where communication policy is being weighed. The report concluded that:

1. The union leaders' program is carefully planned and consistent. It deals almost exclusively with "breadbasket subjects"; union leaders do not talk in economic abstractions.

2. Communication with rank-and-file members is aided by excellent publications, which are used to promote social goals. From 45 to 65 per cent of the space in some of these publications is allotted for this type of material.

3. Repetitious handling of the same subjects is extremely well done and indicates that editors and staff assistants are top-quality journalists.

4. Many of the union publications follow the same pattern of presentation with little or no deviation in the type of material.

5. Management did not counteract union activity among employees on realistic "breadbasket" subjects, such as union leaders use as levers to promote national social legislation.

6. Employee publications frequently took a negative approach to challenging problems—more often resorting to "sniper tactics" against the opposition than to clear, logical statements of management's case. Management often seemed to be "maintaining its dignity" when the audience it wished to reach understood "toe-to-toe" slugging better.

7. Controversial subjects were avoided, but at the same time, attempts were consistently made to stimulate pride in the virtues of the "American way of life." A steady reading diet of such "flag-waving" stories could prove an insult to the average worker's intelligence, for he too believes in the American way of life. The futility of communicating in this manner has been noted several times in leading business publications.[3]

8. Constructive action by management, resulting in a better understanding of an individual company's economic problem, frequently was taken during a particularly trying labor-management negotiation—usually

[3] Edward C. Bursk, "Selling the Idea of Free Enterprise," *Harvard Business Review*, May, 1948, p. 372; also "How to Play the House Organ," *Fortune*, October, 1952, p. 144.

in the form of letters to employees explaining the company's position. In addition, annual reports to employees have proved highly successful in dispelling misinformation about the company's financial position. The report deduced that the same tactics would result in the same success on controversial issues affecting the nation.

Silence—the losing strategy of businessmen

An associate of the author, C. J. Dover, consultant, employee communication, General Electric Company, in an address before the Public Relations Society of America, enumerated four reasons why the majority segment of American business management has preferred to take refuge in silence in the face of persistent attack. Two of them are particularly pertinent to this discussion: [4]

Too many executives believe [he states] that to take a position on a hot issue involves risk—perhaps the risk of losing prestige among employees if a given issue finally is resolved in a manner not to [their] liking—or perhaps the ever-present risk that to be openly partisan may boomerang, and solidify employee opposition to the management stand.

The most glaring fallacy of this alibi is the *false* assumption that there is *no* risk in keeping quiet. To the contrary, the evidence is terrifyingly abundant that the greatest risk of all is silence. In this modern, industrial society there is no such thing as a communication vacuum. Employees are regularly exposed to hard-hitting, anti-management arguments. Some of the anti-business spokesmen are honest men. But most are irresponsible demagogues who quickly rush into the void created by management silence. They fill the eyes and ears of employees with lies and distortions. Their aim is to generate discord, to create class conflict and to convince all concerned that management consists of hideous creatures who have dollar signs for eyeballs and a secret desire to make every office and every plant a sweatshop. But the point is that, regardless of whether the anti-management tirade comes from honest men, do-gooders, or demagogues, *by our silence we too often stand convicted as charged.*

When an institution remains silent in the face of years of flaying, smearing, and condemning of its actions and its intentions, common sense should tell us that many people will become convinced that the charges

[4] "Silence: An Employee Relations Pitfall," *Vital Speeches of the Day,* Feb. 1, 1957, pp. 249–252.

are true. . . . But, if more objective evidence is needed, let's consider a conclusion which may be clearly drawn from an extensive study at Yale of factors influencing attitudes:

"From the moment an untruth is aimed at an institution, it must be attacked vigorously and revealed for what it is, for if it is allowed to go unchallenged, in a short time, it is likely to be accepted as the truth."

Mr. Dover next concludes that:

Many companies which deal with unions seem to believe that for management to communicate directly and forthrightly with employees on controversial subjects somehow abrogates a right held exclusively by union officials. Where this kind of curious thinking predominates, it's not unusual to find a situation where a union official can press a button today, and paralyze production in all of that company's plants tomorrow—with or without giving the employees a reason. And if he does give a reason, and it's *not* a good one, the company often seems powerless, even with truth and logic on its side, to persuade the employees to ignore the walk-out order and come to work. Those of us who are in such a situation should be pondering Lord Acton's warning that "Power tends to corrupt, and absolute power tends to corrupt absolutely." There are many elements in the accumulation of power. But apart from a past record of deeds, perhaps the most important single factor is a freely-used system of communication with the people whose direct actions are decisive in any controversy. The only basic power which exists at the bargaining table is the support of the employees. And how can management expect employee support if it has never communicated its stand on the issues? This silence, in effect, gives the union a virtual communication monopoly on the truly important issues. Bernard Berelson, one of the nation's top social scientists, warns us of the clear and present danger of a communication monopoly. Here are his words:

"This is of central importance: communication has effects upon converting opinion under conditions of monopoly which are much greater than its effects under conditions of competition. . . ."

In plain English, this warns us that if we shut up, we'll probably be shut out. To be forthright is not being anti-union. It is being pro-employee. No responsible businessman or union official would seriously deny the other's right to state honestly his view on employee-centered issues. But management is waiving that right, when it justifies its silence with the pious statement that "We mustn't go over the union's head." Indeed, we are abdicating our moral responsibility to act in the best interests of our employees. Surely, our generation should need no reminder that appeasement is scarcely a workable formula for meeting controversy.

Silence is indeed the losing strategy of businessmen.

Regaining a valuable birthright

There is increasing evidence that a new generation of American businessmen is recognizing that an "essential quality of leadership is courage," and that "communication has effects upon converting opinion under conditions of monopoly which are much greater than its effects under conditions of competition."

Consider this rebuttal, for example, by the B. F. Goodrich Company of Akron, Ohio, to a charge by the unions that a price increase in its products was a basic contributory factor in feeding inflation.

Commenting on remarks made by L. S. Buckmaster, president of the Rubber Workers Union, the company's four-page documented commentary addressed to all employees said, in part:

"We will not remain silent to the implication that B. F. Goodrich is raising its prices unnecessarily and merely to gain unjustified profits." The letter went on to explain that although tire prices had risen about 55 per cent since 1948, the average Goodrich worker had received an 84 per cent increase in wages and benefits since that time.

The letter, after presenting hard-hitting supporting facts, figures, and charts, concluded by observing:

BFG employees do have fine wages and employee benefits. We resent the insinuation that the B. F. Goodrich Company is deliberately making them worth less through inflationary profit policies. . . .

Inflation is a serious problem. No one—not you personally, nor the company—improves financial position as long as it continues to creep onward. Certainly we welcome suggestions to help curb this trend.

However, we do not feel that "blaming it on the other fellow" is an answer. Such public denouncements can only unjustly shake customer confidence; they cannot build good will. We sincerely regret Mr. Buckmaster's release and the attendant misunderstandings that it caused.

One final but significant example must suffice. Walter Reuther hit the headlines in the summer of 1957 with the proposal that the auto makers reduce the price of their 1958 models $100 below the average 1957 price. In return he said, in effect, undoubtedly with the smile of Mona Lisa, that in the UAW 1958 negotiations such a price decrease might temper the union's economic demands.

Immediately, Ford, General Motors, and Chrysler all replied with such public vigor and effectiveness that Mr. Reuther quickly dropped this specious prenegotiation argument, designed to soften up management before the start of collective bargaining.

The following is quoted from an "open letter to Walter Reuther," signed by Henry Ford II and distributed to all employees, share owners, and distributors:

Your proposal fails to recognize the simple economic facts of life. The sharply rising labor costs we have been incurring as a result of the labor contracts negotiated two years ago are already built into the very products on which you now suggest that we cut prices. And additional labor costs will be added to these products in September under the contract's cost-of-living formula. Since the introduction of our 1957 models—and including the 3-cent rise in wages in September—our hourly labor costs have increased 18.6 cents per hour.

The problem of inflation affects everybody—the wage earner as well as the employer; school teachers, lawyers, doctors, dentists, clergymen and all professional people; government employees; the proprietor of the country store and the clerk in that same store; the farmer, the small business man, the manufacturer, the retailer, the distributor, the service company. The problem is assuming serious proportions and poses a grave threat to the stability of our economy. We will not solve the problem with propaganda broadsides. We will not solve it by resorting to unsound economic practices.

True labor statesmanship today would consist, it seems to us, in labor leaders resisting pressures, from whatever source, for excessive and inflationary wage increases. It would consist in union leaders acting for the common good and refraining from the use of the extraordinary leverage and monopolistic power of today's big industrial labor union.

We commend this course of action to you.

Much of the current evidence would indicate that the business community is beginning to abandon the posture of defensive silence that has characterized the past two decades.

Of one thing we may be certain, however. Astute trade-union officials will continue to keep management off balance by hit-and-run proposals, by negotiating in the newspapers months in advance of the actual collective bargaining meetings; by vigorously and skillfully communicating their goals and their economic ideology.

If a balance is not restored in the communication process, businessmen face an endless retreat and an accelerated trend to a collectivist society; and history will record ironically that they were the principal contributors to their own liquidation by failure to utilize the one skill at which they could have been most adept.

Employees respect leaders who speak up

Businessmen must speak up, must go on the offensive in the communication area across the country. They must accept the risk in risk-taking communication. It is just one more of the risks involved in conducting a profitable and growing business in a free economy—and it is indeed a minor risk.

The following observations by the author are based upon a decade of successful use of risk-taking communication by the General Electric Company:

1. The head of any successful business, if he is a man of integrity, enjoys an enormous latent respect and prestige with his employees and the community neighbors.

2. The head of such a business, even though he be not the owner but the manager of a branch plant, has great credibility with his employees. Management simply doesn't know its own strength. It *is* a fact that employees are *overwhelmingly* inclined to believe forthright statements by the head man to a far greater degree than those of any other so-called representatives or spokesmen.

3. This prestige and this believability are nontransferable. Nobody else, no association, no group of employers can do as good a job as the boss man in the plant.

4. The average employee wants his boss to be a leader, not a follower; he wants *his* boss to express *his* viewpoint so that the employee can be helped to form better judgments as to the pros and cons of the complicated social, economic, moral, and political issues which bombard him.

Above all else, employees admire a fighter who will stand up to union officials, the politicians, and the demagogues whenever the interests of the business, the employees, and the share owners require such action. Risk? Yes, some, but the rewards are great. Where there is no risk, there is no progress—and "Progress," in the author's company, "is our Most Important Product."

CHAPTER 23

Long-term Communication Planning

The difference between a dynamic enterprise which offers steadily increasing values for customers, unusual growth potential to prospective investors, and job security and opportunity for employees, as contrasted with a static enterprise which is barely breasting the tide, is often the difference in the ability to plan ahead.

There is widespread acceptance of the urgent need for intelligent, resourceful planning in all the orthodox areas of managing a business, such as research, engineering, manufacturing, marketing, personnel administration, and financing. But you may examine hundreds of enterprises before you find one which has the prescience to appreciate the need for long-range communication planning.

In the author's company, intensive and continuing research is devoted to the subject of planning. The following observations concerning planning as a distinct and vital type of work of a professional manager is excerpted from *Professional Management in General Electric,* "Book Three: The Work of a Professional Manager":

In the broad sense, plans represent the transformation of general objectives and policies into specific working documents. Detailed plans for work to be done should be accompanied by realistic, achievable time schedules of expected performance.

These plans should be in quantitative terms with respect to the performance of all people involved, and also with respect to all physical and monetary resources required to accomplish the stated objectives. Such

288

quantitatively stated plans constitute self-imposed standards against which to measure performance as a function of time.

Thinking ahead is one of the indispensable parts of a manager's work. Astute anticipation of obstacles, and taking requisite steps to avoid or to overcome them, will often result in major savings of time and money, and may even make the difference between success or failure of particular ventures. The greater the scope and importance of the particular projects, the greater the importance of anticipating and making the favorable situation rather than just being ready to meet what comes, or put out fires.

Assuredly, reasonable allowance needs to be made for unforeseen circumstances . . . a degree of flexibility needs to be built into planning, and predetermined ways need to be provided for taking care of minor changes which result from unforeseen events.

However, the other and more important side of this coin is that the more thoroughly and imaginatively the planning has been done, the more study and weighing of alternatives and consideration of consequences of proposed actions, the less the probability of being caught unprepared by unforeseen circumstances. Adequate planning and thinking ahead can greatly decrease the necessity for continually putting out fires. Furthermore, by anticipating needs, unnecessary margins should be avoided. Through thought and study, factors of uncertainty can be decreased, and padding for unforeseen circumstances can be eliminated, over-all efficiency improved, and profit margins raised.

There is more than one way to accomplish any specific objective. However, a factual approach based upon adequate data, together with resourceful, wise analysis will often indicate the most efficient (least costly) way.

Needs should be recognized early enough to allow time for adequate analysis of existing data, and for whatever additional research is required to arrive at the right (most favorable) way.

Thinking ahead is indeed one of the indispensable parts of a manager's job—and all signs and portents indicate that the ability to think ahead three to five years on the communication needs of the business will be an increasingly important factor in separating the men from the boys among managers in the next decade.

In order to emphasize the need for long-range communication

planning let us examine the anatomy of the communication process as illustrated by the language of graphs.

The specific goal of all employee communication is to achieve mutual understanding and confidence between employees and management on all matters of common concern, so that there will be eager, enthusiastic, and productive cooperation in attaining the objectives of the business and satisfying the work-connected needs of the employees.

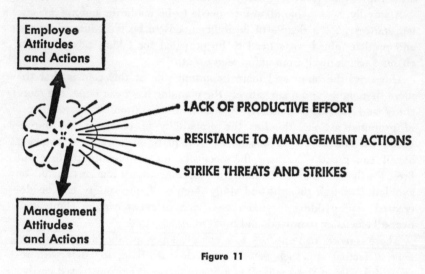

Employee Attitudes and Actions

• LACK OF PRODUCTIVE EFFORT

• RESISTANCE TO MANAGEMENT ACTIONS

• STRIKE THREATS AND STRIKES

Management Attitudes and Actions

Figure 11

The barrier to the achievement of this goal is the gap (Figure 11) which exists between the attitudes and actions of employees and attitudes and actions of management on many matters which are vital to the success of the business.

Too many employees come to the work place with negative attitudes—lacking confidence in management, misinformed on management's motives, policies and practices, feeling that their interests and those of management are diametrically opposed. Under the stresses and strains of the job, these differences become acutely magnified. Cooperation breaks down and the business suffers from lack of productive effort, and symbols of outright resistance to management such as walkouts, strike threats, or strikes are manifest.

The entire employee communication process can be represented by two converging lines (Figure 12). Here we see true two-way communication operating to narrow the gap between employee and management attitudes and action and then attempting to merge them to achieve the unity of purpose requisite for attaining the objectives of the business and the satisfaction of employee needs.

We attempt to accomplish this through good downward communication by management to gain employee confidence and trust and

THE COMMUNICATION PROCESS

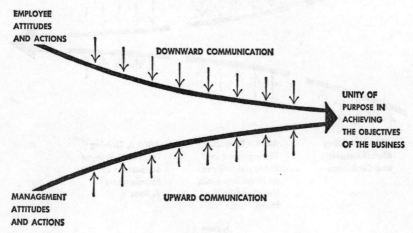

Figure 12

through truly effective upward communication by means of which management may be kept informed of employees' needs and desires in order to readjust its planning.

In this way, we build mutual confidence and common understanding on the part of both employees and management of the needs and interests of each other. Only in this manner can the attitudes and actions of both be modified sufficiently to achieve unity of interest and purpose.

But the process is not so simple as Figure 12 might indicate. In order to determine the distinct types of communication work required to achieve this desired result, we will next arbitrarily divide the area between the converging lines, which somewhat resembles a trapezium, into three separate areas. Only in this way can we fix in mind the kinds of communication work we must perform in order to achieve our goals.

Figure 13 graphically depicts the three distinct kinds of communication work required. Area 1 will represent the kind of com-

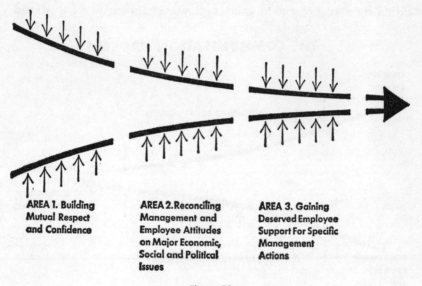

AREA 1. Building Mutual Respect and Confidence

AREA 2. Reconciling Management and Employee Attitudes on Major Economic, Social and Political Issues

AREA 3. Gaining Deserved Employee Support For Specific Management Actions

Figure 13

munication work—based on good deeds, of course—we must do in order to build mutual confidence and respect between employees and managers. Area 2 will represent the communication work we need to perform to bring about mutual understanding on the many controversial issues which tend to keep employees and managers apart. Area 3 will represent the familiar type of communication work we have to do in order to obtain employee support for some particular management action, such as planning a major change in plant facilities, introducing new technology, changing the method of wage payment, etc.

Now why must three kinds of communication work be performed? Because, whenever the employee has to make a decision on whether to give or to withhold his cooperation, he is influenced by one or more or all of these three factors:

If we fail to develop mutual respect and confidence through good deeds, properly interpreted (Area 1), our whole business concept of working together in the balanced best interests of all contributor-claimants to the business is founded on sand. If we fail to come to grips with and forthrightly to explain the economics on which our policy making and decisions are based (why we must operate the way we operate) (Area 2) we run the grave risk of allowing our employees to be taught by others that our goals and actions are narrowly self-centered and opposed to the goals and best interests of the employees and customers.

And obviously, if we fail to communicate well in advance of specific management actions (Area 3), we are headed for the customary disruptive employee actions inherent in misunderstood motives and in resistance to unexplained changes at the work place.

This book has thus far dealt primarily with Areas 1 and 3; so, in this concluding phase, let us examine Area 2 which might well be termed the missing link in employee communication as practiced by most business institutions today.

This missing link is the failure of managers to lay out a three- to five-year plan to develop understanding of the basic economic principles involved in the operation of a successful business—principles on which managers and employees and other groups in society have markedly different attitudes and frames of reference.

Despite spectacular successes in building understanding on particular current issues and practices, the job of developing a mutual frame of reference in which to view our economic system, the problems of operating a business, and the motives of businessmen has hardly been started.

It is significant to note that the popular misconceptions about business and the major criticisms of our free-enterprise system are virtually the same today as they were twenty years ago. This is not surprising. Indeed, we businessmen should have lost much ground in view of our paralyzing silence in the face of much better organized critics.

At the risk of being dismissed as a long-haired theorist, the author will state with deep conviction that only planned long-range communication in Area 2 can reconcile the differences in basic attitudes between managers and employees.

In the first place, the objectives and goals of a business enterprise are of necessity long range. They are affected not only by day-to-day developments in the market place and by the quality of management planning but perhaps more importantly by erosionary outside forces whose strength rests upon public opinion.

In the second place, as in politics or in military operations, it is possible to win most minor skirmishes and still lose the crucial battle.

Thirdly, without the framework of long-range communication planning it is difficult to conduct employee communication much above the level of crisis or fire-fighting activities.

Some dangerous misbeliefs

What are some of these issues which, if not explained, pose a grave danger if managers and employees remain hopelessly split? They will, of course, vary from enterprise to enterprise, but can we not pick the following as being a minimal list of importance to *every* enterprise?

The belief that managers cannot achieve the economic purposes of a business and simultaneously satisfy the legitimate needs and aspirations of its employees.

The suspicion that managers do not share fairly the rewards of production with employees.

The attractively specious belief that profits should be frozen at a percentage of sales.

The too widely held idea that technological advances—or their synonym, automation—are inimical to the best interests of employees.

The fallacy that wages can be raised without a corresponding increase in productivity.

The demagogic cliché that the way for everybody to live better is to divide up the production pie more equitably rather than to increase the size of the pie.

The specious union claim that the welfare of the economy and of our society can be enhanced by complete unionization and by making union membership a condition of employment.

The socialistic dogma that the standard of living and the security of employees can best be achieved through national planning, Federal subsidies, and increasing Federal control.

The economic fairy tale that we can all have a four-day work week immediately at the same take-home pay with no increase in productivity, with no increase in prices, and with a higher standard of living.

The fallacy that people can have "something for nothing."

There are, of course, many others, but these will suffice. It is the obligation of the mature management team to look ahead—to analyze those issues on which the most divergent attitudes prevail and which, if not reconciled, threaten to undermine the health of business and the national economy in the immediate years ahead.

The perceptive manager, having isolated the basic issues on which he must develop thorough understanding, proceeds to plan his communication on these issues with the same care and skill as he might plan his five-year forecast of manufacturing facilities and marketing strategy.

The advantages of determining a company's major communication themes for the next two, three, or five years are substantial indeed. For, once a theme has been selected, countless opportunities present themselves week by week and month by month to the alert communicator to interpret and advance the theme.

Let us assume that a major theme is to demonstrate management's deep concern and determination to provide greater job security through sound management rather than through presently economically unsound crutches such as the so-called guaranteed annual wage or the shorter work week. Once this theme is planned, every management action to achieve employment stabilization can be opportunely utilized to explain the progress being made. Likewise any temporary failures are forthrightly admitted, and the difficulties of stabilizing employment in a free market are reviewed. Additionally, each new order, new product, cost reduction, quality improvement, etc., is utilized in communication as another example of the economically sound way of making jobs steadier.

The determination of basic long-term communication themes will vary between individual enterprises. There are specific areas of misunderstanding, however, that are common in practically all organizations. Listed below in the left-hand column are some of these common areas where, because of a lack of a common frame of reference, management is being too often denied the employee support its motives and actions deserve. In the right-hand column are indicated typical recurring communication opportunities for building mutual understanding in these areas.

Areas of Misunderstanding (major themes)	*Opportunities for Interpretation*
Steady work—steady pay	Announcements of research findings Installation of new equipment Changes in methods of production and distribution Plans for plant expansion and changes Changes in advertising and sales campaigns Loss or acquisition of orders for particular items Changes in products Changes in product mix: additions to and deletions from the line Inventory shifts up or down Hiring, upgrading, and shifting of employees Long-service employee awards Changes in billing or other sales procedures
Automation	Changes in methods of production Installation of different equipment Modification of work plan

Areas of Misunderstanding (major themes)	Opportunities for Interpretation
Automation	Contrast of old and new production methods: physical effect, cleanliness, safety, employee opportunities Contrast of old and new products: quality, quantity, cost, convenience Job changes and upgrading
Profits	Annual report "State of the business" meetings Additions to plant, equipment, or research New and improved products Growth or decrease in employment Price changes New and additional orders Emergency service demands Financing of necessary community services
Productivity	Loss or acquisition of orders Introduction of new materials Waste and spoilage Promotions and job changes Machine and method changes Price changes Employee suggestions
Responsible unionism	Examples of "peaceful progress" in comparison with union violence and corruption Strikes and the public interest Union organizing campaigns Jurisdictional disputes Mass picketing and secondary boycotts Changes in methods of production and distribution Loss of orders
Business climate	Movement of industry from or to the community Local job situation for young people Municipal services and needs Effect of state and local taxes on business operations Results of business-climate appraisal

Areas of Misunderstanding (major themes)	*Opportunities for Interpretation*
Big business	Effects of subcontracting
	Defense contributions through research
	Jobs and taxes made possible by business growth
	Research and new products
	Pioneering in employee benefits
	Contributions to charitable and educational institutions
	In-company training and self-development programs

Now why is it important for managers to achieve mutual understanding and tolerance, if not full agreement, on matters such as these—even when they seem to have no immediate bearing on any particular operating problem being faced at the moment?

It is important because these are fundamental economic principles which are the bases for so many of the specific decisions managers must make, and actions they must take, for the survival of the business and for the greatest security for the greatest number of employees.

Du Pont, whose life blood is new technology, seems to have chosen the need for constant technological improvement as a basic theme. Having done so, it then proceeds to develop understanding and acceptance for this business way of life in a variety of media and with refreshing originality, as this single example will illustrate:

Du Pont's justly famous employee publication, *Better Living,* January–February, 1956, published a group photograph of the wives, sons, and daughters of employees at a certain plant, giving the name of each. The article then pointed out that when the babies shown in their mothers' arms enter the work force in 1976 at twenty-one years of age, the United States will be two centuries old and may face one of its greatest problems. Du Pont's article then lists the alternatives facing these babies in the following compelling terms:

For the simple arithmetic is that if the trends of the past 80 years continue, then the anticipated 216 million U.S. population of 1976 will demand twice the quantity of goods and services available today. Yet the work force 20 years hence will be only about 30 per cent larger than it is today.

What this means is that, at today's rate of output, the nation would be able to produce only about 70 per cent of the goods and services demanded. Translated into time, there would be a shortage of 76 billion man-hours of labor in 1976.

This leaves three choices: Work 11.5 hours a day, or 57 hours a week. Attempt to recruit more labor among students, retired persons and housewives. Or increase individual output.

Since the first two courses are clearly unlikely by present American trends, the real answer lies in the third—in utilizing every technical advance, every ingenious invention, every new tool to increase productivity so the available labor force can fill the 1976 demand for $750 billion of goods and services. The basis for achievement exists; the question is how the nation nurtures its prospects.

In sum, this chapter which is written for the mature manager puts communication in its proper perspective as one of the greatest undeveloped resources of the business. It presents the communication process as a dynamic process (1) which starts far upstream in the development of mutual respect and confidence, earned by a good code of conduct consistently practiced and vigorously interpreted, (2) which isolates through attitude surveys and other observable data those basic misunderstandings or lack of knowledge which threaten the future welfare of the business and its employees and reconciles these differences through carefully planned long-term communication, and (3) thus paves the way for specific employee communication to gain support for specific management actions that may be required three to five years hence.

This is assuredly the mature manager's method of getting his communication on target, of harnessing his communication to move forward the short- and long-term objectives of the business to enhance the welfare of the employees—of *managing by communication.*

Index

300

Supervisor, first-line, job-related communication work of, order giving, study, 119–120
  orientation of new employees, 112, 113
  selection interviewing, 110–112
  transmitting of policies and procedures, 115–117
  (*See also* Foreman's informative conference; Performance appraisal)
Sylvania Electric Products, Inc., 57

"Take ten" meeting, 166
Telecommunication, 172
Timken Roller Bearing Company, 47
Training courses, for advanced management, 10
  for appraising performance, 127
  for foremen, 102
  for improving assignment making, 118
  for interviewing, 111, 112
  for Job Instruction Training, 114, 115
  for listening, 201, 202
  for political effectiveness, 94, 95
Training Within Industry Foundation, 114

Union relations, 50–65
  collective bargaining, communication in, 50, 51, 57–60
   "new look," 51–65
    attitude toward strikes in, 55
    key to, 65
    mature approach to, 52, 53
    objective of, 53
    offer, making and publicizing, 54, 55
    in small company, 60–65
    taking issues to employees, 57–60
   orthodox pattern of, 51, 52
   pre-negotiation communication in, 58
  employee relations different from, 57
  union influence, growth of, 10, 11
  (*See also* Strikes)
U.S. Rubber Company, 253–255
Upward communication, 194–209
  acceptance and discharge of responsibilities, 197, 198
  clean organization structure, 197
  counselling, formal, 200, 201
  employee-attitude surveys, 209

Upward communication, employee round tables, 204, 205
  exit interviews, 208, 209
  grievance procedure, employee, 198–200
  listening, 201–204
  management responsibility, accountability for, 197
  manager-employee luncheons, 205
  obstacles to, 195, 196
  performance appraisal, 207, 208
  planned shop contacts, 209
  plant panels, 204
  post-employment interview, 208
  prerequisites for, 197
  problem-solving procedures, 198–200
  question boxes, 203, 204
  rumor clinic, 202, 203
  suggestion system, 205–207
  techniques, check list of, 196
  (*See also* Oral communication)

Walking the shop and office, 173, 174
Watson, Brantley, 29
Weirton Steel Company, 171
Weisenfeld, Allen, 51, 53
Words, misunderstanding of, 20, 21
Workshops, 93, 94
Written communication, 181–193
  for employees, 184–193
   audio-visual media, 193
   benefits report, individualized, 191, 192
   booklets, special, 189
   bulletin boards, 192, 193
   bulletins, 184
   channels of, 160–163, 180–193
   financial report, annual, 191
   house organ, monthly, 185, 186
   letters to employees' homes, 187, 188
   news digest, daily, 186, 187
   newspaper, 184, 185
   pay envelope inserts, 189
   posters, 193
   reading racks, 189–191
  for management, administrative, 180
   bulletins, special, 180, 181
   handbooks, 182
   newsletter, 181
   publications, special, 183
   reports, formal, 181, 182
Wuerthner, J. J., 93

Yale University, 103, 104